Craven rugby handbook

Dr. D. H. Craven rugby handbook

EP Publishing Limited
1977

First published 1970
Tafelberg Publishers Ltd
Cape Town, South Africa

First published in New Zealand 1975
A. H. & A. W. Reed Ltd
Wellington, Sydney & London

First published in Great Britain 1977
EP Publishing Limited
East Ardsley, Wakefield
West Yorkshire WF3 2JN, England

by permission of the copyright holders

Copyright © A. H. & A. W. Reed 1975, 1977

ISBN 0   7158   0616   5

British Library Cataloguing in Publication Data
Craven, D H
  Rugby handbook – [New ed.]
    1. Rugby football
  I. Title
  796.33'32   GV945
  ISBN 0-7158-0616-5

Please address all enquiries to EP Publishing Limited
(address as above)

Printed in Great Britain by
The Scolar Press Limited
Ilkley, West Yorkshire

Contents

Part I
THE GAME OF RUGBY

Chapter 1
RUGBY ANALYSED. Structure 3. The player 11. The forward battle 14. The battle of the backs 19.

Chapter 2
SET-PIECES. Tight play: the scrum 24; the line-out 34. Broken-down play; the ruck and the maul 44. General play 50. Broken play, including tactics 70. Good balls and bad balls 78. Special play 87.

Chapter 3
THE SKILLS AND SUB-SKILLS. The skills 90. Importance of skills according to positions on the field 113. Grading and sub-skills 114. Time required for skills according to positions 115. The measuring of skills 116.

Part II
EXERCISES FOR RUGBY

Chapter 4
EXERCISE RECOMMENDATIONS 123. Rugby for schoolboys 125. Schoolboy Rugby policy 127. Laws for primary schools 128. Using the exercises 132. The practice programme 136.

Chapter 5
THE EXERCISES. Games for the primary schools 142. Big or biggish games 165. Exercises for power, stamina, speed, and strengthening 166.

Chapter 6
SKILL BUILDING 185. Exercises to acquire technique 190. Advanced technical exercises 194. Exercises without equipment 204. Exercises with equipment and individual exercises 206.

Chapter 7
ROUNDING-OFF OF SKILLS 223. Line-out and line-out formation 225. The scrum and scrum formation 229. Ruck, ruck formation, and loose play 230. Handling against defence (and attack) 233. Kick-offs and drop-outs 235.

Chapter 8
APPLICATION OF SKILLS 236. A pattern of Rugby and exercises for it 244.

Preface

THE ROAD LEADING TO international colours is difficult indeed. Without hard work, sacrifices and dedication, the ideal of becoming a Test Player will never be realised. Hard work has made Springboks or All Blacks or Wallabies of players who did not have the required talent. On the other hand, some of the most talented players have failed as a result of indifference or ignorance. This book is an attempt to point the way to becoming a top-line Rugby player.

I am convinced that if the methods shown in this book are followed, our talented players will in the majority of cases reach the top and thus add lustre to the game. Not a single facet of the game has been omitted, and no age group has been ignored. In fact, I go so far as to predict that even if no actual coaching is given to players, but all the exercises in this book are followed, those players will still come out on top. No coaching at all is better than poor coaching, but it is nevertheless remarkable the way talent can be developed if the right guidelines are laid down.

For many years I have advocated the idea that practice matches should be limited. I am still saying it now, because this is the only method many coaches use. Practice matches should be held only if all the other exercises have been done and if one has worked up to them from the bottom. If the latter method has been followed I have no objection, but to use practice matches for getting players fit and for getting them to acquire and round off skills is doing an injustice to the game. I have also discovered why practice matches are used so excessively: some coaches have no other skills at their disposal. In this book a sufficient number of exercises is given to take the place of practice matches; so practice matches need be used only to establish that the exercises have served their purpose and to allow players to play according to what they have been taught before the practice match.

This book is divided into two parts: Part I deals with the player and the theory concerning the game.

We start by analysing the game and explaining the aim of forwards and backs in each of their positions. This will show us what requires attention, e.g. the different kinds of fitness. Once we know what the aims are we have to know how to set about acquiring them and thus achieve far more than mere physical fitness.

I am not offering any apologies for coining new terms or for substituting new terms for old terms. Nor do I offer any apologies for repetition, because this helps to keep the great truths of Rugby in mind. The greatest art in Rugby is to keep the old truths alive, and to keep on emphasising the important things so that they overshadow the less important aspects of the game.

After the game has been analysed, there follows a description of the plays – tight play; the play which follows it, general play; broken play; loose play, etc. The basic principles have often been described, but there are still coaches who would like to learn more about them. Without a sound knowledge of these no coach will be able to pinpoint mistakes or devise effective remedial methods. For these reasons the basics cannot be stressed too much.

After the fundamental principles we proceed to the most neglected aspect of Rugby, and without which no one can play well – the *skills*. Year after year at my university at Stellenbosch we get students who still have to be taught those Rugby skills which they should have mastered at school. It is remarkable however, how quickly players improve once they have acquired these skills. But how much better would they have been if they had been trained properly at primary school? Skills are both a player's equipment and ammunition, and anything he attempts without them will be of a hit-or-miss nature.

Next we proceed to analyse the skills, taking the important points from each skill and putting them tobether again after supplying each with a definition. We discuss their importance, as well as the importance of the sub-skills for every position.

Part II contains all the exercises: physical exercises and skill exercises, including skill building, rounding off of skill exercises, and exercises for the application of skills. We start with very young boys, who are given exercises which will be the basis for their development as Rugby players.

We discuss when and how youngsters should start playing Rugby; how they must learn progressively, until they can do everything. Suggestions are offered about what each group can do both during and after school. It is also suggested how their coaches can make every player feel important. In addition, a completely new organisation of school and club teams is advocated.

For the very young, games are offered, developed through years of experience and containing the origins of the skills. Primary-school boys should still play as many games as possible, and we give them the opportunity to do this. Only later do we teach them actual techniques followed by skill building. These exercises will help both to develop technique and to ensure that the physical requirements for such techniques are not neglected.

After this we let the players apply the skills in situations which are similar to, but not exactly like, match conditions. They must use the skills while playing with others and they must use them in situations where the skills must be employed. This we call rounding off of skills. Only after this are the skills used precisely as in actual play. This we call the application of skills. All relevant exercises are given for the acquisition of technique, skill building, rounding off of skills, and the application of skills. How these exercises are to be used and the time to be allocated to them are contained in a practice programme.

This manual will assist coaches to build players according to their capabilities, and this is our purpose, not the winning of trophies. Up to the present no such guide has been available.

My thanks are due to Mr H. C. Duckitt for the diagrams.

Stellenbosch, May 1969. D. H. C.

THE GAME OF RUGBY   I

Chapter 1
Rugby Analysed

THE RUGBY STRUCTURE

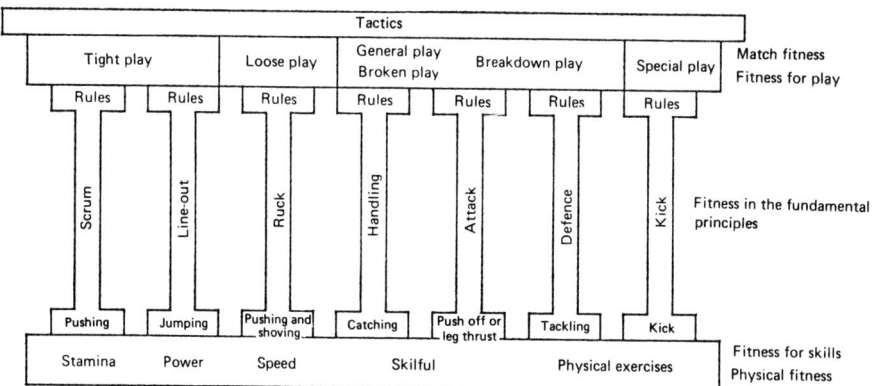

The Fundamentals

Central to the game are the fundamentals. What are they? They give the game its specific characteristics and they have conspicuously emerged as integral elements in its evolution. Consequently they are the pillars supporting the game and this is their function in our Rugby building. Remove one of them and the game is no longer Rugby. Neglect one of them and the game suffers. Our game is based on the fundamentals. They are:

The scrummage: Remove this and what remains of Rugby?
The line-out: Is there another game with this kind of fundamental?
The ruck: What other game has a ruck and, in addition to it, an attacking, a defensive, and a neutral ruck?
Attack: In no other game do we have a side-step, a swerve, a dummy, slackening and acceleration of speed in exactly the same way as we have them in Rugby.
Handling: In what other game is the ball passed as frequently? Rugby also has the falling ball, the diagonal ball and the scooped ball, each with its sub-skills.
Defence: In few games do we find the crash tackle or the tackle of a player with the ball.

Kick: In no other game is there such a variety of kicks as in Rugby: in the air from the hand, the touch kick, the high kick, the cross kick, the hook kick (by the fly half to the blindside lock), the centre kick, and the short kick. Next we have the ground kicks – the drop kick, the grubber kick, and the place kick.

When considering these fundamentals closely we see that some of them stem from the game's origins. Rugby is a game in which attack is opposed to defence. This is basic and is tied up in the very roots of Rugby.

The other fundamentals spring from attack and defence. In fact, in the early days of Rugby there was only attack; defence came much later. We must therefore never lose sight of the fact that attack should be the watchword of the game. The aim of defence was first of all repossession. Only if this could not be achieved were players to be stopped. Possession thus constitutes the basis of attack, and repossession should form the basis for defence. In time, other fundamentals were developed from attack and defence. Only after attack had failed, and the ball carrier fell on it and the other players closed on it, did the scrum originate. Later on handling came into being, with the result that more possibilities of attack were created. Initially, falling on the ball was considered a coward's act. Today, when the ball is on the ground, a ruck is formed and this can be the finest ally of attack.

In former days there was no kicking except to the posts; but then players became cautious and kicked the ball away from their posts to the sidelines, so that it would be more difficult for their opponents to attempt a drop kick or succeed with a penalty kick. As a result of this the line-out came into being.

So strong was the urge to attack that kicks were also used as an attacking aid. First of all there was the cross kick, followed by the punt, the diagonal kick and the grubber.

Today handling is the best ally of attack, while kicking is the best ally of defence. Bad handling, however, leads to the majority of scrums while kicks cause line-outs. The conflict is consequently between attack, supported by handling, and defence, bolstered by kicks. The game is also a struggle between handling and kicking. In this conflict the scrum, the line-out and even the maul take place when attack or defence either fails or succeeds.

We realise that kicks can also play a part in attack and that similarly handling can play a part in defence, but at the same time kicking and handling have identical basic functions to fulfil.

Plays in the Game

As said before, we play within the fundamental principles, and there are different plays within the game. Pillars support the lintel on which a roof is placed; so if we play with the scrum and the line-out, we have tight play; if we play with attack and defence, of which handling is a part, we have general play.

General play follows upon tight play, and if a team in possession wishes to get the ball out to their wing as a platform for attack, this is called general attacking play. If the other team attempts to prevent this it is called general defensive play. General attacking play is basic because every team ought to get the ball to their wings without a hitch. If general play is used as a platform from which any back-line player can launch an attack, and the attack is successful we have broken play (the so-called first-phase attack). If the attack fails, we have broken-down play (the opposition has repelled the attempt, or has broken it down). If play is broken down, there are usually loose balls and/or rucks and mauls, giving us loose play.

Loose play connotes everything which is "loose": loose balls, rucks, and mauls. Loose play also occurs when any loose ball which, after being kicked, lands in-field or in the hands of a defender – thus again causing a breakdown in play. We prefer making, or creating, tight play from rucks and mauls because the forwards tighten up as they would in scrums and line-outs. Possession from a ruck or a maul also leads to general play, or broken play (second-phase attack), broken-down play, or even loose play.

There is still one more kind of play – special play. This entails the kick-off and the drop-out, and when penalty kicks are taken. The following diagram will illustrate the different plays in the game:

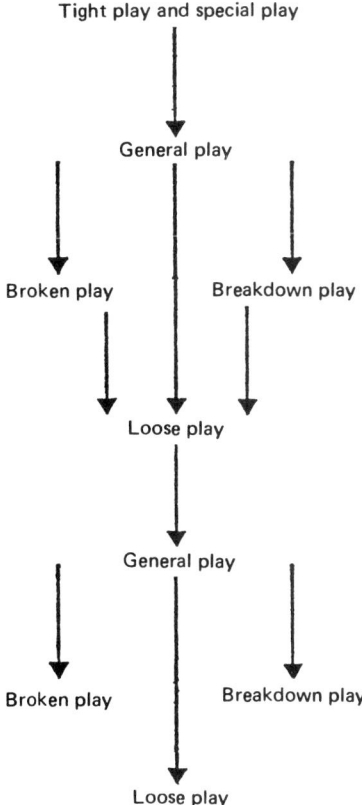

Notice the part played by tight play and loose play. No wonder that Rugby must suffer if one of these aspects is neglected.

The laws
The laws prescribe how the game is to be played. In other words, they prescribe how the fundamentals are to be used. For this reason the laws also deserve a place in the general structure of the game. It is imperative that we know the laws, otherwise we do an injustice to ourselves, to our team and to the game itself.

Tactics
The extent to which use is made of the various plays in a match will determine what tactics are used. If the accent is on tight play, it means that a team's scrummaging and the line-out work are superior to those of their opponents. If a team makes use of general play, it means that it has the backs, and especially the wings, for it. If a side concentrates on broken play, it means that the team's scrum half and inside backs are good attacking players, or that it is capable of tactical moves which could lead to broken play. Tactical kicks could be used to bring about loose play. A team may also decide not to pick up loose balls but to concentrate instead on mauls because it has good loose forwards for the task. A tactic consists of making full and correct use of your strength in one or other type of play. Your strength can, moreover, be enhanced by tactical moves. It also means that you can depart from the usual and come to light with the unexpected. Tactics provide spice and adventure to the game, rounding off everything, and thus forming the roof of the Rugby structure.

The Skills
A player's abilities are judged on his performance in the plays of the game. He may be judged to be playing well, or below standard, or even to be playing poorly. He is assessed on whether he pushes only in the scrum, or whether he is too weak for scrummaging; or if he does not jump high enough in the line-out; or if he is stationary in a ruck; or if he is incapable of taking a gap or if he permits his opponent to slip past him; or if his kicking is ineffective, or if his handling is not up to standard.

When these and similar pronouncements are made, something more than the plays of fundamental principles are involved. We do not study how the player masters the basic principles or the plays, but how he copes in what he *has* to do in these. The individual is merely a link in those plays or fundamental principles. This again supposes that we expect certain things of him, certain capabilities. We call most of these capabilities "skills". This is the term used for expressing the player's capabilities of performing, well or badly, in the plays, i.e. his genius, his capabilities, his effectiveness, or whatever else we wish to call it.

Each fundamental principle has its own skill:

Scrummage:	pushing.	*Handling:*	*catching and passing.*
Line-out:	jumping.	*Defence:*	tackling.
Ruck:	pushing and shoving.	*Kicking:*	kick.
Attack:	push-off or leg-thrust.		

Skill consists of movements. To execute these movements correctly, many things are required, but it is most important that they be acquired and *correctly* acquired. It is quite true that some players can apparently perform these complex movements in a natural way and do them well and correctly. But other players are less successful; the fact remains that every player must acquire skills which do not come naturally. Somewhere and at some time players must have first seen and imitated skills, very often as children, when imitation is spontaneous. Even in these cases it is essential for them to learn how a particular skill is executed and the correct way to execute it. This will help them to analyse and rectify the mistakes they make.

One can, as has been said, easily acquire skill by observing an expert. Hence the value of demonstration, in which a mental picture is formed and imitated. This is one of the best ways of teaching young boys how to acquire skills.

The complex action which we call a skill requires what is known as control which, in turn, contains elements of power, reaction time, motor time, coordination, balance, accuracy, etc. Control is a neuro-muscular action. It is something which one either has or does not have. By exercising the elements of control repeatedly, one will improve the action up to the limit of one's potential.

Using the elements in the correct proportions for the task can be likened to the baking of a cake. If the ingredients are correct, the cake is a success – but the mixture, without the correct oven temperature and the time required for baking, is not a cake. Skills, likewise, require both the correct mixture and its preparation. The correct proportion of the controlling elements forms the basis, and the application of these elements becomes the determining factor which leads to a skill.

The controlling elements in their correct proportion are the nucleus, or the focal point of the game. The movements or adaptations leading to this focal movement are the preparatory or the satellitic. Each skill therefore consists of movement, of which some is the focal movement, and some permit the focal movement to come into its own. Neither of these aspects can be neglected, but the focal movement must first be perfected before the entire action itself can succeed in all situations. This focal movement is aimed at what is called technique, and the way in which a player carries out the entire action is known as his style. It is doubtful whether the focal movement can be performed in more than one way, but this can vary from person to person without being detrimental to skill.

In order to be able to control a skill, one should repeat it frequently. This is because at the outset many muscles are used which are not involved in the skill, and because muscles which are involved are used either too much or too little. By means of repetition, however, one acquires the knack of using only those muscles required for the skill and only to the extent that they are needed. This means that relaxation of different muscles takes place at different times. Thus techniques must be practised repeatedly until differentiated relaxation has been attained.

It is easy to have command over control and technique if no opponent is there to challenge them. If however an opponent is involved, the movements must be performed in a specific space and period and with the necessary strength.

Even the best technique will not amount to much if wrongly executed. To allow the focal movements to come into their own, the three requisites mentioned above must be kept in mind while acquiring the skill. First, the satellitic movements must not be neglected; in Rugby they are used to apply the focal movements in the fundamental principles or plays. Both satellitic and focal movements are needed, and must be practised regularly. When scrummaging, all the bent joints are fully or partially stretched to the extent required. Here I stress that the focal movement is represented by technique, and the satellitic movement by the way in which we pack down or stand.

The focal movement of pushing will not amount to much if the player does not bind or binds weakly. Nor will pushing amount to much if the player's stance is incorrect, or if he is pushing too late or too soon. All these are satellitic movements. Likewise it will not help the line-out jumper if he does not turn his body after catching the ball, or if he does not jerk his arms down forcibly, or if he does not land with his feet apart and in a bent position. In addition, he will need help from his fellow-players, which we call consolidation. The latter, too, is a form of satellitic movement.

In a ruck a player's shoving will be of little avail if he does not apply it at the correct place, or if he steps on the ball, or if he is upright, or if he does not bind, or if he goes in with his back first.

No matter how good a player's leg-thrust or push-off is, if he fails to straighten, the focal movement will be squandered. The same applies to a player who catches a ball while his attention is fixed on his opponent instead of on the ball. He is then performing some kind of a satellitic movement which is incorrect. A player may be famed for his tackling prowess, but should he come up incorrectly for defence or with his eyes closed, he will lose his reputation as a tackler. A player may have a wonderful kick, but if he kicks too late or his run-up is wrong, his kicks will be valueless to his team. These examples indicate the importance of satellitic movements.

Skill building consists of acquiring the technique and of making the muscles which are involved in it attain their object. In order to apply the satellitic movements correctly, we practice rounding off of skills in sections, with backs and forwards separated for tight play and general play. However, skills are executed in particular situations, and the problem of employing them to the best purpose in different situations demands sound judgment or instinct – i.e psychometric actions.

Players must, therefore, be taught how to act in certain circumstances and how to apply their skills. This we call application of skill.

In order to develop the skills of Rugby to the full, we require the following: skill building to achieve technique, which represents, in the main, focal movements; a knowledge of exercises to develop the power for their execution; the ability to cope adequately with time and space; the rounding off of skills in order to use the satellitic movements, either in a section exercise or against fellow-players in situations which are not entirely match situations. This is best done by means of section exercises or team exercises; or the application of skills in order to sum up play situations and to act correctly when play takes place in games or in practice matches. If practice for the rounding off of skills is done in sections, it is assumed that players have already attained their peak in skills, i.e. that they are fit as regards their personal skills. Skill fitness presupposes that they know the technique and have completed skill building.

As soon as the rounding off of skills in sections has been done, the players are ready for the next step. They are therefore fit as far as the fundamental and principal functions are concerned because the basic principles are rounded off in sections. Skill fitness is also known as motor fitness.

Physical exercises

Fitness is the foundation of the Rugby structure and of the game. Without it the entire building must collapse. And when we speak of fitness we mean physical fitness, whose component parts of power, stamina and speed are sufficiently developed to comply with the demands of the game. It also means that the body is adequately fit to continue with the next step of skill building in the practice programme without fear of injury when the skills are practised explosively.

Rugby is a game of power. It is a game in which power plays a major part in scrummaging, rucking, and mauls, even in line-outs and push-offs and tackles. Without the required strength a player had better not even aspire to become a forward. A back can still rely on agility and speed, but he will soon realise that power helps him to play better and that his chances of injury are minimised.

Because Rugby is a power game, it is also said that "Rugby is a man's game." This means that power must be correctly applied. A player must also be hard, because he is expected to play against hard men and he must make contact with hardness. A player will experience bumps and jolts, and he will fall or be flung aside like a rag. Players will fall on him and even tread on him. Elbows, knees, or even hard heads will strike him without pity, and if the player has a faint heart these things will hurt him and even frighten him. Rugby is a game for a man with a stout heart. A faint heart cannot be accommodated.

Thus we begin with power exercises which will, at the same time, contribute towards hardness. Power is necessary not only for acquiring skill in Rugby, but also for the prevention of injuries. As part of skill, power prevents injuries because, in power training, attention is paid to all the muscles which cause the joints in the body to function. It must be borne in mind that in Rugby the joints tend to meet the greatest strain. Exercises for the following joints have been devised: the feet, ankles, knees, hips, back, shoulders, neck, pectoral girdle (clavicle, scapula), elbows, wrists and hands.

To gain specific power for the execution of specific skills, the muscles must be harnessed in the same way – and preferably more comprehensively – as they would for their tasks in a match. Consequently, the exercises should have a relationship with the skills for which power exercises are carried out. If the exercises are identical with the skills, so much the better. If exercises for general power are done the entire body is harnessed for a task, and these exercises need not have any relationship with the tasks that will be demanded of a player in Rugby. Overall power or strength is nevertheless required. In the same way that general and specific power must be built, general and specific stamina and speed must also be built. If a player has general stamina he will be able to run for miles without getting unduly tired. If, however, he has only stamina power, he will soon tire if he has to start doing side-steps, or start jumping or pushing. If a player has specific stamina, he will be able not only to run for miles, but his skills can also be practised at intervals and he will still recover quickly if he becomes tired. Nor will he be stiff the following day. The time taken to recover when tired determines how much stamina a player has.

Stamina also includes muscle stamina. At the centre of general and specific stamina are the heart, lungs and blood-vessels. By practising exercises similar to those on the field, muscles provides muscle stamina to a player. These can be used in some exercises for acquiring differentiated relaxation. To acquire power, we work with a maximum effort – or near-maximum effort – and with repeated exercises, as is done for improving muscle stamina.

When referring to general speed, we refer to the fact that a player runs as fast as he can, i.e. as fast as his capabilities will allow him. To possess speed he should practice sprinting regularly. However, to possess specific speed, a player must be able to stop in his tracks, turn around quickly, take off quickly, and push-off at full speed.

We repeat: to be physically fit is to have, next to power, sufficient stamina and speed to acquire skill before the skills themselves are practised. If the skills have been acquired, the player is sufficiently fit to start practising the fundamental principles. If he has made sufficient progress with the fundamental principles to practise the plays he is fit in the fundamental principles. If he has mastered the plays, if he is fit, and if he can apply the laws while playing, apply tactics and do justice to matches, he is match-fit.

The means for acquiring these kinds of fitness consist of:

Physical fitness: physical exercises, stamina exercises and speed exercises.
Skill fitness: technique exercises and skill building exercises.
Fitness in the fundamental principles: rounding off of skills by means of team exercises.
Play fitness: rounding off of skills and application of skills by means of two teams practising every aspect of the game, thus encountering every type of situation to be found in a game.
Match fitness: further skill application as it would be encountered in a match and in which the plays of the game flow into one another in a natural way.

Methods
The term "exercises" should not be used when we come to the rounding off of skills and to the application of skills, because by then we are dealing with training. When doing exercises we are building. First of all we build the body, and so speak of physical exercises. After this we build the body for the execution of skills and for speed and stamina. We can then still speak of physical exercises, but to give skills their specific place in our programme, we use the term "skill building exercises". Under this heading we also have "technique exercises".

After these the built-up body is prepared for executing the skills in order to do good work. We now speak of rounding off of skills or training – the skills are brushed up in relation to their functions in the game. We are now not so much concerned with the preparation of the body (in physical exercises and in skill building) as with the execution, performance and achievement in a team in which the individual merges into the whole, even if he plays an important part in the team effort. We now speak of "rounding off" or "training". Rounding off or training is also used in the plays if these are practised separately or in pairs. Training consists of drill or repetition. The play in the game is repeated by a section or by the entire team until it has been completely mastered.

Only if we wish to see whether all the preparations are satisfactory and we prepare the players to carry on by themselves – as they will have to do in matches – do we speak of practice matches. By this time the coach evaluates on the touchline, while the referee controls the match and the captain leads his team. These practice matches must not be used in excess or as a means of developing the types of fitness we have already described. To get to the top of a tree one has to start at the bottom, and this is more or less what has been attained by the players. For this reason their practice matches should be considered as only a small part of their programme; they are a means for testing how the physical exercises, the skill exercises and training have progressed, and to determine whether they have produced the desired results or whether adjustments are still required. Mistakes occurring in practice matches are rectified by means of the correct remedy, be it rounding off of skills, skill building, physical exercises, the building of stamina, etc.

It will be seen that the expression "practice matches" is used in a different sense to current usage.

The practice programme
Provision is made in a practice programme for physical exercises, all types of skill exercises, and for practice matches. Not one of these or their sub-sections should be omitted or neglected. Progress in one of these exercises will indicate if the players are ready for the next exercise. A roster should be used for this purpose. Players must be afforded time to practise one exercise after the other until they are match-fit. All the exercises, however, should be included, i.e. physical exercises, skill exercises, and practice matches.

THE PLAYER

The importance of the player
Why do so many players stop playing Rugby? Because they no longer feel important; because they do not find something in Rugby which gratifies their ego. Why do so many players play halfheartedly or practise irregularly or listlessly? Because they do not think that an important task has been entrusted to them.

What is the solution? Make each player, whoever he may be, feel important and make him feel he is doing an important job when he plays for a team. There was a time when practically every man in South Africa played Rugby, when playing the game meant something, when you were important if you played Rugby, and when you were performing an important job in doing so.

Today things have changed. We must nurture Rugby, and this can be done only if we take care of each and every player as if he were the most valued member of the club.

How is this to be achieved when such a player plays in the lower grades, as a member of a side already stigmatised as an inferior team? How can such a player feel important, and how can he be aware that he is playing an important part, if he knows full well that there are others above him playing a more important role? How can such a player hold forth on Rugby when others are in a better position to do so? And how can he boast of his tries if they are scored in a less important match?

There are so many instances in life where persons drop out or feel inferior that we must do everything in our power to prevent this in Rugby. But as long as we continue to grade players in a club according to teams, we shall drive them away. If a club can guarantee that it gives full attention to every player in every team along with good coaching, good facilities, competent referees and touch judges, good balls, good support and good publicity, it will retain its players.

But how many clubs achieve this?

We suggest that the grading system be abolished, except for top teams and, in big clubs, for first and second teams. We propose furthermore that in its place a system be applied which will make practically every player a first-team player. To bring this about, we suggest that players be divided into groups or sections which have other common interests besides Rugby.

In schools the division can take the form of classes, residential areas, hostels, etc.; or the division can be artificial, as was the case at my school, when those of us who were not in the school team were divided into the Rogues and the Rascals. We were proud of being a Rogue or a Rascal – and did our numbers increase!

In athletics they use colours. At Stellenbosch we use residences. People who work together, live together or share something in common, be it colours or a name, are more closely knit in small groups than in the name of a club or a town to which everyone can belong. I am going to describe our system at Stellenbosch to indicate what has been achieved by doing away with the old grading system and to suggest what might be done elsewhere.

At Stellenbosch we have a first team, a second team (above 21 years) and a "young" team (under 21) playing in the competitions. After them we have 11 College clubs. The first teams of these 11 clubs consist of 165 players. And every player has a chance of playing in the second team or in the "young" team. Had we graded these 165 players, some of them would have played in our 14th team, some in the 13th, 12th, etc. But would they still have played? They certainly did not play when we were still applying the grading system. Sometimes we even had to cancel second-team matches.

Each residential club, however, still has a second team, and for those players the first team is just around the corner. Making the first team is a tremendous honour in a place where everybody knows and is interested in each other.

Consequently we have another 165 players who feel important and are doing an important job for their college, i.e. $(2 \times 165) + (3 \times 15)$ players are content – 375 players. If we were applying the grading system, some of them would have turned out for the 25th team! But one problem now arises: playing for the third team of a big college is not too bad, but it is no longer an honour in the case of the smaller college, so we also have to look after such players. One of these 11 residential clubs is comprised of "oppidans". They have now divided their numbers according to boardinghouses or college areas and thereby keep an additional 16–18 teams satisfied. Residential clubs, on the other hand, divide their residences into sections and players turn out for their section's first team, so that each player is really a somebody in a smaller group. With this system we have between 60–80 teams – I do not know how many there are, and the under-19s are not even included.

Neither are the non-members that we allow to play. These are players who cannot or do not want to practise but nevertheless wish to play Rugby. Matches are arranged for them too, on the system of residences. The laws are simple: they play 10 minutes a side in any kind of rig-out, even barefooted should they prefer it. The match is over before they are tired. But they have become a part of Rugby, are members of a club and have satisfied their appetite for the game. Many of them become members of the club and among them are many talented players who soon get promotion. Some of them have even made our top teams.

Of course the system has its disadvantages. If things are going badly with the second team, it is no honour to be playing for it and a player would prefer playing for the first team of his college. In such a case discipline is required. A player who cannot or will not play for the second team should not be playing at all. A solution might be to give the college clubs representation on the central committee. The club is then theirs and they will not "hide" or keep players away.

This is what we have done, and it works. By organising such groups, or their colleges, into clubs, more people become involved in the game as chairmen, secretaries, vice-presidents, etc. In this way Rugby gains. Referees are given more opportunities for handling matches, and selectors of the central club are more important because they have to select the best players.

Another important point: to ask a player in a lower team nowadays to play on a Saturday is tantamount to asking him to play during his holidays. And this he has to do from March to September! This is expecting too much from many a first-team player, so how can we demand it of a player who already feels inferior but has other interests, or wishes to visit friends or relax?

For many reasons we arrange for these teams to play their matches during the week, generally on Friday afternoons, thus keeping their weekends free.

Why is this system not more widespread? Because people cling to the things they know, and because there are those who are not prepared to work, or are in fear of their positions. Fortunately there are also people who *are* prepared to work. Let us hope that their influence spreads everywhere, so that social Rugby will automatically be absorbed by these groups. Indeed, social Rugby groups could be taken over, as they are, by clubs.

We must not, however, suppress social Rugby altogether. Its existence demonstrates that there are still many people who wish to play Rugby, but because they fail to get what they want from a club, they look for it among their own groups. These people clearly indicate that the group system, or hostel system, works.

From the point of view of schools, this means that most players play during the week, so that considerable expense in connection with transport and jerseys is saved, and parents can have their children at home during the weekend, and teachers can relax. Only the school's first team or age group participates in competitions while the others "fight" it out among themselves. Playing for the first team will then be a greater honour than is the case today. If neighbouring schools also apply such a system, winning teams may tackle each other on a particular day – and make an occasion of it.

Thus all our players are made to feel important, because *the more important they feel* the harder they will practise – the harder they will strive, and the more they will sacrifice. Both club spirit and team spirit will be improved, and the easier they will play together on or off the field.

The player's place in the game
The functions of forwards and backs are here discussed as units in the game, and the function of every player in these units.

We are so accustomed to speaking of winning and losing that we often forget what the separate functions of the backs and forwards actually are. Rugby is often described as a team game, so that the accent is placed on the team without allocating the rightful place to its two separate units.

It is true that Rugby is a team game, but the forwards and the backs have divergent places, and although it is the team which wins or loses a match, it is actually one of these units which lays the foundation for a victory or has to take the blame for a defeat. It seldom happens that the entire team really plays together, although the forwards must battle for possession and the backs must use this possession. Actually, a team plays together only when both forwards and backs have won their separate "battles". The aim of a team should therefore be to gain the upper hand both in the forwards and the backs so that the two can link up, or so that both can act in combined movements. When this happens we see the finest Rugby that one can see, and tries come automatically.

To win in the forwards and backs and develop combined play, the forwards must first get the upper hand in the tight play, the scrum and line-out, as well as in the loose, the ruck and the maul. Similarly, the backs must know what is involved in their own clash against opposing backs.

Each player has his position and duties and he must know what is expected of him in his position. What follows is an attempt to describe the aims of the forward play and back play, and thereafter the function of each player or position in the game.

The forward battle
Hypothesis A
1. If the forwards win the battle against the forwards of the opposing team, their team is victorious as a rule.

2. (a) If the tight forwards concede victory to the tight forwards of the opposing team, the loose forwards are also defeated. In other words, a pack defeated in the tight play is also beaten in the loose – in rucks and mauls and in the cross-defence of the loose forwards. Again, if the tight forwards of a pack are superior, they and their loose forwards also win the loose, while their loose forwards keep on obstructing the opposing team's backs.
   (b) No matter how good the front row of a pack of forwards may be, the locks are also defeated if that front row is outplayed by its opponents, in which case the line-outs are lost as well.
   (c) If one of the front-row forwards fails against his opponent, the whole pack loses.
3. If a pack of forwards is defeated, their backs will have forwards of the opposing team in the path of their attack. In other words, if a pack of forwards is superior, then their backs have more often than not to contend only with backs.
4. Even if a pack gains possession, but it is bad possession, they lose the battle for their backs. Bad possession is, *inter alia*, a ball coming from a scrum or a line-out in a slovenly way.
5. If forwards are forced back on to their heels in a scrummage, not only are they defeated, but their backs are also forced back and consequently cannot gain the upper hand in their part of the game.

Hypothesis B
Where do the forwards win? In the scrummage. But this does not only mean good possession and that the ball on a team's put-in – and a number of tightheads – is won. It also means that the battle of shoving-power is won and leads to bad possession for their opponents, who are, as we have said, forced on to their heels and become fatigued. This, in turn, results in a fatigued pack arriving last in the loose, because a pack which sags in a scrum cannot break up quickly. Nor can they jump well in the line-outs, and loose forwards, assigned to take on defence, are bound to fail. This means that supremacy gained in shoving in the scrum yields results in the loose, in line-outs and in defence. Hence the scrum is always the place where the battle between the forwards is decided.

Hypothesis C
How do the forwards win?
1. If a pack is victorious, it is mainly the five tight forwards who bring this about. They accomplish supremacy in shoving-power. But momentum comes in the first place from the lock forwards. Only when they have won the shoving contest can the props put more force into the momentum of the pack. The loose forwards obviously contribute their share, but the flankers are on the extremities of the scrummage and shove with one shoulder behind one prop.
   The lock forwards are in the middle of the scrummage, forming its nucleus. As such they push against the entire front row. Should a pack thus lose the shoving contest, all other things being equal, the battle is lost by the lock

forwards; and if we say that the forwards are beaten, we really mean that the lock forwards have lost.

The shoving-power of the lock forwards may, however, be better than that of their opponents, but their front row may fail in acting as conductors and complements of this power. Props must therefore be able to hold their own, have powerful spines and necks, and they must not swing out. Their principal aim is to provide a platform for the locks to shove; their second task is to pour power into the shove-stream supplied by their locks. The flankers help the lock forwards by ensuring the complementary streams along the sides of the scrummage, while the number eight helps the lock forwards in supplying the main shove-stream. By their contribution to the shove-stream, the flank forwards simultaneously help the props in front of them to assist the hooker with his hooking, and the number eight helps the lock forwards to be straight *after* the shove, so that they are locked with concomitant advantages.

(N.B. Pushing-power starts with leaning-power, and the transition stage between lean and shove is the heave.)

2. Forwards win or lose in the line-out, but even line-out work suffers if the shoving-power contest is lost. Good mauling can also soften opponents, but this happens very seldom in comparison with the number of scrummages in a match. Good consolidation by a pack of forwards, who occasionally hold the ball before letting it out, also soften the opponents as they struggle in vain to get at the ball.

3. Forwards also win or lose in the loose, but even here victory depends on supremacy in the scrums and on the softening process by the pack winning the shoving-power contest.

4. Forwards also lose when the loose forwards are unable to execute their defensive tasks, as when flankers are compelled to work too hard so that they cannot, for example, harass the opposing scrum half if he dawdles or makes mistakes; or they cannot stop him from breaking or stop him before he gains advantage; or if the number eight, for the same reason, cannot harass the opposing fly half or keep his breaks in check, partially or completely; or if he (the number eight) fails to plug all the gaps.

(N.B. Softening in the scrums, in the first instance, supported by softening in the line-outs and loose play, should be the aim of forwards.)

Policy with regard to forward play

The policy of forward play is to soften the opposing pack of forwards in the scrummage by means of better shoving-power, which will not only nullify the opposing backs' play in the loose, in the line-out and in defence, but will also soften them further by ensuring that the opposing forwards are not in the way of their own backs.

Forwards are like a boxer in a ring taking on an opponent who *must* be beaten: they *must* look upon their opposing forwards as opponents who *must* be beaten. The hard struggle in the scrummages is felt in the line-outs, in the loose, and in defence, where the struggle is continued.

The place of the individual forward in the forward battle
All forwards must be strong.
All forwards must possess leaning power and shoving power.
All forwards must be able to drive.
All forwards must be able to pile into the ruck.

Props and hooker
The scrum
1. Good conductors or complements of weight. This also applies to the hooker.
2. Good shovers at the precise moment when their locks are supplying shoving-power, so that they not only push away their opponents, but also enable themselves to break up quickly for the loose play. The same applies to the hooker.
3. Support for the hooker. He must have a fast strike.

The line-out
After doing their job in the scrummage, they must be good at consolidating and one of them must be able to start a "churning" movement in the front of the line-out. Should the opponents obtain possession, they must break up their consolidation or make it ineffective. The hooker becomes one flanker of the line-out and the same is expected of him as of a flank forward in respect of loose play.

Loose play
After completing their tasks in the scrum and line-out they must be good in loose play. They must see to it that they arrive at loose play before the opposing fron-row forwards. In this way they ensure that the time-gap between their loose forwards and themselves is just sufficient for them to continue the spade-work of their loose forwards. They must be able to drive while the loose forwards are still moving forward with the ball, and they must push their loose forwards ahead when a loose scrum is formed in order to get over the ball or to gain the advantage in a maul.

The lock forwards
The scrum
They must be powerful pushers – the best in the pack – and must still be moving forward, thereby softening their opponents and helping themselves as the scrum breaks up. Apart from being the best shovers in every scrum, they must also be the best jumpers or get the better of a superior jumper by pulling him through the line-out, getting hold of his arms on the way down, knocking the ball from his hands, etc.

(N.B. Props can straighten their legs for shoving only when their locks' shove is more powerful than that of their opponents.)

Loose play
After performing their duty in the scrum and line-out they must contribute to good play in the loose by seeing to it that they arrive at the loose play before

the opposing locks. By so doing they ensure that the time between themselves arriving, and their loose forwards arriving, is just sufficient for them to carry on the spadework of their loose forwards. Obviously they must know how to do it, and this means they must be able to drive while the other forwards are still moving ahead with the ball. They must also push their loose forwards ahead if a ruck ensues, in order to get over the ball or gain the advantage from a maul.

The flankers and number eight
The scrum
The flankers see to it that the sides of the shove-stream, initiated by the lock forwards, are maintained. In this way they assist their props with the hooking (who, in their turn, have to assist the hooker) while at the same time they attempt to dominate the loose game. The number eight helps the locks in supplying the shove-stream, which will result in the locks being straight after the shove.

Should the opposing team gain possession, the loose forwards must exploit any mistake made by the opposing scrum half and see to it that he does not break or make any progress with his breaks. It is the special task of the left (loose-head) flank-forward to stop the scrum half. The tight-head flanker must not only harass the opposing scrum half, but he must neutralise the fly half from the inside, or – should the fly half make mistakes – he must capitalise on them. The number eight covers, in particular, his loose-head flanker from breaks by the scrum half. He also has to cover both sides of the scrum for mistakes and breaks by the fly half, and cover the entire back-line from inside gap to inside gap. He covers, as well, his own back-line in order to rectify mistakes, or to be on hand when they run into trouble.

Line-outs
They disrupt their opponents' line-outs by ending them as soon as possible, by getting possession of the opponents' bad balls, and even by making the opponents' good balls look bad. One of the flankers must be able to do line-out work; both must be able to consolidate, and the eighth man must be able to do line-out work at the back for "peeling off". Should the back-line of the opposing team gain possession, the loose forwards must be up with the ball as far as possible so as to exploit mistakes, or nullify breaks, especially inside breaks.

Loose game
They must arrive at loose play before their opponents and be able to pick up loose balls and either pass or drive with the ball. If it is impossible to do either and a loose scrummage is formed, they must get over the ball and move ahead at once. If they fail to get over the ball or over a player lying on the ball, they must push and keep on pushing so that their tight forwards can "jock in"* to

---

* "Jock in" is an idiosyncratic expression used by the late Mr Markotter, *doyen* of South African Rugby coaches. His expression is preferable to colloquialisms such as "climb in" or "get stuck in".

form a moving basis. If it is impossible to drive and there is a maul, they must see to it that the ball, when in their possession, is on their side of the maul and that they drive forward. If an opponent, however, has the ball, they must force him onto their side of the maul or see to it that he is grounded.

General
They must be good tacklers.
They must have skilful hands and feet.
They must be able to fill other berths in case a back-line player is injured or is out of position, or if a forward is injured.
One or all of them must be able to fill a berth in the back-line or play in other positions in the scrummage.

The Battle of the Backs
Hypothesis A
1. Backs lose if they fail to round off what has been started by the forwards and, in consequence, do not help their forwards. Stated in another way: back-line players who make the fewest mistakes – and especially mistakes behind their forwards – win the battle. Backs win if they take care that their forwards advance or advance more frequently than retreat. They also win if they help their forwards in their "conflict", especially if this can include linking with the forwards to form a combined attacking front. This happens if the backs succeed in launching an attack which will take them beyond, or as near as possible to, the advantage line.
2. Backs lose when they play into the hands of their opponents, and this can happen if they are concerned only with doing the orthodox. Their opponents will then know exactly what they are going to do. Stated in another way: backs win if they sow uncertainty among opposing backs and if they can disrupt movements by their opponents.
3. Backs who can close all the gaps and who can render their opposing numbers harmless behind the forwards must win.

Hypothesis B
By what means do backs win? By handling (the basis of everything they do)-
1. In order to cause uncertainty amongst their opposing backs, thereby disrupting their opponents' line of defence and methods of attack, i.e. preventing the backs from coming up straight and fast, causing them to falter in defence and not being able to close the gaps.
2. In order to take care that their own defensive line is adequate and that it cannot be disrupted.
3. In order to create sufficient space or elbow-room for manoeuvring and thereby affording time for action to every back-line player.
4. To increase the softening-up process of the opposing forwards by striking where it is least expected.
5. By taking the inside gap to link up with the forwards; i.e. by striking deeply.

To sum up: to be in possession of all the weapons of attack, using handling as a basis, in order to disrupt the opposing backs.

Hypothesis C
How do they achieve their object?
1. Uncertainty among the opposing backs causes disruption of their line of defence, and this uncertainty spreads when they do not know the following:
   (a) Which side of the field – blind or open – is to be used.
   (b) Which player – the blind-side wing, the full back, the number eight – besides the usual back-line players – is being used.
   (c) Which method of attack – usual breaks, tactical movements or tactical kicks – is to be employed.
2. Vacant areas occur behind a back-line and in front of the full back and are most effectively used at their extremities, on the wings. These gaps are closed mainly by the wings themselves, the full back, the number eight and the flank-forward on whose side the movement is launched, and by the back-line itself. The number eight and flanker see to the open side, the wings see to the touch area and the section immediately in front of them, the full back to the rear section, and the back-line to the front section. The forwards must force their opponents' number eight and flanker to work harder than they are accustomed to or than they are fit enough for, so that they cannot adequately close the gaps or prevent them being widened. The open-side wing and the back-line cannot do their share if they have to come up fast – they must hang back – and the blind-side wing cannot do his share if he has to cover-defend. The open-side wing and the back-line wait for the opposing fly half to pass before actually enlarging the vacant area by coming up in defence, and when the inside centre gets the ball the area is further enlarged. In order to force them to come up faster, either the fly half or the inside centre may use the dummy pass before short-punting, which includes the grubber kick and stab kick. The blind-side wing and the full back also wait to see whether the fly half is going to pass the ball before they start covering. A dummy pass by the fly half, followed by a hooked kick, will cause the vacant area on the blind side to enlarge. In the case of a midfield scrum, both vacant areas are in effect blind-side vacant areas, but the above principles are still valid.
3. Sufficient space for movements.
   (a) This is accomplished by judiciously running, with and without the ball, running before receiving the pass, running when once the ball has been received, and running when it must be passed. Every yard taken without the ball means a yard closer to an approaching opponent, and every yard run with the ball means the same. These yards must be confined to a minimum, without neglecting (b) below.
   (b) Every back-line player must draw his opponent and as many other defenders as possible. This is achieved by enticing a defender to the player carrying the ball in such a manner that he is eliminated after the pass, i.e. he is unable to function in cover-defence.
   (c) By crisp passing. This includes:
      (i) To go and "meet" the ball with the hands – to "fetch" the ball – and letting it go through the hands on its way to the next player in one movement.

(ii) Passing the ball at the correct height.
   (iii) Passing the ball in front of the receiver, not directly at him.
4. "Striking deep" means stretching out the opposing back-line so that the gaps in their line of defence, which will be small initially, will be extended. This extension is the more effective the further it progresses from tight play. Consequently the extra man in the back-line is effective, as are the outswing pass, long passes, and the so-called "circumnavigation" when one or more of the back-line players receives the ball on the outside of the wing. By taking or manipulating the outside gap and playing to the outside, play is transferred further away from the forwards, compelling them to cover a greater distance.
5. Linking up with the forwards entails taking the inside gap, or, should this fail, running into the tackle there.
   (N.B. Breaking by means of taking the inside gap or the outside gap and drawing your man, straightening the line remains the basis of attack and handling is the hub. If the inside gap has been put to the test a few times, the outside gap will widen because uncertainty will prevail amongst the defenders.)

Policy of back play
By means of variable play, sow uncertainty amongst the opposing back-line players.
By disrupting their line of defence and methods of defence, force gaps.
By proceeding near to the line of advantage, which will assist the forwards to link up with them.
By seeing to it that the plan does not rebound on them.
   (N.B. Disrupting the opposing back-line players means what softening-up means to the forwards.)

The function of each individual back-line player in the back-line battle
Every back-line player must be able to break with power or with speed.
Every back-line player must be able to run into a tackle without losing the ball, and if he lands on the ground, he must see to it that the ball is on his team's side.
Every back-line player must be able to straighten the line and keep it straight, both on attack and defence.
Every back-line player must be skilful with his hands and feet in any situation. He must be skilful in punting, kicking for touch, and grubber kicking.
Every back-line player must be able to use his speed correctly.

The scrum half
1. He must have quick and accurate hands to give a fast and accurate pass from any kind of situation which may arise from the loose exchanges or set pieces.
2. He must be able to break to link with his forwards – and sometimes with his backs – and ensure that they take play forward. His breaks should include both opportunistic breaks and forced breaks. In this way he must keep focussing the attention of the opposing loose forwards on himself, thereby keeping them away from his backs.

3. He must be able to cover and defend, which means that he must be able to kick defensively with either foot from any situation. He must be able to harass not only his counterpart and exploit mistakes made by him, but the opposing fly half as well.
4. He must arrive as soon as possible at the loose play, to be in a position to act according to its demands.

The fly half
1. He must keep the opposing team guessing so that they do not know from which side of the scrum attacks are to be launched, or whether he is going to break, pass, or employ tactical kicks. He is therefore the general in the battle; he is the tactician who, apart from his own game, will have a share in most of the other tactical moves.
2. He lays the foundation for time and space for his backs by his positioning, by running with and without the ball, by his quick hands, and by the way he draws not only his opposite number, but also all the defensive streams from the scrum.
3. He must be able to break – opportunistic and forced breaks – for which he needs to be agile and fast, especially quick off the mark. He must be able to launch his forwards or his backs from his breaks.
4. He must be able to spot weaknesses in his opponents' line of defence and see to it that vacant spots or boxes are created or enlarged.
5. He must be able to defend and cover-defend. He therefore dictates the game by means of his hands and feet, his breaks, and his unpredictable play.

Centres
1. They must be able to take inside and outside gaps and send their wings and their forwards away. They must therefore possess a dangerous method of breaking, preferably by means of a side-step, and they must be able to execute opportunistic or forced breaks.
2. They must help to create vacant spots or boxes and use them themselves.
3. They continue the work of their fly half in straightening the line, creating time and space, and causing uncertainty by their varied play and tactical moves, which include stretching out the defence and "playing concertina". They dictate whether the attack is to be launched deep or down the centre, with or without the use of tactical movements in which the distances of the passes to them and from them vary.
4. They must never run obliquely except when tactical moves are initiated.
5. They must be able to defend.

The wings
1. They must round off, partially or completely, back-line movements which are well and correctly executed. If they have time and space, and if the defence-streams have been drawn on the inside players, they must make progress with the ball; and if they cannot get past their opponent, they must at least get round him partially or make a dent in the defence.
2. A distinguished kind of break must be founded on speed, usually a swerve,

but often a side-step. They must be able to execute this break either on the inside or outside.
3. Their specialised play includes throwing the ball in accurately at line-outs, good cover-defence across the entire field with the full back and by cross-kicking. Their covering includes vacant spots (boxes) on the blind side and the field side.

The full back
His prime needs are:
1. Faultless handling of all kinds of flight-balls and grubbers.
2. Good positional play for dealing with kicks and breaks.
3. The capability of turning defence into attack and linking up with the back line on the attack.
4. Solid defence.

Additional qualifications
The abovementioned qualifications expected of players in their positions can serve as a guideline for the selection of teams. It can happen that a tight forward has at his disposal a first-rate attribute such as, for instance, the gift of running exceptionally well with the ball, or being a good place-kicker. Such excellent qualities then become an additional qualification, making him a preferable choice to another player in the same position. If their qualifications are equal in every other respect, or if a team particularly requires such an admirable qualification, the player who has this attribute must get preference over a player without these qualifications. Even though such a player may be somewhat weaker than the other, but more valuable on account of this quality, he must be given preference. The same holds good for a player who can play in more than one position; this is also an excellent qualification.

Chapter 2
Set-Pieces

TIGHT PLAY: THE SCRUM

OUR TASK in this chapter is to determine how the shoving-power of eight forwards can be harnessed better and faster than that of their opponents. We want to give the first shove before our opponents. In order to do this we must be stronger and apply our strength in such a way that all the available strength is used and nothing is lost. There are two important satellitic movements which must be executed in order to achieve this. Without these, full justice cannot be done to the shove. They are: 1. Forwards must bind or pack down correctly; 2. Their stance must be correct.

Binding or packing
Eight forwards are banded together by their arms, necks, shoving direction, and their own power so that they form a unit which will be capable of acting as one. At the same time all unnecessary internal movements must be eliminated. A scrum must be tight, which is why we speak of a tight scrum. It follows that a scrum must not be loose. In this tight unit, however, certain subtle internal movements take place and they are mainly aimed at assisting the hooker in his task and at keeping the scrum stationary. Actually, it is one of these binding elements, the arms, which facilitates these movements. The shove also fits into these movements. Here follows the method of binding as we recommend it:

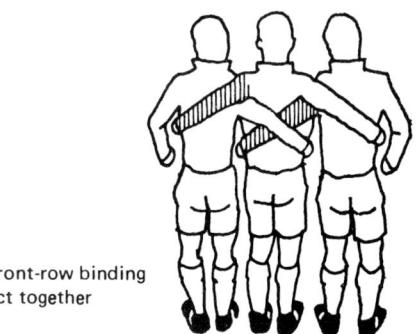

Method of front-row binding
Dark arms act together

The shoulders of the two prop forwards are placed under the hooker's armpits to get his shoulders as far forward as possible. In other words, to get him closer to the ball. The hooker binds over the arms of his props and his hands get a hold under their armpits. This allows him to pull with his arm on the side on which he is hooking, preventing him from pulling his own shoulders down, as he would do should he pack lower than the armpits. The forearm of the tight-head prop is underneath that of his partner because he (the tight-head prop) must also pull when the ball is put in on the loose-head side. This he does to help his hooker with his pivoting movement when hooking.

The hands of the prop forwards' inside arms grasp the hooker's hips because the front row must form a solid unit and any movement between them is thereby reduced to a minimum. The loose-head prop does not pull with his arm, as such action would entail counteracting the pivoting movement needed by the hooker for hooking the ball.

(N.B. Sometimes the hooker binds with his left arm over the arm of his loose-head prop and with the right arm under the tight-head prop's arm in order to swing better when hooking.)

When the scrum has gone down, the opposing props bind with each other and the loose-head prop gets the so-called "inside track", i.e. his left arm is on the inside and his opponent's right arm on the outside when they take hold of each other's jerseys.

Method of second-row (lock-forward and flanks) binding
All four arms pull

The loose-head lock forward's shoulder is placed underneath the armpit of the tight-head lock forward so that the latter's shoulder is pushed forward as far as possible to adapt to the hooker's position. The loose-head forward gets hold of his partner's hip in order to form a solid unit and eliminate any movement between them as far as possible. At the same time, the tight-head lock forward gets hold of his partner as low down as possible without pulling down his inside shoulder in the process. When the scrum has gone down, each lock grasps the crook of the prop forward's hip in front of him with his outside arm. These are the only two arms which join the second row with the first row, and consequently this coupling must be effective. When the ball is put in by the opposing side, that is on the tight-head side, the tight-head lock can place his inside shoulder in the armpit of his partner. This often helps to win tight-heads.

Flankers
They bind with the inside hand on the back of the lock next to them so that they can give an oblique shove. If necessary they can bind completely round the forward next to them. Once the scrum has been formed, they can keep their outside arm completely free; or they can place it on the ground or bind with it on the prop in front of them. The latter, however, leads to a tendency to twist their backs awry.

The number eight
He grasps the outside hips of the lock forwards in front of him once the scrum has been formed.

The part played by the arms
At the moment the shove begins, the hooker pulls with his arm on the hooking side. If it is on the loose-head side, the tight-head prop pulls with his inside arm. The locks pull with both their arms in order to forge themselves into a solid unit and to keep the prop in front of them on their shoulders. The flanks do not pull, and the number eight sees to it that the locks maintain their unity.

The Stance
Object
The object of the correct stance is threefold. First, to ensure that the maximum power of all eight players is used. Second, that all shoving-power is fed through to the point of contact, i.e. where the shoulders of the two packs of forwards come in contact. Third, to leave a passage through which the ball can pass without obstruction.

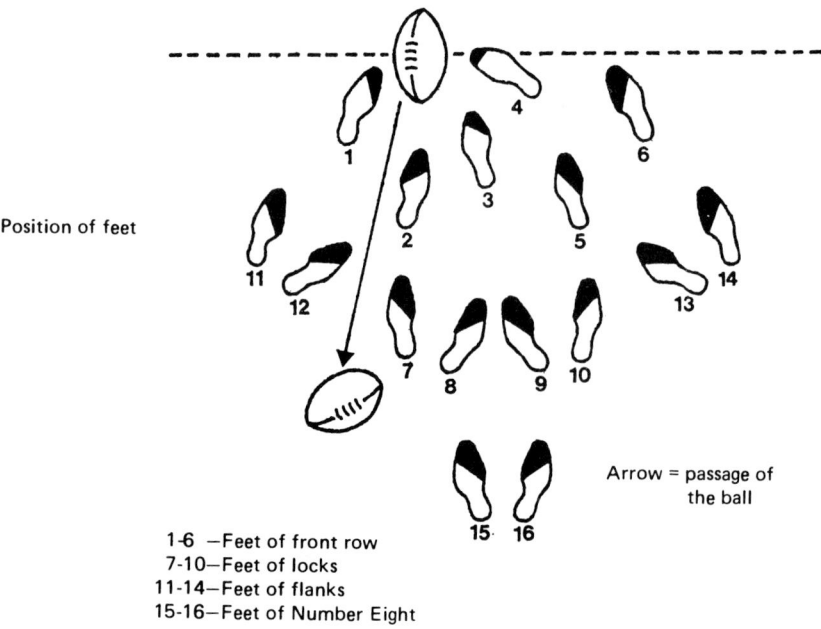

Position of feet

Arrow = passage of the ball

1-6 —Feet of front row
7-10—Feet of locks
11-14—Feet of flanks
15-16—Feet of Number Eight

Body position

Front row — Before pushing / After pushing

Other rows — Before pushing / After pushing

Front row
The feet of the prop-forwards must be placed in such a way that their non-pushing legs come as near to, and as quickly at, the ball as the laws permit, and their pushing legs in such a way that the second row of forwards have a suitable leg to push against. To comply with these two requirements the angle, passing through the body and legs of the front row, must be smaller than that of the rest of the forwards.

A second difference between the front row players and the other forwards in the pack, is that the legs of the former are bent to a greater degree. This gives rise to another difference, viz. the backs of the front row players will be more parallel to the ground than the backs of the other forwards. This, in turn, entails another difference, viz. that the seats of the front row forwards will be raised higher than those of the other forwards. Another difference is that the position of the heads of the front row forwards differs from that of the other five forwards. Whereas all backs, including the necks, must be straight, the front-row forwards must be able to lower their heads without bending their necks. The head is thus bent at the top of the neck. Should they find this impossible, they bend their necks in the usual way and, as part of the shove, they lift their heads. In this way they will see the ball better.

Explanation: for hooking on the loose-head side
The feet of the loose-head prop forward are turned slightly inwards to give the movement of the outside leg more swing inwards; the left foot is in front of

the right foot because the right leg pushes and the left leg blocks the opening of the scrum and even assists with the hooking of the ball. For this reason also, only the point of the foot rests on the ground while the front part of the right foot is used for shoving. The locks must push against the props and the hooker, and for this reason the right feet of the front-row forwards are not placed far back and the legs are not bent too much. The hooker must have sufficient space without his hips losing contact with his props. We call this "getting under" his prop.

The hooker pushes from the front part of his left foot, which is turned slightly towards the opening of the scrum to "open" the left hip for the pivot when hooking. The right foot is placed lightly on the ground in line (front to rear) with the hind foot.

The tight-head prop also adopts a stance with his inside foot behind his outside foot, but leans towards the inside without swinging out or pushing askance. If he can supply more weight to the inside in this way, he can place his left foot in front and his right foot behind.

The locks push off both feet, particularly from the inside of the front foot. Their feet remain close together.

Should the ball shoot out too quickly the loose-head flanker may shove straight ahead, or the loose-head lock may advance his left foot slightly to block the ball. He can also deflect the ball to the other side of the scrum, for tactical reasons, so that it emerges between him and his partner. This allows the scrum half to break, or gives him a better chance to do so.

Flankers and number eights
They push off both feet, particularly from the inside of the front foot. If the scrum twists, the tight-head flanker can prevent the twist more effectively if he moves his right foot behind and his left foot in front. In this way he can push harder. This should, however, not be necessary because two legs always push harder than one. Flankers who push with the outside foot from behind usually do so because they are accustomed to this method. However, the sooner they abandon this idea the better.

Putting in the ball on the tight-head side
The feet remain in the same position but a few changes are necessary or can be introduced in an attempt to attain better results. The hooker places his right or his hooking foot as near as possible to the hooking point below the face of his tight-head prop, and his feet are slightly turned in that direction. The stance of the tight-head forward is like that of a loose-head prop for putting in the ball on the loose-head side, as is the stance of the loose-head flank. If, however, the loose-head prop finds he can give more assistance to the hooker by switching the position of his feet, then he should do so. He then places his inside foot in front of the outside foot.

The push applied in the scrum
We now come to the essential purpose of the scrum, i.e. pushing. A push must

be sufficiently powerful to push away another pushing stream by heaving harder and quicker.

The binding of the scrum and the stances are precisely worked out so that the maximum shoving-power is attained. All that now remains is the straightening of bent joints. It is, however, not as simple as this because a number of principles are involved.

The tendency of the scrum to swing

The scrum must be stable. It must be poised that way for the ball to be put in. A stable scrum entails a number of things: the arms must do their work, and leaning-power must ensure that the scrum as a unit does not swing or veer. The tendency of every scrum is to veer to the loose-head side, and unless a counter-move is consciously applied, the scrum will swing time and again. The reason for this must first be determined before a counter-action can be found. In order to do this we must first of all study the diagram below, in which the feet in a scrum are indicated by numbers.

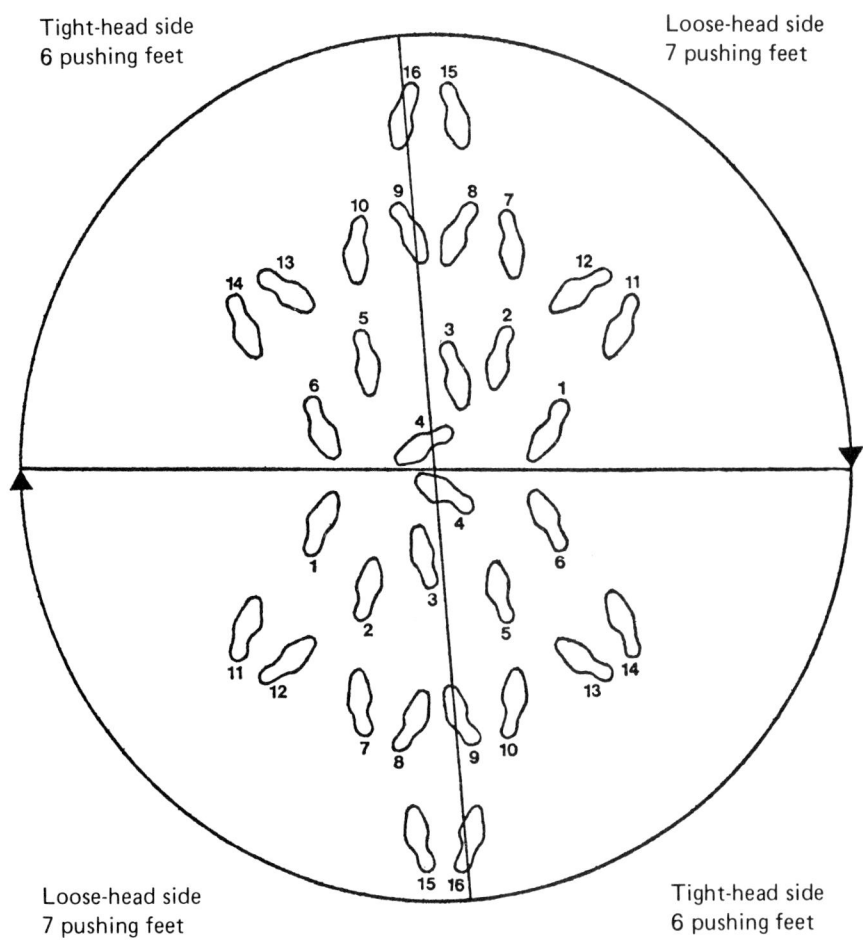

It will be seen that there are at least 14 pushing feet on the loose-head side of a scrum when divided from front to back. At the most there are 12 pushing feet on the tight-head side. Having two more pushing legs on the loose-head side of a scrum may seem slight, but if one measures the pushing power (as can be done nowadays) it will be seen what a great difference is made by those two legs. In addition they push against the so-called protruding points of the lateral axis. This explains why a scrum swings so easily to the loose-head side. This means that the tight-head side of the scrum must push much harder than the loose-head side. Yet we expect that every forward will push as hard as possible. How can more weight be lent to the tight-head side with two fewer pushing legs? The answer is simple. The forwards on the tight-head side must be heavier, stronger, and taller than the forwards on the loose-head side. Their knees must be bent slightly less and they must moreover, use a wedge to check a swing, should there still be one. This is achieved by having the tight-head flank pushing inwards more obliquely than the loose-head flank.

Shove directions: This wedge which the tight-head flank forward forms must not be confused with the expression which is currently against raising its head, viz.: "you push on to your hooker." This expression died out, but has recently been revived. One wonders if this is not one of the reasons for the deterioration of our scrumming. Let us indicate the thrust direction of every forward by means of an arrow and let us see what we will have if we comply with this slogan.

Eight shove streams flow towards the hooking side, because the hooker also pushes in this direction, four push straight ahead and four try and stem

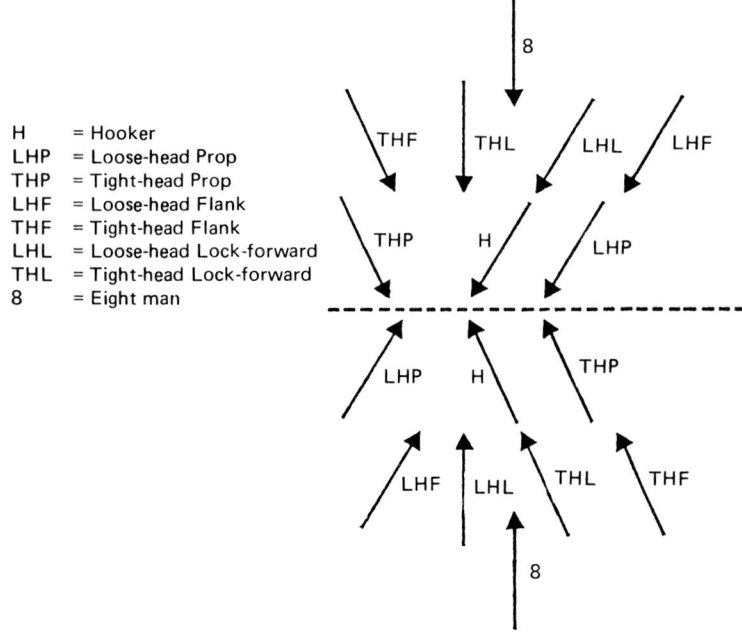

H = Hooker
LHP = Loose-head Prop
THP = Tight-head Prop
LHF = Loose-head Flank
THF = Tight-head Flank
LHL = Loose-head Lock-forward
THL = Tight-head Lock-forward
8 = Eight man

the eight so that the scrum does not collapse and disintegrate. If the two straight-pushing lock-forwards also have to deflect their thrust slant-wise to the inside, one can imagine what will be left of the hooker and how the arms will struggle to bind the forwards together. It is attempting the impossible, and the sooner we can get away from this slogan, the better. With the correct shoulder positions of the hooker himself and that of the tight-head prop it is quite sufficient if the thrust is straight ahead, except in the case of the two wedges (the flanks). Their thrust streams can be pushed into the main stream far more easily laterally than directly against it. The following thrust streams are consequently recommended:

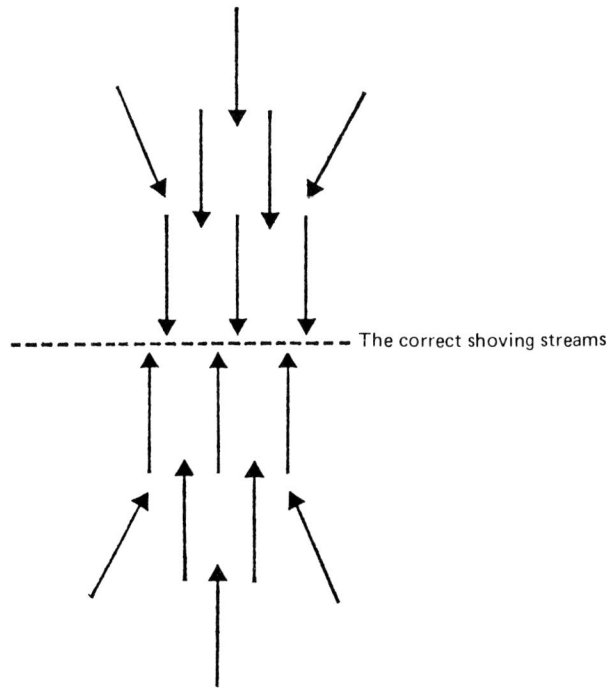
The correct shoving streams

Shoving, the focal movement
We now know what the satellite movements are and can thence proceed to the focal movement, viz. pushing. Pushing from a solid basis against a movable object is not very difficult, provided there is sufficient shoving power for pushing the object away. In a scrum, however, the object also pushes. Thus pushing does not only entail pushing your opponent away but achieving this after overcoming his shoving power. Two kinds of shoving power are to be taken into account, viz. leaning power and pushing power. Leaning power plays a more important part than is generally realised. The weight of the two packs and how low they pack down are of importance here. How low they pack depends on flexions of the body which are eliminated or diminished. Should a pack struggle against leaning power, i.e. against a pack all set for shoving, its own pushing power would have to be formidable indeed to overcome that of its opponents.

Leaning-power also depends on how many feet are used for shoving. If locks push off one foot and the pushing leg is sharply bent, the leg will not supply nearly as much leaning-power as would two legs which are slightly bent. Leaning-power also depends on the solidity of the scrum and on how securely the arms of the eight forwards are linked. Leaning-power presupposes that the pack must be immobile, to which they are helped by the flankers who supply the wedge element.

If we accept that the leaning-power is correctly used, pushing is a continuation of this power, because every push is preceded by the former. Leaning-power is part of the bending of the leg, which is entirely removed by pushing. If there are no flexions, there can be no shoving. Flexion in the longitudinal axis can be that of the neck, the entire back, the hips, the knees, and the ankles. Leaning-power, however, compels players to "remove" some of the flexions before shoving. Consequently all the flexions are extracted from the back and, as far as the locks and eighth man are concerned, also in the flexion of the neck. In their case, as in the case of the front row, their backs now become the conductors of pushing power; consequently their backs must be absolutely straight.

The degree to which the back is straight is often determined by the neck. If the neck is bent, the back is inclined to buckle. If the neck is straight, the back is inclined to be straight as well. Locks can straighten their necks in advance, but front-row forwards usually do not find this easy because they have to keep their eyes on the ball. They must therefore learn not to bend their necks at the base, but at the top; failing this, the neck must be straightened as part of the shove. The first method, however, is better.

The flankers can bend their backs slightly if the opposing leaning-power does not overwhelm the prop forwards. Should they straighten their backs, together with their knees and hips, they will make a tremendous contribution to the shove-stream. Of course, everything will depend on which side gains the upper hand. Mastery will determine to what extent the knees, and also the hips, are bent. If the leaning-power is too strong, the losing pack has no choice: they either unflex all the pushing legs and hips – the second and third row become as inflexible as oaks – or they attempt the intermediate stage by "taking the leaning-power straight from the shoulder" on one straightened leg. This has one disadvantage, as such a pushing stance does not facilitate the straightening of the hips if the pushing leg, the foremost one, pushes so strongly that the rear leg can be moved up to it. Obviously the foremost foot must be very slightly forward to bring about such a movement.

But pushing also implies that the parts which are straightened must be fully stretched after the shove. If this does not happen, the frontal pushing power will "break open" the joints. In order to assure that the pushing power is retained, care must be taken that the joints which are involved in pushing are entirely straight afterwards. It is clear that the front-row forwards cannot do this by means of their hips. Should they straighten their hips, they will assume the position of lock forwards. The measure to which the hips are straightened is determined by the measure to which the second row behind them becomes straight. Straightening means that no pushing-power – and thus no energy – is lost. Should the scrum become "undone", or should it wheel, or should a single back or a single joint buckle, this will happen. If the second row and the number eight push from the front of their feet and the opposing shoving-power proves too much, the ankles will give way and shoving-power will be lost. This will not happen, however, if the front foot is diagonally placed.

Shoving means that you do it faster than your opponents. If your scrum could start pushing before your opponents, a shoving-stream would be generated which they would hardly be able to resist. Unfortunately this cannot be done. Something similar, however, can be applied. This is to shove explosively, so assuring that your shoving-stream is generated before that of the opposing pack.

Usually the push is given too late and, above all, too slowly. As soon as the scrum half, when putting the ball in, starts the forward movement with his hands, the ball is in play again and the shove can be given. It is necessary to wait until the ball leaves his hands or touches the ground.

Hooking

Everything described here is aimed at enabling the hooker to move forward, to have his hooking leg free – and not pinned down by too much frontal shoving power. This is how he operates: the lower leg is fired like a bullet from the knee which, at the same time, serves as a gunsight for determining the height and distance of the shot. The hooker's primary aim is to get his foot behind (on the far side of) the ball before his opponent. The hooker who wins this duel "cuts off" the other's foot.

The second contest concerns the ball itself – how to get it out. For this, one of two things can happen:
1. The prop sees to it. He will not succeed, however, if the scrum wheels or if it does not have the assistance of his flanker – unless he changes his feet, which is undesirable. And he will not be able to do it if he or his scrum is beaten.
2. The hooker himself does it. The moment his heel touches the ground on the other side of the ball, his foot – with the heel as basis – recoils like a lash. This action requires exact timing because if the hooker strikes too soon, his foot will not get behind the ball but against it, resulting in the ball being kicked out of the scrum. It also happens if neither of the hookers wins possession – or if the hooker is fighting a lone battle against overwhelming odds, having only his leg as an ally but no superiority as far as shoving-power is concerned.

The heave

Because the heave is of such vital importance we conclude this section with it. The first shove means that all the pushing legs are straightened explosively, that five bodies are straightened and that three others are partially straightened. Eight heads are lifted in the process and eight arms pull, while one – that of the loose-head prop – pushes. In addition it means that the following is done simultaneously:

There is no wastage of effort in eight bodies; no unnecessary internal movement in the scrum; no swinging or moving of the scrum; no wastage at points of contact (shoulders of front row) where the pushing power converges;

and
The whole scrum moves forward.
The hooker is actually pushed over the ball.
The front-row's outside foot can easily help with the hooking.
The ball comes out exactly far enough and fast enough.
Breaking up from the scrum will be easy.

Mistakes
1. (a) The heave is not given simultaneously. *Correction:* Let the forwards scrum with closed eyes and react only when the scrum half calls out.
   (b) The first shove progresses satisfactorily but brings no advantages. *Correction:* The front-row forwards lift their chins as part of the shove and all players pay attention to the positioning of their seats.
2. The scrum swings too much. *Correction:*
   (a) Switch the locks or flankers if the tight-head lock or tight-head flanker is not as strong as the loose-head lock and loose-head flanker.
   (b) Let the tight-head side lock the scrummage.
   (c) The loose-head lock's shoulder is not placed in his partner's armpit.
3. The scrummage veers to the side at which the ball is not put in. *Correction:* Tight-head forward pushes more obliquely.
4. One of the front-row forwards swings out. *Correction:* The lock forward behind must pull harder on him, and the flanker behind must either push harder or more obliquely.
5. One of the front-row players is too weak. *Correction:* If you have no stronger one, make the weak one stronger by means of more – and regular – power exercises for back and neck.
6. The ball comes out at the tunnel. *Correction:* It is a sign that the prop does not advance his leg and place it inwards as part of the shove, and that the flanker behind him is perhaps not giving him sufficient help.
7. The scrum is too loose. *Correction:* Let two packs push against each other without the ball and compete.

THE LINE-OUT

Use of forwards
It has become customary to use as line-out forwards nos. 3 and 5 and, in recent times, one of the loose forwards at the back. There are also teams which throw in deep only when on attack. Therefore one, or even two of the loose forwards must be tall.

Habit is usually the result of experience – and successful experience for that matter, but it is a fact that South African line-outs, with jumpers at nos. 3 and 5, have become too stereotyped. One of the reasons for this is their practice of always placing the two locks at nos. 3 and 5. They are not trained to take up the nos. 2 and 4 or the nos. 4 and 6 berths. In section work, interchanging these positions is vitally important, so that every forward should be able to act as line-out forward, consolidator, and supporter.

The line-out forward is the one to whom the ball is thrown; the consolidator is the forward immediately in front of or behind the line-out forward. These two pack around him. The supporters are the other forwards who form the solid unit of the line-out before it terminates. When possession has been gained, a team will want to prevent the line-out from terminating because, should this happen, the opposing backs may cross the 10 yards offside line and take up a shallow position.

Consequently the line-out struggle entails more than mere possession. The team which forfeits possession of the ball has to develop a secondary struggle – disrupting their opponents' possession, even if only partially. Possession is made null and void if nothing can be done with the ball. Possession is partially disrup ed if the ball is given to the scrum half after the line-out has ended. If a team in possession terminates the line-out (for instance, by pushing their opponents away, by forming a ruck, etc.) it is done mainly for tactical reasons in most cases, e.g. so that the scrum half may break. Consequently it is important that players should know when the line-out is over. We give the following examples:

1. When the ball is passed to the backs over their own advantage line.
2. When the ball is tapped or deflected over their own goal-line.
3. When the ball catcher progresses forward with the ball immediately after gaining possession.
4. When the entire pack, with the catcher, progresses in such a way that all the feet are across the line through the line-out, or even pushed across it.
5. When the ball is on the ground among the feet of the forwards.
6. When the ball goes over the head of the furthermost forward in the line-out.

The consolidators and supporters bind together in such a way that they can either push together or prevent their pack from being pushed back, thereby causing the line-out to end, and enabling the defending backs to take up a shallow position.

Deflection
Unless the ball is deflected immediately, all forwards must be used in the line-out. Now what is meant by "deflected"? It means that at the moment the ball touches the two hands of the line-out forward he turns and drops the ball or applies just sufficient strength behind it to direct it to the hands of his scrum half or to a forward coming round. Deflection means that only the fingers are used – not the hands and arms.

Passing
Passing in the line-out means that the ball is taken in the air as part of the turn; after the turn the hands are whipped down, and the ball is passed. We always say that when the ball is taken, the hands are behind it. If this is the case and the line-out whips the ball down, his hands will then be in front of the ball. What happens is actually something between having the hands behind and alongside the ball when it is taken, bringing about the minimum changing of grip prior to giving a pass from below.

Tapping
Tapping means that the hand nearest to the opponents taps the ball. In this way an attempt is made to keep the ball from the opponent. It is, however, a method which is no ornament to the game, leading to more tries against than for your team. It will turn your scrum half's hair grey and will make matters far too easy for the scavengers in the opposing side.

People confuse deflection with tapping. If a forward deflects with one hand, they should speak of tapping. Deflection means control which allows the ball to drop slowly between the line-out and the scrum half. If a ball is tapped it travels fast and, in most cases, goes out of reach of the scrum half – often over his head. This, of course, is fatal.

One hand or both hands?
Should a player be opposed by a better line-out forward than himself, he can apply deflection from one hand to the other. The throw-in line is next to the line-out forward. In other words, his inside hand in the air is nearer to it than his outside hand. Taking the ball with two hands would mean leaning over to the opponents' side. When two opposing line-out forwards do this, it becomes clear why we have so much barging in the line-out.

If the inside hand is used for stopping the ball, at least part of the barging would be eliminated, and there is an additional advantage: it is the inside arm which must be whipped up for the body to get the turn in the air. If this arm whips up and the other arm is used only as an aid in taking hold of the ball, the shoulder joint of the whipped-up arm will go at least three or four inches higher. If both arms are whipped up. the two shoulder joints remain equally high. So whether the ball is taken with one hand or two, it is the inside arm that does most of the work. The outside arm is merely an extension, as in baseball, in which the ball is caught with the gloved hand while the bare hand merely assures that the ball does not drop from it.

In this way, with the catching hand somewhat lower than the stopping hand, the line-out forward makes sure that he adds three to four inches to his height. This is the kind of catching with both hands which we recommend.

Tightening
We have spoken of consolidators, and a pack which cannot consolidate, cannot "pull in" or engage their opponents and put them out of action when possession is gained by their own backs. Possession, as we will see later on, must be good possession or good ball for the backs. Best-possession consists of backs opposing backs, without forwards obstructing their path.

The rhythm of good line-out work variation is something like the following order: "Closed" (consolidate), "Closed", "Closed", "Open" (deflect or pass immediately), "Open", "Closed", "Closed", etc. In other words, the opponents must be uncertain whether consolidation is going to take place, or whether the ball will be deflected, or whether it will be passed out immediately.

This uncertainty must be aided by alternating the line-out forward to whom the ball is thrown. We have grown so accustomed to having the ball thrown in to no. 3 in our own twenty-five and to no. 5 on attack that practically no thinking is required. A well-trained pack can use no. 5 with profit in its own territory. Not only will most opponents not expect it, but possession after consolidation can mean a blind-side movement; if a kick is imperative, the blind-side, and even the field-side, will present less interference from opponents.

Stray balls
A ball which has been deflected will drop. This must not be confused with a stray ball, which is a ball which, in the attempt to be taken, lands on either side of the line-out. A stray ball is a scrum half's nightmare and something should be done about eliminating it as far as possible. For this purpose a fourth kind of forward, apart from the line-out forward, the consolidators and the supporters, is used. We call him the "coverer" because he covers the line-out forward so that stray balls do not get the scrum half into trouble.

When the ball touches the line-out forward's hands, the coverer is already behind him and in a position to get to stray balls on either side of him. While on his way into position he will not be able to get to balls behind him. Thus he will already be slightly astride and on his toes when the ball makes contact with his line-out forward's hands. To be able to do this requires quick action. The laws state that he may not leave his position in the line-out before the ball leaves the hands of the wing, so at that same moment he leaves his position. He will then be easily in time for balls coming down on his line-out forward. If the ball is thrown in straight, however, it results sometimes in dangerously stray balls, most of which will, fortunately, be in front of him if he is no. 5 covering no. 3. If no. 3 covers 5, the ball travels far, even for straight throw-ins, and this allows him to be at the ready position when the ball touches the hands of no. 5. The same applies for nos. 6 or 7 when the ball is thrown deep.

Kinds of throw-in
We have spoken of two kinds of throw-in. It has also become customary nowadays to throw the ball straight at no. 3, who lops it on to no. 5. Even this is being overdone. Both methods can and must be used, but in such a way that it will cause the opponents to be uncertain which throw-in will be employed. Regular straight throw-ins to the front of the line-out result only in jostling and pushing, often leading to no possession at all if the two line-out forwards are well matched. Straight throw-ins to the back of the line-out require quick judgment on the part of the opponents, and in this they might be too late. This kind of throw-in also lends itself to deflection, which is used more frequently at the rear than at the front of the line-out. This brings us to jumping and consolidation. First let us take jumping.

Jumping
As in pushing, jumping requires a basis, a fixed point. In point of fact, jumping has much in common with pushing, especially with the quick shove. Jumping means pushing your own weight upwards. Two legs are better than one when in a stationary position, but if you are able to take a running approach like a high-jumper, one leg would perform better than two.

Why is this? Because weight in movement is less than dead weight or weight in the stationary position. Moving weight can be lifted more easily because of the momentum involved. But a Rugby player can, at the most, take one step before jumping off one or both feet. Some forwards jump off the foot nearest to their opponent, but experiments have shown that one jumps higher off two feet than off one.

This may be elaborated as follows: everyone uses one leg, usually the right leg, more often and more effectively than the other. Consequently that leg is either stronger or more adept. In line-out work the strongest leg must be used correctly because, although we jump with both feet, the so-called jumping foot apparently does most of the work. Therefore we step with this foot before we jump. If it is the right foot and our opponents are on the right-hand side, the short step is taken with the right foot to be followed by a little hop or skip on the same foot, practically as part of the short step. When the jumping foot touches the ground after this, the other foot is placed next to it and both execute the jump. Everything is done from the ball of the foot, although there are some line-out forwards who make the little skip and even the jump off a flat foot.

Perhaps it is better that the jump should roll off, as it were, from the entire foot over the ball of the foot so that the toes are pointed directly downward when the jumper is in the air. This little skip creates an opportunity for getting everything ready for the jump. The body is inclined somewhat to the front, the arms go rearwards behind the back and are whipped forward when the left foot moves forward to come next to the right foot. When both feet together touch the ground the jump takes place. In point of fact, this is actually an explosive action with all the bent parts in the longitudinal axis straightened and the arms forcibly whipped upwards. The arms are more or less next to the sides when the two feet come together for the jump. The whole body stretches out. Even the chin comes into action as it is forcibly lifted.

Jumping in Rugby is timing, because when you are at your maximum height the ball must be at the same height – the reach of your hands or hand. In order to perfect this timing, forwards, during practice, will have to alternate, as often as possible, the distance they stand from the winger. In this way they acquire the knack of timing so that they will be able to perform in any position in the line-out. Forwards who jump only at no. 3 or at no. 5, thus playing in only one position, may be able to jump equally well but their timing will be defective.

There is a further meaning to jumping. The jumper's stance is not square but partially diagonal. His inside shoulder is in front of his outside shoulder. This enables him to start the twisting movement on the ground. Should he succeed in getting to the ball, it is best if he completes the twist the moment he starts descending. This is made possible by straining forcibly upwards with the inside arm. It is this whipping arm which enables the line-out forwards to execute the turn in the air with the ball, and it is the hand of the arm which, as we have pointed out, is nearest to the touchline or the centre line of the line-out.

In the same way as the arm is thrust upwards, it is thrust downwards in order to frustrate the efforts of the opposing forwards to get at the ball. The ball is screened by keeping it fairly low down, yet not so low that the opponents will be able to get at it with feet or hands. The player braces himself on landing, and does not bend his back or, if he must, only as slightly as possible.

Jumping therefore means putting the body in motion by a short step and a little hop prior to straightening the whole body, which has been bent in the longitudinal axis; and, in the process, whipping the arms, especially the inside arm, powerfully upwards.

There are forwards who jump in their tracks off both feet or rock themselves on two legs before jumping. There are also players who jump off the foot which has taken the little hop. There will be individual differences, but it seems that the method described above is the best. It is however advisable to be able to jump off one foot so that the jump can be speedily executed, especially if the opponents take the throw-in and there is no time for preparing the jump. Some line-out forwards jump in such a way that they get their inside shoulders in front of their opponents, and they do this quite successfully until their opponents attempt to do the same thing. This is one of the reasons why we see so much jostling and bumping in the line-outs.

Consolidation

Only at the moment that the line-out jumper touches the ball with his hands may his forwards bind on him, otherwise it may be regarded as obstruction.

Should the line-out forward miss the ball, it would in any case be pointless to try and bind with him. The "mechanics" of binding consist of the following: the moment the ball is caught by the line-out forward, the two consolidators place their arms round him so that they guide him, as it were, to the ground with their arms. For this purpose the consolidator in front of the jumper uses his inside arm and the consolidator behind him his outside arm. With their free arms they get hold of the line-out forward's back to prevent his being pulled through. This will cause both consolidators to push somewhat obliquely inwards, but this does not matter much.

As soon as the line-out forward touches the ground, the consolidators take up the position for shoving; in other words, they push upwards and forwards in a bent position with their inside shoulders against his loins while he anchors himself, wide-legged and crouching, to the ground. They face in the direction of their opponents, of course, and their feet are not in the off-side position. In other words, their front feet (preferably the outside feet) are practically in line with the feet of the line-out forward. The inside feet are placed rather far back, so that they can push with them. They are also in a position which allows the other forwards to push against them. As they are on both sides of the line-out forward, his hands will bring the ball over and lower than their arms so that the ball is completely screened from their opponents. The other forwards keep a passage open when they pack round the consolidators.

It must be quite clear that the forwards not only pack round and bind with the line-out forwards, but they do it in such a way that they are able to push, should this be necessary. But let the consolidators beware of going too low when taking up a position for shoving. They must do so for a definite reason: the lower they pack, the more easily their opponents can get to the ball.

The supporters
When the supporters pack they first move towards the ball, with the ball as it were, before packing, and then they do so at specific positions. It is not always necessary to pack. This is because nowadays forwards are so bunched together that their opponents cannot get through their ranks, and because supporters as a rule do not bind if the ball is deflected or passed out immediately. They do so only to consolidate the line-out and specifically for welding a pack of forwards or for tying up opponents in order to keep them out of the way of the backs. The two consolidators, however, always pack when a line-out forward brings the ball down.

We can now proceed to study the following diagrams in order to appreciate better the part played by the line-out forwards, the consolidators, the supporters, and the coverers. Two methods are shown in the diagrams, but the first one only is described, because the second one is obvious.

The numbers of the forwards in the scrummage are used for the diagrams below:

|6|¹|4|²|5|³|7|
| | |8| | | |

Different line-out formations

1. Formation 2 1 ④ 3 ⑤ 6 ⑦ 8   ◯ = Line-out forwards taking part in move

a) Consolidated round ④

|2|¹④³|7|6| | of 2→1→④→3←5←6←7←8
| |5| | |8|

(i) One lock-forward covers the other.
(ii) The forward in front of the line-out forward and the one behind him, the consolidators, always lay the foundation for support.
(iii) The other forwards pack on the outside of the two consolidators.
(iv) Packing is never done behind a line-out forward but at his sides.

b) Consolidated round ⑤

|1|³⑤6|4|7| | of 2→1→4→3→⑤←6←7←8
| |²| | |8|

No. 2 here does not bind on the outside of no. 1 but between 3 and 1 (for better shoving-power); in the same way the lock forward who covers 4, packs between two forwards, in this case between 6 and 7.

c) Consolidated round ⑦

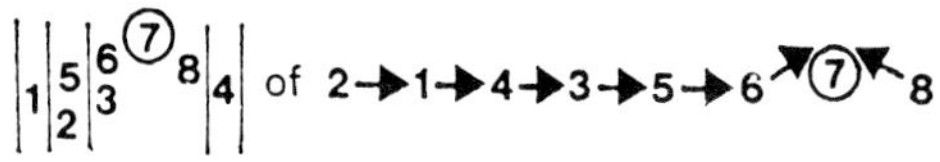

|1 |5 6⑦ 8|4| of 2→1→4→3→5→6→⑦←8
   |2 3

This consolidation can be used for a blind-side movement by the fly half; otherwise the ball is passed out directly. Note that the lock forward who does the covering packs on the outside of eight on this occasion, that 3 packs between 6 and 5, and that 2 packs between 5 and 1.

2. Formation 2④1⑤3 6⑦8

a) Consolidated round ④

|5|2④1|6|3 7|8| of 2→④←1←5←3←6←7←8

The covering lock forward packs on the outside, on to 2; 6 packs between 1 and 3; 7 packs on the outside of 3, and 8 decides whether to pack and where. If he packs, he will choose the outside in order to keep a sharper eye on developments.

b) Consolidated round ⑤

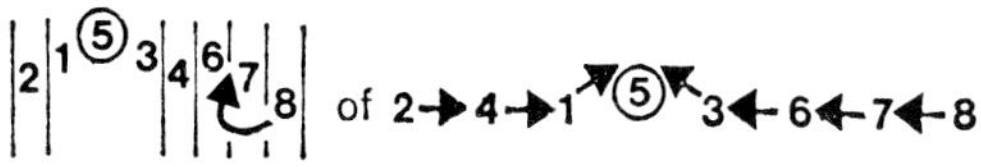

|2|1⑤3|4|6 7|8| of 2→4→1→⑤←3←6←7←8

c) Consolidated round ⑦

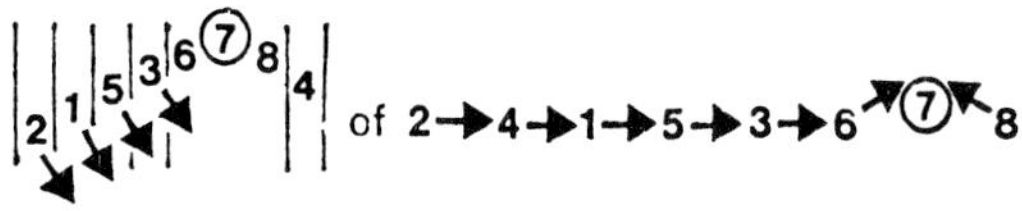

|2|1 5|3 6⑦8|4| of 2→4→1→5→3→6→⑦←8

6 and 8 consolidate; no. 4 covers and packs, and the remaining forwards come round. No further support is necessary because, as a rule, the ball is given out directly. If the ball is kept, they pack where help is required.

3. Formation 213④6⑤78

a) Consolidated round ④

|2|1|5|3④6|7|8| of 2→1→3→④←6←5←7←8

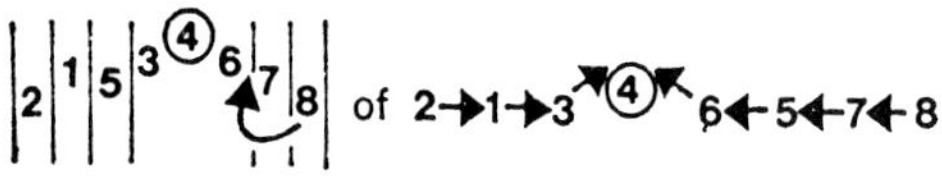

b) Consolidated round ⑤

| | |3|6⑤7| |4|8| |
|1|2|2 | | | | of 2→1→3→4→6→⑤←7←8

c) Consolidated round ⑦

| | |3|6|5⑦8| |4| |
|2|1| | | | | | of 2→1→3→4→6→5→⑦←8

4. Formation 2136④7⑤8

a) Consolidated round ④

| | |3|6④7| |8| |
|1|2|5 | | | of 2→1→3→6→④←7←5←8

b) Consolidated round ⑤

|1|2|6|3|7⑤8| |4| of 2→1→3→6→4→7→⑤←8

Important principle:
The success of consolidation depends on how quickly the forward in front or behind the lock forward who covers is able to take his place close up. The same applies in other instances in which forwards do not pack on the outside of the player in front or behind them.

Opponents throwing-in the ball
The same principles remain whether your own team or your opponents throw in the ball, because this causes the least amount of disruption; and if your team succeeds in gaining possession, consolidation takes place in the usual way.

Should the opponents get the ball, the line-out can be terminated by shoving and your backs can come up on defence. One of the aims of the pack losing possession is thus to terminate the line-out as soon as possible by, as stated above, pushing the opponents away. Another method would be to prevent the opponents' consolidators from doing their work. This is done automatically by your own consolidators when trying to pack round their own line-out forwards. Their eyes are always trained on the ball, and if they see that their own line-out forward is outplayed by his opponent, they only go deeper in, as it were, in the line-out in an attempt to get at the ball when it is brought down, in this way preventing the ball from being passed out. Seeing that this attempt brings the two consolidators next to, or near to, their own line-out forward, whether he has lost the contest or not, these three form a basis against which their own forwards can push.

Whether the hooker and the number eight must push depends on the situation; should it appear that the shove would not come off without their help, they must lend a hand. This means that the opposing scrum half will not easily get the ball, because a retreating pack of forwards does not give out a ball without further ado. But if he does get the ball, and badly at that, the number eight and the hooker must be free to send him flying. Thus the criterion here is for these two players to come nearer to the maul and to see what measure of success has been attained by their consolidators in their effort to get at the ball. If the ball is well and truly held, they can push; if this is not the case, or if it is badly done, they remain outside and they become the two flankers of the maul.

The line-out forward of the team not throwing the ball in, the so-called defender, must here judge if the ball is thrown to his opponent. In this process of judging he is not afforded the same time for the short step and hop as would have been the case if it were his ball. Consequently he will most probably jump from one foot, and this he will have to practise as well. Or, if he does use the short step and the hop, he will have to curtail it. This, too, he will have to practise.

Faults in the line-out
1. Undoubtedly the commonest fault rests with those wings who cannot let the the ball "alight on a sixpence". Even with the best line-out forwards in the world, a wing whose throw-ins are poor will forfeit his best allies. Wings must not only be able to do both kinds of throw-ins – straight and lobbed – but they must also be able to adapt them to the jumping height or the stretching height of all their line-out forwards. In addition, they must not let wind and rain fluster them.
2. The second commonest fault rests with nos. 2 and 6 in the method described, viz. using one of the locks as coverer. They either remain rooted to their starting point or are far too slow in closing up, with the result that the defenders pour through the gap left unstopped by the coverer. For this reason many teams use no. 2 to do the covering. Others again do not use a coverer at all, something which can, of course, be fatal if stray balls occur. In this case the scrum half himself sees to covering, taking up his position in front near the 5-yards line.
3. The coverer moves too slowly to the point of readiness, or he jocks in without making sure that his fellow-player has the ball. Another mistake is immediately passing to his back after collecting a stray ball and bumping against one of his team-mates in the process. A penalty kick inevitably follows. (Actually this player is not to be blamed because the player bumped against should have made way for the coverer.)
4. The forwards, especially the supporters among whom are the three loose forwards, play too loose and do not jock in when their line-out forward holds on to the ball. Deflection does not always entail jocking in, but as soon as the ball is brought down and held, every player must jock in. Or, if

players do still jock in, they do so at the first available place instead of doing it according to plan.
5. The line-outs become too stereotyped with a pattern of throwing-in only to nos. 3 and 5, having only no. 3 on the defence, and with no. 5 on attack. If no. 6 is used, it is always with an eye to attack only, or if a peeling movement is started, it is always launched from the back of the line-out.
6. The ball is tapped.
7. Too frequently the ball is passed out immediately, instead of following the rhythm of "Closed – Open".
8. Consolidators or supporters have not adjusted themselves to catching balls within their reach or cutting them off.
9. If the opponents gain possession, the eyes of the loose forwards are trained more on the man about to receive the ball than on the ball itself.

BROKEN-DOWN PLAY: THE RUCK AND THE MAUL

Broken-down play should actually be treated after general play, but in order to keep the play in which forwards are mostly concerned, it is discussed here, immediately after the tight game.

Broken-down play is that which follows unsuccessful general or broken play if the ball is free. It is loose-ball play, but it also includes mauls if the ball is carried by a player who is held or tackled. Even in this case it is the first task of such a player to get the ball free so that he can pass or drop it; in other words this is another form of loose ball.

Definition: A *ruck* is formed when the ball is on the ground and one or more players from each team are on their feet and in physical contact, closing around the ball between them. A *maul* is formed by one or more players from each team on their feet and in physical contact closing round a player who is carrying the ball. For the sake of convenience we distinguish between static and dynamic rucks or mauls; and these can be attacking, defensive or neutral rucks or mauls.

Static rucks or mauls
The name indicates that this kind of ruck or maul is not preceded by running. They are formed where play is, or near to the tight game. A scrum half is caught either at the line-out or scrummage and a ruck or a maul is formed. The forwards are out of position, but the backs are not; they are drawn up exactly as in the case of the tight game. The scrum half who is not caught, however, has a chance of breaking because the flankers, whose task it is to keep an eye on him, most probably had to jock in first to the ruck.

Dynamic rucks or mauls
These are preceded by running. There has been, for instance, a movement fairly distant or even far away from the tight game. On this occasion, however, the backs are involved. They are either disorganised or one of them may be trapped in the ruck or maul and is thus out of position. If the ruck or maul is formed

completely, the team to gain the advantage of quick possession sends the ball to the wing for the overlap. General attacking back-play thus occurs. Should it take long for the ball to emerge, the opposing backs are afforded the opportunity of taking up their positions. Then the scrum half can break, instead of passing out the ball. The term "completely formed" is used because sometimes the ball emerges from such a ruck or a maul before all the forwards have jocked in to it. When the ball is passed out, some of them are still in the way. But most probably they are also out of the way if the back line moves in the opposite direction.

Attacking rucks and mauls
An attacking ruck or maul takes place in front of your own forwards, and behind the opposing forwards. The advantage, as far as the chance of possession and attack following on this are concerned, is therefore on your side.

Defensive ruck or maul
This is the opposite of an attacking ruck or maul. It takes place behind your own forwards and in front of those of your opponents, who consequently have the advantage.

Neutral ruck or maul
Here neither of the teams has an advantage with regard to the direction of running because the ruck or maul is formed opposite the spot where the tight play which preceded it took place.

How is a ruck or a maul formed?
Like the scrummage, the ruck or maul must have a base. There must be someone to push against because the aim of the ruck is to get the ball free by shoving over it. The aim of the maul is to push your player who has the ball forward towards the opponents' side so that, should he drop or let go of the ball, it will come out at the back. What it amounts to is that the ball must be pushed free. For this reason the skill at the ruck or the maul is one of shove-in movement. This kind of shoving, however, is preceded by quite a number of movements described below.

The attacking maul
The term "loose ball" can be interpreted in two ways: it is a ball which is on the ground, or it is a ball in the hands of a player who is held but not tackled.
   The player is therefore still in a position to pass the ball or release it, i.e. he can still play the ball. The player will pass the ball or let it go to one of his team-mates, whose aim must be to move forward with the ball, or have another team-mate do so. A player will keep the ball himself only if passing or releasing it is dangerous.
1. A maul therefore begins when a player has the ball and is held, or when he has been blocked by a number of players.
2. If a loose ball is picked up, the aim of that player is to go forward. Only

when he cannot advance any further, when he is held but still keeps the ball, is a maul formed round him.
3. A maul is also formed when two players pick up a ball simultaneously and fail to wrest it from each other's hold. In this instance there is no question of a tackle.
4. We can assume, then, that even if a player is tackled on his feet, a maul may in point of fact take place, especially if the maul is on the move as the result of shoving-power.

In each of the above instances the ball is held, and it must be freed so that possession can be gained by the team which succeeds in getting or keeping it loose.

How do they do this?

Let us suppose that there is an attacking maul. If one of the players should hold the ball – usually because he has been checked and has no one to whom he can pass, or because a pass would result in a tackle behind him, or be intercepted – a good maul can assure possession.

If we label the player with the ball no. 1, then no. 2 will be the next player to arrive on the scene. The part played by these two will determine what is going to happen. No. 1 will see to it that he gets the ball, and when he has it he will go forward with it. If he is checked, no. 2 must try to carry on the forward movement, as must no. 3. Only if this movement is checked must the next step be considered, i.e. to tussle and turn round so that the ball becomes loose. The other forwards then bind on both sides of their team-mate who has given his back. They must not bind behind him because the ball must be kept free for passing. Obviously there will be shoving to get the opponents out of the way, especially of the backs if they gain possession from such a maul.

If no. 1 is checked and no. 2 cannot continue the movement, no. 1 will try and turn himself, remaining on his feet, and no. 2 will bind with him. No. 3 will bind on the other side of no. 1 while the remaining forwards will jock in by packing against nos. 2 and 3.

Should the opposing team's no. 1 get the ball first, our no. 1 must smother-tackle him with the ball and immediately start trying to push him forward. No. 2 and the rest will assist him in this. If the opposing no. 1 is well anchored on his legs, as he usually will be, our no. 1 will attempt to turn him to his side or tip him so that a ruck can be formed. He can also try and take the ball from him, but that is actually the function of no. 2. He sees to it that he gets a hand on the ball to wrench it away.

When the opposing team's no. 1 is pushed away, he is starting to lose the contest because he is in the process of losing, or has lost, his anchorage. If the ball is between himself and our no. 1 he can no longer pull at the ball because he will be pulling in the same direction as he is being pushed by his opponents. If he is on the side of our no. 1 opponent and he pulls, he is also playing into our hands because he is easily brought down.

His best position consequently is on his own side of the maul with his back towards his opponents. If shoved against, he can offer resistance and the ball still remains protected. By offering his back, he may also be able to twist himself free and realise his first objective – to go forward. With his back turned to the opponents' no. 1, however, a maul has not actually been formed because the ball is not between them. No. 2 of the opposing team can then jock in from his side of the game and prevent him from passing the ball or letting it go.

And the rest?

There are not many decisions to be taken by the other players if nos. 1 and 2 do their jobs. The only thing they have to do is to push. To do this they begin stooping when still a few yards from the base of the maul, then bind with everyone within reach, jocking in with all their might to generate the shove-in motion. But they should slack off slightly before finally jocking in so that they know where to put in their heads and in order to get more strength into their legs. If they run blindly into such a maul, they may hurt themselves. In the first place, they can bump their own heads very hard; secondly they may injure the other players, and thirdly, if they are running faster than the slower moving maul, they will bounce back off it like a ball.

The shovers, furthermore, see to it that they remain on their feet; yet it is better to push themselves over, as it were, than to remain standing upright. Whereas the shovers had their eyes trained on where the ball was lodged and where they had to jock in, they now have their eyes fixed on the ground to ensure that the ball is pushed "open" without hindrance as soon as no. 1 releases it. If the ball is held, they use their eyes to decide on which side they have to jock in. No. 1 releases the ball as soon as there is no danger of an opponent getting it or holding it, and when his team-mates join him he can, to save time, even roll the ball out. The ball then rolls in one direction and the pack moves in another.

Defensive maul

There is no difference here in the functions of nos. 1 and 2, except that if no. 2 has to push against no. 1, he will have to turn around to be in a position to do so because he and the rest of his forwards are on the retreat. They also do everything as for an attacking maul, except they too will have to turn around. This turnabout allows them to make the check before making bodily contact. They run alongside the maul and when they turn into it they pack against friend and foe alike and immediately start pushing. The short cut to the base of the maul is the only route to be followed. In other words, it is not necessary that some should jock in on one side and some on the other.

Neutral maul

The functions of all the forwards here remain the same, but as a result of the position of the maul they will, as it were, be pushing somewhat obliquely across the field. This would have no advantage. Consequently they must make a slight detour before jocking in on the side of their approach to enable them to push obliquely forward. The ball ought to emerge on the side opposite to that of their approach, and the scrum half will be able to break easily. Otherwise the fly half may do so.

The ruck

The ball is on the ground. How did it get there? It has either been knocked on, dropped, or kicked; or it may be there following a tackle or because a player has fallen on it. It is a ball which cannot be picked up unhampered. If it can be picked up in any way this should be done, because a maul is better than a ruck. Few balls, however, can be picked up unhampered; in other words, there should not be many rucks. Difficult balls to pick up are those which are grounded together with a player who has been tackled or when a player has fallen on the ball. These balls, however, may be snatched up, i.e. a player stoops down and grabs the ball, after which he straightens immediately. He does this by suddenly checking his speed; as soon as he has the ball, he can make tracks again. But if a player or players are still fumbling in trying to pick up a ball from the ground or a ball which is rolling, a ruck thwarts their efforts.

A player's first aim is to pick up a ball on the ground even if it leads to a maul. Once it has been picked up, the ball must be treated in the same way as the one leading to a maul. In other words, it is a race to get to the ball first, to pick it up and go forward with it; failing this, to get it free, turning with it and not letting it get to the ground. One of the most important functions of any player is to scoop or snatch up the ball, and it is not only the job of the forwards but also that of any back. If the race is lost, it may be offset by tackling the winner or by knocking the ball from his hands and getting it loose again. Perhaps a second player will then win the race.

The attacking ruck
The difference between a ruck and a maul is that in the ruck there is usually a player lying near the ball. If it is one of the opponents, you can be sure to find him lying between yourself and the ball; if it is one of your team-mates, he will be lying between the ball and the opponents. This should not be so, but it is what happens in practice. Again you want the ball on your side, and no. 1 must bring this about. But he has more on his hands than this. He must "hide" the ball as it were, or see to it that it is between his feet. He has another task: he will be pushed against from the rear – this he expects – and therefore he must buttress or anchor himself. This he does by running up to the ball, stopping in his tracks, i.e. putting his weight on his front foot while leaning backwards, lifting his back higher in the process than would a prop forward in a scrummage, more like the protectors in a line-out. Immediately after planting himself in this manner, he starts straining forward. In this he is helped by nos. 2 and 3 who pack, preferably on both sides of him. The rest then jock in against them as in a maul, but – unlike a maul – this will take place behind the ball. This means that they bend low and bind tightly a few yards from the ruck and then run into it. Their eyes are fixed on the ball because they have to push across it without touching it.

Something about the footwork of no. 1: if he steps aimlessly across the ball, the opposing no. 1 may kick it away. Usually they are so close together that they never give it a thought, but it is nevertheless better if our no. 1 can place himself between the opposing no. 1 and the ball. He achieves this by seeing to it that his left foot is in front if the race is from the left-hand side, and his right foot behind and hard up against the ball. If the race is from the right-hand side, he places his right foot in front and his left foot behind and hard up against the ball. If a player lies between him and the ball, he steps across the player with his front foot so that this foot is between the ball and the opponent. Should the player lie on the other side of the ball, he steps across the player and the ball with his front foot against the ball.

Defensive ruck

This requires the same movement as an attacking maul. The footwork of no. 1, however, is somewhat different. He need not turn around and step across the ball on his side. If, however, a player should be lying on the other side of the ball, he places his rear foot against the ball and his other foot across the player. Should the player by lying between him and the ball, he places his rear foot against the player and his front foot across him. He will thus have his back towards the opponents' side. Nos. 2 and 3 link up with him, also with their backs turned to the opponents. Should they turn round to face the opponents' side, they would expose themselves to serious injury. They brace themselves for the bumps coming from behind, keeping their bodies somewhat straight, so that their own forwards, making the slight detour and jocking in, do not bump against their heads.

Neutral ruck

As far as the footwork of no. 1 is concerned, this is the same as in the defensive ruck. For the rest it is identical to the neutral maul. The forwards must make a slight detour in order to push obliquely ahead.

Mistakes

What follows is supplementary to the previous section in which the ruck and the maul were treated positively. Here we shall enumerate the things which occur so frequently in practice, the mistakes that are made and which spoil the game of Rugby.

Nos. 1 and 2

1. They do not distinguish between loose balls which are to be picked up and those which are to be won by means of rucks.
2. They lack purpose in fighting for a base.
3. They do not hide or screen the ball.
4. They do not stiffen their backs.
5. They do not start the shoving movement.

The rest of the forwards

1. Nos. 1 and 2 have to make a decision, *inter alia*, whether the ball has to be picked up or whether it should serve as a base for the ruck. Furthermore, how is the ball to be screened in the most effective way? The other forwards also have important decisions to make and, as is the case with all decisions, these depend on certain circumstances. First they must decide what kind of ruck it is, and then act accordingly. But we see the same fault today in all rucks: all the forwards jock in in the same way.
2. Their second task is to look where the ball is: on the ground or in someone's

hands. How often do we not see forwards jocking in when the ball is handed to them on a platter: in other words, they can take it from the hands of a fellow-player.
3. They want to pick up balls when only a ruck can be formed.
4. They do not run into a ruck and, if they do, they forget to slacken their pace for a moment beforehand, to enable them to jock in with determination and greater shoving-power.
5. They jock in on the wrong side of the ball at a neutral ruck or maul, and in this way fail to hide it from their opponents.
6. They want to hook the ball instead of pushing it clear.
7. They go in with their backs first as if they could then push.
8. They do not bind, or bind too late.
9. They are upright when going in instead of stooping low.
10. They jump into a ruck or maul.
11. They bump their heads hard against players in the ruck because they do not look for openings.
12. They do not look where the ball is but step on it, causing it to bounce, so that the scrum half has difficulty in getting it.

GENERAL PLAY

General attacking back play: from the scrum, line-out and ruck
Before we discuss general back play, there are a few terms to be understood. But before giving them, let us repeat the definition of general play.

General play is that which follows tight play and loose play, and can be divided into two subdivisions: general back play and general forward play. Each of these can again be divided into two subdivisions – general attacking front play or forward play, and general defensive front play or forward play; and general attacking back play or back-line play and general defensive back play or back-line play. General attacking and defensive back play are basic to back-line movements, because possession gained by the forwards is given to the backs. They must be able to get the ball faultlessly out to the wing if necessary (attacking back play), and the aim of the defenders is to prevent this, or, should it reach the wing, prevent it from proceeding any further. In these two aspects of general back play the forwards also take part, either as attackers or as defenders.

Backline formation at line-outs and scrums
Because the back must take up a position at least 10 yards from the touchline at the line-out, but on a line through the rear foot of the rearmost player of the scrum, we must distinguish between the back-line formations at scrums and line-outs. Obviously the defenders can and may line up shallower at scrums than at line-outs, and the attackers, if they want to attack, must accordingly line up deeper. Thus we speak of a line-out formation and a scrummage formation for a back-line.

Starting point or positioning line
This indicates the position of the attackers and the defenders in the tight game.

Defensive line: the line halfway between the starting point of the attackers and the defenders is consequently the line at which the defenders join battle with the attackers.

Safety line: this is the hypothetical line in depth where the attackers pass the ball and where they are out of reach of the defenders, thus on their side of the defensive line.

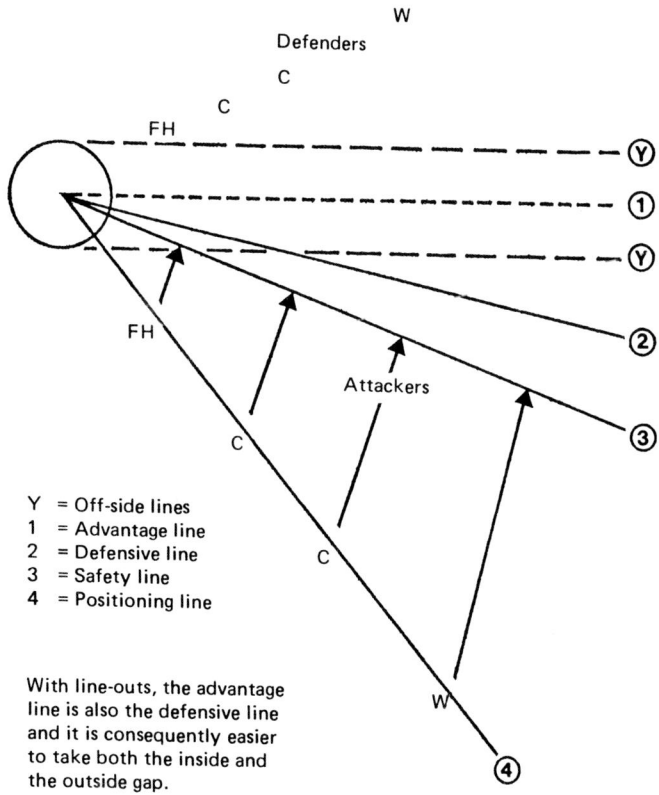

Y = Off-side lines
1 = Advantage line
2 = Defensive line
3 = Safety line
4 = Positioning line

With line-outs, the advantage line is also the defensive line and it is consequently easier to take both the inside and the outside gap.

As we have seen, different skills are linked here, and each must be correctly executed for them to blend as a unit. The principle of general back play must be understood and put into practice.

Thus we must know, as in life, where to start, which road to take, and where and how that road is going to end. These questions are considered in the principles that we are going to mention. What is the position taken up by the backline in relation to the scrum and the line-out respectively? When do the backs start running? How far do they run, how do they draw their opponents, and why? How is the ball handled?

Here we have to remember the following:
1. It is more important where a back passes the ball than where he positions himself.

2. His position in depth is determined by the positioning of his opponents. He can be on the same spot when he receives and passes the ball, or while he is running.

Aim
1. The aim of general back-line play is to get the ball to the wing.
2. It is also basic for movements from rucks when there is an overlap.
3. It is, furthermore, a launching pad for attack. For this reason every player, from the scrum half to the wing, must receive the ball in such a way that he has room for using his weapon of attack and making preparations for doing so.
4. It causes the opponents to spread.
5. It takes the ball to the place where there are the fewest number of defenders.
6. It affords the attackers an opportunity of discovering the defensive methods of their opponents and of studying them.
7. It gives all the players a chance of getting the feel of the ball.
8. It causes opponents to get accustomed to the way in which you draw an opponent.

Later this becomes the foundation for breaking.

Positioning
If the defenders are lined up deeply, the attackers take up a shallow position to the extent that they can still get the ball to their wings. If the defenders' line-up is shallow, the attackers' position is deep. Hence, the shallower the defenders lie, the deeper the attackers position themselves; the deeper the defenders lie, the shallower the attackers' line-up. In senior grade matches, however, it is taken for granted that the defenders will line up as shallow as the laws permit, and on this assumption training sessions are conducted.

Three hypothetical positions are of cardinal importance for an attacking back-line: the starting position of the backs; the point where they receive the ball; the point where they pass the ball. Of these, the passing line is the most important because it must be beyond the range of the defenders. Thus we can also speak of it as the safety line.

But how are these points, especially the passing line, determined? It is done by observing the opponents' starting position and their speed, and by adapting yourself to both. It is done, furthermore, by acting correctly from your own starting position by taking off at the correct moment, by not holding on too long to the ball, etc. One usually judges the starting position which, according to one's type of play, will ensure that the receiving line and especially the passing line, are safe. As stated previously, the shallower your opponents are lined up, and the faster they are coming up, the deeper your back-line will lie. But the deeper your back-line is stationed, the further away you are from the advantage line and from your own forwards. The danger is therefore increased if a mistake is made with regard to these lines, or if you mishandle, or if you are caught in possession, i.e. if your judgment concerning the receiving points and the passing points is at fault.

One of two methods may be followed for making sure that your place of passing is truly safe. The first method is to judge your *starting position* and then move from it, complying with all the rules of attacking back-line play. If successful, your judgment has been correct. If it is not, you must position yourself deeper until it is corrected. Consequently any attacking back-line must have a mental picture of its starting position. The second method consists of judging the position of the *passing line* and then making the starting position, the receiving line, and the passing line one and the same. In other words, your back-line remains stationary while waiting for the ball, on receiving it and when passing it. Teams can decide for themselves which method they wish to follow for determining their formations at the line-out and the scrum. This presupposes that you have a good back-line at your disposal. If this is not the case, you need not be concerned about the three lines; instead, the fly half will see to it that his receiving position and his kicking position are safe.

Individual positions
We start with the fly half, the pivot around which everything revolves. His position behind the scrum or the line-out is determined by his duties in general play. It may seem incongruous to think about defence while discussing attack. Nevertheless it is appropriate.

The fly half must not be concerned solely with himself, but he must consider all his back-line players who have to receive the ball in such a way that they have time and space at their disposal. The fly half must not only draw his opposite, but he must also draw his opposing loose forwards and possibly their scrum half as well. The deeper he can take up his position behind a scrum or a line-out, the straighter they will have to converge upon him. The straighter they do so, the more easily they can be drawn.

Authorities of the game are of the opinion that the fly half need not position himself more than two yards, at the most, behind the scrum. The distance in depth behind the scrum at which he has to take up his position is determined by the length and speed of his scrum half's pass and to what depth his opponents are lying. It has been calculated that if a fly half wishes to give his wing 5 yards for manoeuvring with the ball, he must be 19 yards from his opponent when passing the ball. From a line-out there are 20 yards between the fly halves. This means that the attacking fly half must *pass*, not receive, the ball on the so-called 10 yards off-side line. At a line-out, the 10 yards off-side line, or beyond it, is therefore his passing line. At a scrum his passing line is right behind it and as far out from it as is made possible by his scrum half's pass. The longer the scrum half's pass, the better. As a rule the fly half starts running only when the ball is near him and not when the ball emerges from the scrum or when the scrum half takes it.

Running straight
What about the backs? We expect that they, like the fly half, will run straight, or as nearly so as possible. They must not run diagonally, because they will then neither be able to draw the defenders nor to make their "push-off" or thrust, as part of their attack, effective.

If all the different attacking and defending streams are put on paper, the following conclusions will be reached:
1. The shallower the defenders' line-up, and the more obliquely they come up, the more difficult it is to beat them on the inside. The more diagonally the attackers run, the more difficult it is to beat such defenders.
2. In order to beat a defender coming up diagonally on the inside, one need merely use the straightening technique.
3. The more diagonally an attacker runs, the more his thrust will land in the defensive stream. The straighter he runs, the less the danger of this. This applies to both the inside and the outside gaps.
4. The straighter an attacker runs, the more difficult it is for the defender to turn round if the attack succeeds, and the sooner therefore the attackers will have cut right through the gap.
5. The faster an attacker runs, the smaller his side-step push-off will be, and the closer he will thus be to the defender. However, the slower he runs, the more time the defenders will be given for cutting across, consequently he will run into more defenders.
6. The more diagonally the attackers run, the further apart the defenders can position themselves and the more gaps they will be able to plug.
7. For the outside gap the following requirements are needed: ability to keep the defender on the inside (dummy in that direction); and, necessary speed. If speed is harnessed to straight running, the attacker's task is an easy one.
8. The straighter an attacker runs, the easier it is to beat a defender on his inside through the outside gap, or even to beat him through the inside gap by catching him on the wrong foot. It will also be easier to beat an opponent who is on the attacker's outside, on his inside, and to beat a defender who is right in front of him, on either side. The more diagonally an attacker runs, the more difficult it is for him to beat an opponent in the three positions mentioned above. It must be added that the greater the distance, as far as depth is concerned, a defender is from the inside hip of the attacker, the more easily can the defender be beaten on his inside; the further the width, the more easily he is beaten on the outside.
9. The straighter an attacker runs, the more he can see of other players. He can also link up better with his forwards, and will be able to spot boxes or gaps more easily.
10. The straighter a player runs, the more easily he will be able to break through a tackle.

A player must teach himself not to run straight at the outset only, but to persevere in doing so. Should he start running diagonally later on, he must straighten again. If a player can do this, he need not rely on the starting position in order to straighten.

A back will find it difficult to straighten on his own because if his partner, who runs diagonally, passes the ball to him, he will have to take up a position quite a distance from him if he wants to run straight.

In the diagram (next page) the inside centre (C1) will be on the inside of his fly half if he starts running straight from the outset. Alternatively he will also have to run diagonally at first and only then straighten out (C1). Centres should

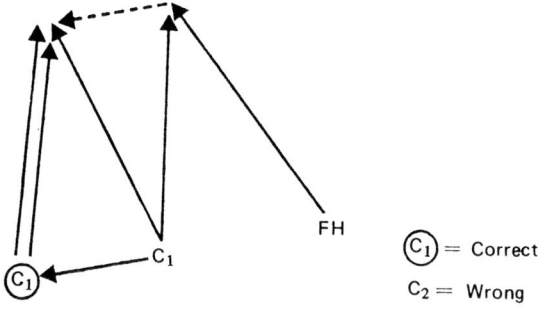

C_1 = Correct
C_2 = Wrong

learn both methods, as well as concealing their starting position, especially as regards (C1) above. In order to do this they can vary their positions. But when it suits them, they must "pick up the trail".

Length of passes

Backs must also learn to "play concertina", i.e. they must vary the length of the pass they receive from their partner. This means they must never take a pass always at the same distance from him. They must take it sometimes close to him and sometimes moderately far from him. As regards their position in depth, centres must pay close attention to space. If they have to cope with shallow-lying opponents, especially at a scrum, they must not receive the ball in line with the passer but behind him. In this way each of them will increase the distance separating them from their opponents by three or more yards.

Lining-up in depth by the back line

The degree of lining-up deeply by the back line must be commensurate with passing in depth.

Starting off

The inside centre should now also set off only when the fly half's pass is already on its way. The outside centre does likewise in relation to the inside centre, as does the wing in relation to the outside centre. They may also start off simultaneously with the fly half. Should they do so, they must bear in mind that they will receive the ball in a shallower position because, while the ball is on its way to them, they will move a yard or two. In general play the aim of the backs

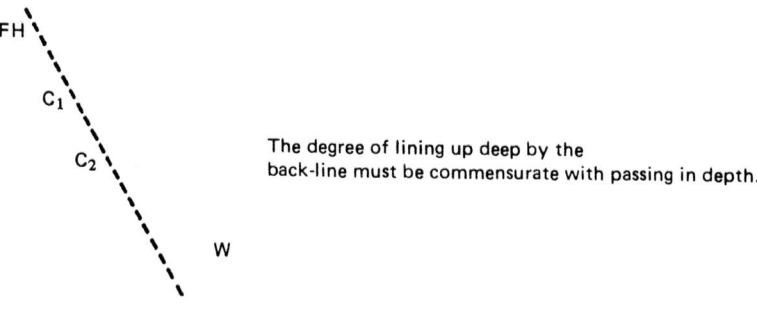

The degree of lining up deep by the back-line must be commensurate with passing in depth.

should indeed be to run as little as possible while the ball is on its way to them. If centres start running with their fly halves, they must lie very deep by taking up a position far behind them.

The centres and wings can also take up a position in a straight line two or three yards behind their fly half, starting to run only when the ball is on its way to them. In this way, no space is lost by running without the ball and they will receive the ball behind the passer, not in a straight or near-straight line.

What distance must the ball be carried?
The answer to this is straightforward. In general play the ball is not carried. All that a player does is to send a ball, already on its way, further on its course. Running is thus a side issue. A player need not even run, as has been pointed out. Running is merely a means of varying the game and for being at full speed when a gap is in the offing – something which hardly ever occurs in top-class Rugby. A player in this grade of Rugby must make his own openings, and running is a means of creating openings. If punts are used as an attacking method, running is a means of getting to the ball sooner. If being stationary helps a player to kick more accurately, and he is quick off the mark, then being stationary can even be effective for this purpose. If, by being stationary, he can cope the better with his drop kicks, he will be unwise if he runs.

The abovementioned methods are recommended because backs must get out of the rut in which back-line players tend to find themselves. If players are running at full speed while the ball is on its way to the wing, they need not always receive, and this is often done. If, however, they do wish to attack by means of running, they must conceal their speed and then use it to beat an opponent. The faster an attacker runs, the less he sees; if his speed is decreased, the larger his field of vision will become. Moreover, your opponent attunes himself to your speed. Should you therefore be in possession of reserve speed, your opponent becomes an easy prey: you know when you are going to accelerate, but he doesn't know. Of, if he is running full tilt, he will not be able to change direction when you start turning on your speed. If a player cannot conceal his speed, all eyes will be focused on him when he starts decreasing his speed and he will become a common target. What must not happen is that a player's speed is broken by a bad pass. This causes him to concentrate on the pass and his range of vision is thus cut off, and this can hardly be regained in the space of time at his disposal.

Flawless passes
For the reasons mentioned above, passes should be flawless, i.e. in front of players at extended arm's length. In order to save time, receivers of the ball must go to meet the ball with their hands, they must go to "fetch" it and pass it in one movement. This means that a pass may be given off either foot; in other words, from the foot which is in front when the passing movement is rounded off.

Drawing an opponent
Here running serves a very useful purpose: it is not easy to draw an opponent

but it can be done by looking up at him – especially at his eyes or even towards his inside – immediately after the hands have made contact with the ball. One can even deviate from the usual rule by deliberately holding the ball briefly on the inside; or, if the ball is taken in front of you, moving towards the inside, looking in that direction, i.e. a kind of short-cut dummy. If one of these actions is coupled with straight running or running on the inside of an opponent, he will still be drawn even if the other things are not done. Running up to an opponent in an attempt to draw him, or passing the ball from the opposite hip, however, is but half the matter.

An opponent is drawn by causing him to run in a direction contrary to the one in which your pass is going to go. In this way he is prevented from helping his team-mates on defence, or being nearby when one of your team-mates is tackled or is forced into making a mistake. It is quite true that an attacker sometimes compels a defender to tackle him because at the moment this happens, or shortly before it, he can send a co-attacker on his way. As a rule this happens if you wish to put a man over.

A scrum half, for instance, breaks round the blind-side and draws the opponents' wing in order to send his own wing on his way. Or an outside centre draws both his opponent and the opposing wing in order to send his own wing away.

As stated, a back-line player must "play concertina", but when the ball is sent to the wing it is advisable to give long passes. In this way the opposing players are drawn out – a good preparation for broken play. If this happens a few times, the gaps between them are increased and their formation is disrupted.

Following-up the ball

General play assumes that a back will follow up the ball as soon as he has passed it, but a warning must be given about this. We have stated that a back passes the ball from either foot. Suppose the foot nearest to his team-mate is in front when passing, and suppose he follows up his pass, the result can easily be diagonal running. Consequently the ball must be passed before it is followed and these two distinctly separate actions must not be blended into a single one.

Catching a ball and passing it requires great skill. Even more skill is needed for passing the ball at the correct moment. The old golden rule that you should pass a ball to a player in a more favourable position (on attack and in defence) than yourself, still holds good. It is also true that a ball travels faster than a player can run; that possession is nine points of the law; that matches are won by the team making the fewest mistakes; that if one wishes to win one must see to it that loose balls behind the opposing forwards are exploited; that if you are defeated, you must seek the culprit responsible for having caused loose balls to be exploited behind your forwards.

Summing-up

Attacking back-line players line up as deeply as they are allowed to do by their opposing numbers, and as deeply as is required for getting the ball to their wing. They position themselves in such a way that they can draw their opponents and straighten the line, which is a method for drawing opponents. They line up so deeply that their passes can be given behind them.

Attacking backs need not start running when they receive the ball; by being stationary their receiving position and passing position are at the same spot. Backs do not run with the ball; the ball is merely sent along on its way. For this reason the ball is "fetched" and sent on its way in one movement, being passed off the foot which is foremost in the process. If this is done, running is a side-issue of the process, although it can be usefully applied for drawing an opponent without running right up to him or forcing him into tackling. As soon as the ball has been passed, it must be followed up.

Mistakes in general play
As attackers
1. Players take up an identical starting position in width, both for attack and defence. If they are too closely bunched for attack they will run diagonally and not be able to draw their opponents.
2. The backs run too fast, instead of two yards at the most.
3. They always pass off the furthest foot instead of passing off either foot, thus forfeiting speed in passing.
4. They do not follow up the ball.
5. If there is a loose ball, they wait for a forward to try and get possession of it.
6. If they are tackled, they do not try and break the tackle or, if this is not possible, try and turn round to keep the ball in play.

General attacking back-line play from a ruck or maul
Although it is impossible to lay down any law regarding general play following rucks and mauls, there are nevertheless some hints and principles that can be mentioned.

It may be said that a planned ruck or a maul can be regarded as tight play; in other words, it becomes a scrum, as it were, and if this is the case it also means that we have some form of general back-line play. There is, however, a difference between general back play after a scrum and after a ruck or a maul. Whereas a back-line positions itself deeply at a scrum when it is their put-in, it lines shallowly for some rucks and mauls. With a static ruck or a static maul, both back-lines lie so shallow that the ball cannot get to the wing. Hence our recommendation that the scrum half should break. From a dynamic ruck or maul we advise that the ball should go out to the wing because, in most cases, there will be a man over. General attacking back play therefore originates from a dynamic ruck or maul. In recommending that defenders should also position themselves in a shallow line for any kind of ruck or maul, it should be pointed out that things happen so quickly at dynamic rucks and mauls that the recommendation is not always practicable. It pays a back-line to employ general attacking back play from a static ruck or maul if neither the scrum half nor the fly half breaks.

As a rule, the backs line up too deeply if they anticipate getting the ball from a ruck or maul. If they have attack in mind, it is perfectly in order to do so at a static ruck or maul. However, should they be deeply positioned at a dynamic ruck or maul, they fritter away the advantages of possession. After all, it remains the aim of every back to cross the advantage line (the hypothetical line running through the tunnel of the scrum or through the centre of the line-out). If a back achieves this, his forwards will be back in the game, and even if mistakes are made, they will occur in front of his forwards and behind the opposing forwards. It is possible to cross the advantage line quickly with possession gained from a dynamic ruck or maul. This is one of the few occasions when attackers can take up a shallow position and have the advantage line between themselves and their opponents. If a deep-lying position is taken up, the opponents will be given the opportunity of rectifying or reorganising their disrupted ranks.

In a dynamic ruck or maul your forwards will be moving ahead. Backs must advance with their forwards in order to line up shallow if possession is gained. In most cases it is the forwards who advance with the backs before a dynamic ruck or maul is formed. It remains a fact that whoever may be responsible for the movement leading to the formation of a dynamic ruck or maul, forwards and backs must move up in line in order to do full justice to possession.

The above holds good not only for any advancing movement but also for kicks ahead. If the defenders check such a movement by the back-line and launch a countermove, they will be successful if the forwards have been left in the rear. And if the forwards move ahead and the backs lag behind, the opposing backs will be successful if they can start a counter-move, for instance when a team takes a kick-off or a drop-out. Suppose the forwards run up while their back-line hangs back. The opponents will gain possession and attack with their back-line. Where will they be stopped? Certainly not in front of but behind the forwards. This will not be to the advantage of the side taking the kick.

It sometimes happens that a kick ahead does not go into touch. Usually only the forwards follow up the ball. The opposing full back gets the ball and cuts infield. If the back-line of the kicking team does not go up with their forwards, the movement started by the full back may succeed. This will not be the case if the back-line moves up with the forwards.

We are here discussing advancing movements and also kicks ahead, because these often lead to dynamic rucks and mauls. As stated above, there are few occasions when the advantage line is between the opposing back-lines. From a scrum and a line-out the advantage line is behind the defenders. But apart from the dynamic ruck or maul, this is also the case if a pack of forwards hook from the tight-head side or if a tap penalty kick is used. If a team has a strong back-line, these two chances must be exploited, just as in the case of possession gained from a dynamic ruck or maul.

General attacking forward play
From the scrum
In order to understand attacking forward play it is best to divide the scrummage into two sections: the loose-head side consisting mainly of the loose-head prop, the loose-head flanker and the loose-head lock, and the tight-head side consisting of the tight-head prop, the tight-head flanker, and the tight-head lock. The hooker and the number eight belong to both sections.

Furthermore, we dub the movements going to a team's loose-head side, a loose-head movement, and a movement going to the tight-head side a tight-head movement. What is a loose-head movement for one team is a tight-head movement for the other. It must also be borne in mind that a scrum is inclined to swing towards the loose-head side. In fact this happens with almost every scrum.

The first phase of general attacking forward play is the breaking up from the scrum. The second phase begins when the first phase has been completed. Breaking up determines which forwards will first catch up with the ball, and this again determines many other things. Therefore breaking up must not be neglected.

If we know what facilitates breaking up, we shall also know what to do: a pack of forwards moving ahead breaks up more easily than one on the retreat. The pack getting in the first shove can thus break up the more easily. We have earlier stressed that the first shove must be retained.

The first shove therefore helps a pack of forwards to break up sooner than their opponents because while the opponents are breaking up, they must still feel the pressure from up front. Breaking up is therefore part of moving ahead; it is the end of the first shove.

But the first shove does more than this: the scrum usually swings to the loose-head side. Consequently the tight-head side of a scrum is at a great disadvantage when a tight-head movement takes place. Their immediate opponents, the loose-head side, already having the advantage of the loose-head side for breaking up more quickly than they can, are already nearer to the ball. For this reason a tight-head side must not swing for a tight-head movement. The first shove must also take care of this.

If it is a loose-head movement, then the scrum is swung for this very reason. This assures that the loose-head side gains a big advantage. The first shove ends after all the joints of the body have been straightened, or straightened to the extent demanded by the scrum. But a pack may decide to push their opponents more than is required for the first shove. If they succeed in this, their scrum half, their fly half, or entire back-line can attack without having to contend with loose forwards in their way. In fact, a pack will be wise if it follows up the first shove with another shove with the specific aim of helping its backs.

For the second shove, one foot of each player in the second and third rows is advanced while the front row transfer their entire weight on to the foremost feet in order to be able to step forward with their rearmost feet. Consequently they push with their foremost feet. Every forward therefore pushes off one foot, and if the second and third rows do so with their right feet, they will prevent the tight-head side from slewing round.

Because the loose-head side can break more easily from a scrum, they can easily pull out their team-mates to get them on their way to the ball sooner.

But pushing in the scrum, using all available power for breaking up, going in hard pursuit of the ball and keeping up for 60 to 80 minutes is expecting too much of any player. For this reason a team may decide that the type of movement determines on which side of the scrum the fast running will take place. If it is a tight-head movement, the tight-head side players move at full speed;

if it is a loose-head movement, it is their turn to go at full speed. Immediately their help is needed, however, the forwards who are coasting along will increase their pace and go into top speed. If the scrum has come to an end, the road of the tight forwards is the shortest one towards the ball. For the loose forwards, however, the matter is not so simple.

When later we discuss general defensive forward play, we shall see that the number eight breaks up as soon as the opposing hooker strikes the ball. If his own hooker strikes the ball, his own scrum ought to be locked, his lock forwards remaining in a straight position so that the number eight's pushing power is no longer required. He can therefore withdraw his head without letting go with his hands or adjusting his feet. He must be able to see in which direction he has to set off. His aim is his own fly half, because he wants to be on his inside. From this position his aim is moving from inside to inside and closely hugging back after back. Should a back make a mistake, the number eight should be on the spot to rectify it. Should one of the backs be tackled, he takes play forward or sees to it that his team maintains possession. The flanker on the side from which the movement originates, runs close behind, following the identical track. Loose forwards always work in pairs and the one must depend on the other while the backs must rely on both of them. And the flankers are assisted by the blind-side wing should the ball travel infield. The best path of the blind-side wing also is hugging his back-line players. He serves as a reserve strength whose help may be depended upon at any time.

The flanker on the other side of the scrum either follows the ball too, or takes up the position of his blind-side wing until it becomes clear that none of his own backs, or those on the opposing side, will come his way and that his help is more urgently required where the ball is.

The line-out
The way line-outs are today, the forwards take the shortest cut to the ball. Loose forwards still try their utmost to do the same as they do from a scrum.

General defensive back-line and forward play
Tight forwards make loose forwards
We have become accustomed to using our loose forwards in general play. This is indeed right. Although their first and most important tasks are in the tight game, it remains a fact that they push least in the scrum and as a rule are less subject to the hardships endured by the tight forwards. Locks push with both shoulders, the props push and get pushed from front and behind, but the flankers push only from an outside leg. This is an important duty, however, which must not be neglected, yet it is not such an exacting task as that of the five tight forwards. Actually, the number eight pushes harder than the tight forwards because he must help the locks in front of him to straighten out completely with his push. His shove is practically like that of a lock forward. For this reason locks are often used as a number eight because in this way the weight of the scrum can be increased. The number eight's shove is of even shorter duration than that of the flanker because, as soon as the locks in front of him are straightened, his task is completed and he can withdraw his head

from the scrum. The flanker, however, must remain straightened after the shove in order to assist the props in retaining the advantage gained.

We often hear the claim that the better the tight forwards perform their tasks, the more their loose forwards can achieve in the loose. This is true. It is because South Africa's tight forwards have always been so strong, and have confined themselves to their main tasks, that she has had so many great loose forwards. This feature has caused present-day loose forwards to try to emulate them. They will not, however, succeed in their efforts unless South Africa's tight forwards revert to what was done by their predecessors. The tight forwards determine what can be achieved by the loose forwards in the loose play. The loose forwards can break away from the scrum sooner than the tight forwards. For this reason they can also be used for defence, on condition that this will not adversely affect their tight play.

Defence of the loose forwards round the scrum
We start with the most important duties of the loose forwards, i.e. round the scrum, where they and their half-backs form a defensive front. How the forwards are used is actually a tactical question, because it is not basic. What follows is the result of many experiments.

The number eight
We have said that the number eight may withdraw his head after giving his first shove. The supposition is that the locks are straightened, that every forward has fulfilled his task and that the scrum is thus locked. A scrum is "locked" as soon as a forward has straightened his pushing leg or legs and the second row of the scrum and the number eight have also straightened their bodies. In this position they cannot be pushed away. It is like a straight post lying on the ground – if it is not picked up at one end, not even Superman will be able to push it away, unless the post slides. Pushing away in this sense does not mean sliding but bulging. Bulging, again, means that straightened or partly-straightened joints bend and forfeit what has been achieved. If forwards push until they are locked, they might perhaps slide, but there is no danger of bulging. Nor will they slide if their feet are placed correctly and if they have seen to it that the studs of their boots are in order.

A number eight who pushes after his lock forwards are locked, or after he himself is locked, places an additional burden on the locks who are already holding on with their arms to their front row. The moment the opposing hooker strikes the ball, the number eight withdraws his head from the scrum because at that moment he has already given his first shove. He also lets go of his lock forwards so that he forms no part of the scrum at all. By doing this he transfers the off-side line from his feet to the feet of the second row. The other advantage will be that the flankers can get into play. Even if they do break up before the ball emerges from the scrum they will not be off-side. This also brings the backs slightly nearer to their opponents.

To the backs, defence means to tackle or stop your man as deeply behind the opposing forwards as possible and as far as possible from your own side of the scrum or line-out. The nearer they come to their scrum line or advantage line, the more easily their forwards will come back into the game. The further they are away, the more difficult it will be for them. Therefore "Hit them up front" is the expression (obviously "hit" is not used in the literal sense of "striking" but is synonymous with tackle, win, or beat). Or, as old Maestro Mark always used to say: "Close the gate up front and not behind."

The backs thus make use of every inch of ground which will bring them closer to their opponents. The opponents are thus taken on "up front". Should an opponent beat or "hit" one of them, there is still sufficient space in which the loose forwards can stop them, which is another advantage attached to "hitting up front".

Flankers

The number eight breaks as soon as the hooker has struck the ball. The flankers break when it suits them. They are on-side if they remain on or move along the off-side line.

But they will not leave their scrum just like that. First of all they must know that their tight forwards are locked and not able to be pushed away. Secondly they must know whether their opponents are going to hold the ball or not. They, unlike the number eight, break with their heads turned sideways, but they still hold on to the locks with their inside arms. Should the opponents hold the ball, the flankers simply slide their shoulders back in position. Should the ball be hooked quickly, they are in a position to sum up the development on their side of the scrum and to act accordingly. Should the scrum slew round, the loose-head flanker lets go with his arm so that he does not go with the swing. He is also then in no way off-side because the swing takes the feet of the locks forward. Should the opposing scrum half or fly half come up with a break, then the flanker is on hand. Should the scrum half break on his loose-head side by means of a swivel break, for instance, the tight-head flanker will easily stop him. This is another reason why the tight-head side of the scrum must not yield an inch in such a situation.

The three loose-forwards are thus at the disposal of the defence as soon as they have broken up, and from this moment onwards there must be order and system in their actions. We illustrate these actions and those of their scrum half and fly half diagrammatically for a scrum with the blind-side next to the right-hand touchline, one in the centre (the so-called centre scrummage) and one with the blind-side next to the left-hand touchline.

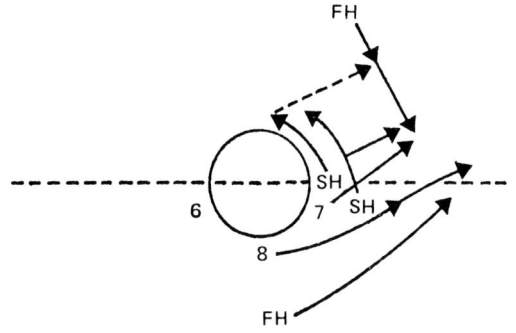

Scrum next to right-hand touchline—fly half of the opposing team takes the blind side. The same method of defence is followed if the opposing fly half moves to the left from a centre scrum.

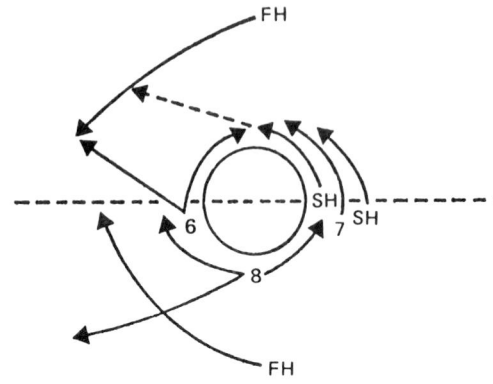

Scrum next to the left-hand touchline—fly half of the opposing team takes the blind-side. The same method of defence is followed if the opposing fly half moves to the right from a centre scrummage.

The halves and loose forwards

There are always four defenders on the right-hand side and three on the left-hand side of any scrum. The defenders, consisting of the scrum half and the flanker on the right-hand side and the fly half and flanker on the left-hand side, are the nearest to the opponents and they form the foremost line of defence. Then there is the second line of defence, the coverers. On the right-hand side they are the number eight and the fly half, and on the left-hand side the number eight.

It will be noticed that the fly half never takes up an entirely shallow position, but somewhat to the left-hand side of the scrum. The reason for this is obvious: he remains responsible for looking after his own opponents and he must take up position in such a way that he will be able to lend a hand on either side, whether or not he is in the first or second line of defence. He can see from the way in which the ball is struck on which side danger threatens and must be in a position where he can arrive there in time. But because there are three defenders on the right-hand side and only one in the first line of defence on the left-hand side, the fly half takes up his position with an eye to this side. Should the opposing scrum half break round that side – and actually it is his breaking side – and draw the flanks, he can easily send the fly half on his way. The fly half also lines up somewhat deeply in the event of his pack gaining a loose-head scrummage.

We notice that the scrum half takes up his position behind his opposite number. This is in order to get on to his opponent's back more easily and to cut off his opponent's pass. A pass from scrum half to fly half on this side is extremely difficult because the scrum half has his back towards the fly half. It is therefore easy to prevent this pass. The defending scrum half can do this more easily if he takes up position behind his opponent. Many scrum halves are chary of their passes from this side. That is why they prefer to kick than attempt to pass.

If the scrum half does not cut off his opponent's pass and the fly half moves on the right-hand side, the scrum half, supported by his flanker and covered by his number eight, goes for the fly half's inside hip. Should the fly half attempt to break, his opposing number is at the ready, supported by the number eight, and if the ball is passed immediately, he is supported by the loose-head flanker.

If a scrum has no blind side, the defence remains the same, but the fly half takes up a shallow position on the side. He therefore always positions himself shallow on the open side if a scrum has no blind side. Should his team win a tight-head ball, he is in a good attacking position because he crosses the advantage line even if his break is not successful.

There is one disadvantage attached to all these kinds of defensive methods round the scrum – a scrum next to the left-hand side touchline. We have said that a defensive line must be straight, and that the fly half is the pivot round which such a line moves. If a scrum on the left-hand touchline has a blind side, the fly half's position is too much to the left for defence. There must be another pivot, and this is simply the foremost player on his way to the opposing fly half, either the scrum half or the flanker.

The centres
The centres line up as shallow as possible, in front of the fly half at a right-hand side touchline or with a centre scrum. They stand close together if it is a side scrum. Whatever method is followed, the centres must be assured that there are players who will see to the opposing fly half so that they will not have to hesitate. Such hesitation is fatal.

The pivot
To get back, however, to the pivot of defence. If it is the fly half, and his opposing number passes the ball, the inside centre instead becomes the pivot and the defensive line from him is straight but at an angle to the rear.

If the outside centre becomes the pivot, he and the wing must be in a straight line. This "straight line", however, is more than just straight; it is at an angle to the rear and then just sufficiently so.

At first, the wing stands far from his outside centre, but his three partners are positioned close together and at an angle to the rear. If the opposing fly half passes the ball, this formation is maintained by the inside and outside centres, while the wing also comes closer. If the opponent's inside centre passes the ball, the outside centre continues the movement and he and the wing form the line.

Before discussing the position of the wings, we must say something about the line drawn up at an angle to the rear. Why is this done? The answer is simple: to close the outside gap. Should an attacker beat a defender, he will run into trouble from the next defender in the line. If the defensive line is straight, but not at an angle to the rear, both outside and inside gaps are vulnerable.

It is this oblique formation which is maintained throughout. For this reason a defender not only keeps an eye on the attackers but also keeps the pivot in sight. If the line does not remain straight, and one of the players goes up before the rest, a gap will be created behind him, and this can be exploited for a break or punt. Another important point: a defender is not exclusively responsible for his own opponent but also for his partner's opponent if the latter uses the extremity of the inside gap.

It also shows a defender what he must do when his partner takes over the defence. He closes the extreme part of the inside gap, and only when he has done this may he proceed to help. Before he crosses – or, as we say, before he covers – he first of all goes a short distance forward, with his team-mates on his outside, running slower to get behind his partner. This will ensure that his partner's inside gap is closed.

The wings
Before describing the line of approach, something must first be said about the task of the wing in defence.

The blind-side wing positions himself as far up in front as possible. The open-side wing hangs back far from his inside centre. The blind-side wing is positioned for a blind-side movement which must be met as far up in front as possible, i.e. he does not wait for the movement. As soon as the opponents' scrum half passes the ball (even before he does so) everybody already knows if the fly half is going to work the blind-side or not. If the blind-side wing sees that his services are not required up front, he must go over to perform his second task of removing the empty space (box) behind him. For this reason he will fall back as soon as possible, but obliquely to the back in order to close the box should the opposing fly half kick into it. Thus, while the scrum half's pass is still on its way to the fly half, the wing is on his way to the vacant spot (box). If the fly half passes, the wing covers, and his path goes obliquely ahead in order quickly to render harmless any possible danger.

The open-side wing also has his eyes trained on the opposing fly half, who might kick to the empty spaces (boxes) in his area. Therefore he not only closes the box but keeps it closed. He merely trots while coming up for defence as long as the fly half still has the ball. Should the fly half pass, the wing increases his pace but does not run full out because the opposing inside centre may test the box by means of a punt. In such a case the wing must get to the ball. Only when the inside centre passes does he run as fast as he can, seeing to it that he keeps the line straight. His path and that of his team-mates then converge.

Which directions do those defensive paths take?
There are two kinds of path, but their ultimate aim remains the same – the opponent's inside hips. The first method consists of keeping speed in reserve from the starting position until the inside gap is closed, i.e. until the opponent's inside hip is on the outside – to put it differently, until the opponent can test only the outside gap. Now the taps are turned on and the running is at full speed. Whether the opponent is going to break through or not, there will be no hesitation and a beeline is made for that inside gap. For any defender, that moment when he decides on going for the inside hip is the point of no return.

Judgment and defence
We may be pardoned for deviating somewhat from the subject under discussion by saying that judgment plays a very important part in Rugby, and that most of the mistakes on the field are the result of incorrect judgment. Application of skills is thus varied as much as possible with the aim of helping players to make the correct decision in the numerous situations which may crop up in the game. If a defender's judgment is wrong when going for the inside hip, he can rest assured that this will not be the only occasion and that he will not be

the only player to make this mistake. The best player is one who makes the fewest mistakes regardless of the many situations in which he may find himself.

The method of defence we have described here is based on speed control. The route taken is actually straight and at an angle to the front, and it is speed which controls the inside hip.

In the second method speed is used precisely the other way about. At the outset it is flat out, but then becomes slower. When running flat out, care must be taken that the defender is on the inside of his opponent and consequently

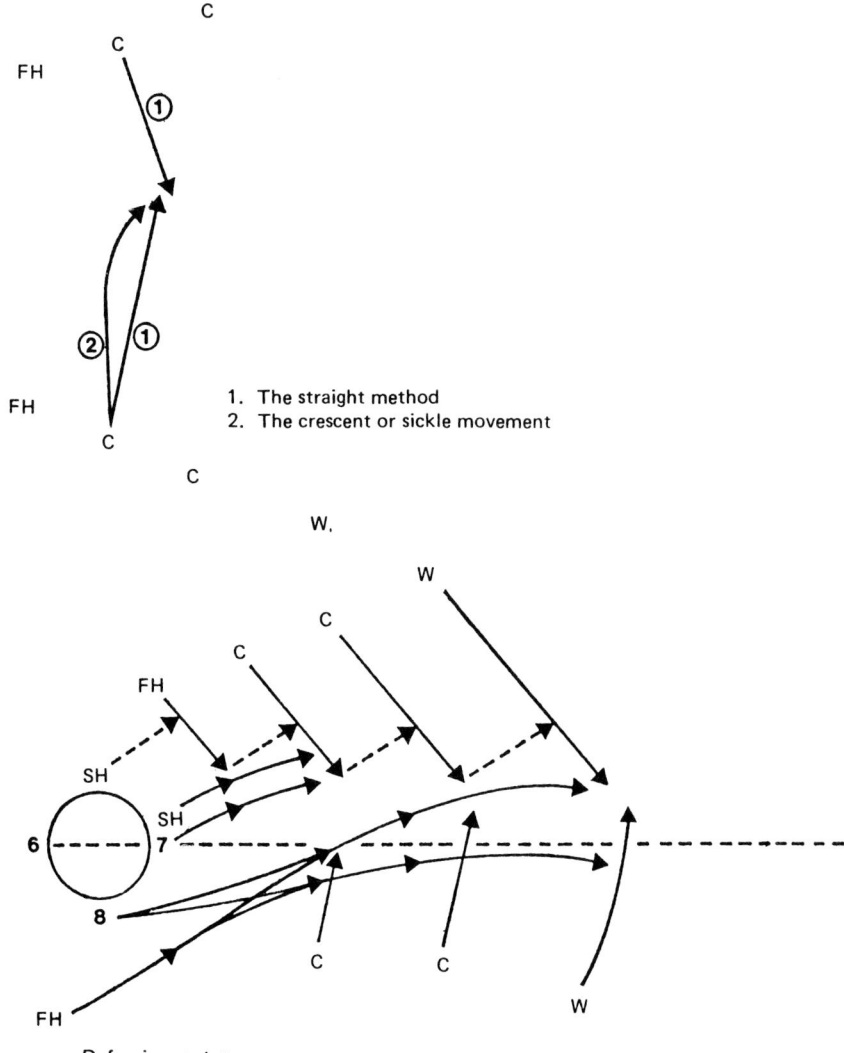

1. The straight method
2. The crescent or sickle movement

Defensive routes

8 indicates the two routes no. 8 can follow;
7 indicates the field-side flank's route when following the ball

this method is more straightforward than the other. At a particular spot – again a matter of judgment – a deliberate curved run is followed while the speed is considerably diminished by taking shorter steps. The outside gap is practically offered to the defenders and they are taunted to the rhyme of "Try and take it, mate, or you're too late". The two methods are illustrated diagrammatically:

In the diagram the first method described is called the "straight method". The second is the "crescent" or "sickle" movement, so called because a sickle has a straight handle and a curved blade. The first is recommended if there is a possibility of tackling the man with the ball in possession, as we have in a movement from a scrum when the centres and the wings are concerned. The second method is recommended when the opponents have space for movement, as is the case from a line-out.

The second method may also be used against opponents showing an inclination for taking either the inside gap or the outside gap, because the inside gap is closed and the outside one can be blocked when an opponent attempts taking it. It can also be used for selfish attackers when it becomes clear that they attempt to break on every possible occasion. It has the disadvantage that you leave the outside gap open for punts, but it has the advantage that you can easily turn round and render such punts innocuous. The way we play today depends on whether a player is left-footed or right-footed and which foot he is going to use for these punts. If he has to use his left foot, one knows in advance that he will not attempt a grubber kick or a punt. This is indeed a sad state of affairs. With this method, however, to the right-hand side of your tight play, such punts need not be taken into consideration.

Routes

We know now how defence is undertaken around the scrum and how a back line comes up on defence. The next question to be discussed is this: what do the defenders of the scrum do when they need not defend? What paths do they now follow?

The diagram will show that the blind-side flanker plays forward as if the scrum half is going to break on that side. In fact, all the defenders around the scrum play forward time and again. If the blind-side flanker's services are not needed up front, he may follow one of two courses: he either goes round the opposing scrum and follows the ball, or he takes up the position of the blind-side wing. The first course is determined by the position in depth taken up by the opponents. Should the movement go open-side, the opponents will definitely still lie deep, and it is advisable that the flank should go round their side of the scrum and not round his own side. If one of them is tackled, blocked or makes a mistake, then he is at hand to give assistance.

Should his pack lose a loose-head scrum, he is well advised to go round his own side of the scrum because the opposing back-line players are lined up shallow in such cases.

The second course of taking the blind-side wing's position can be followed if the opponents are very good and play with their backs, bringing the ball back to their forwards when the back-line movement breaks down on the other side of the field. This is also a measure for countering an opposing team that has a predilection for hooked kicks into boxes. But today this happens so seldom that very few flankers need follow this course, consequently it is advisable not to remain in the wing's position, but rather to move across to the other side of the field. If the blind-side wing returns to his usual position, the blind-side flanker takes up his position among the other forwards and he and his wing cross on their way to their respective positions. However, as long as the blind-side wing can do useful work, he remains on the playing side of the field.

The other defenders of the scrum take the shortest route after the ball because every player's assistance is needed should broken play occur or should a ruck or maul take place. The open-side flank is at the forefront and follows the ball as fast as he can. His course is determined by the course of the ball. The course taken by the fly half, on the other hand, determines the course taken by the number eight, who can do one of two things: he either moves close to his own backs from inside gap to inside gap, or he covers a short distance behind them. The advantage of the first method is that he is in front for any eventuality; secondly, he can render punts ineffective, or help with them. These two courses are illustrated in the diagrams on page 67.

The full back
The full back must be able to depend on his two wings, who still have to defend a section of their touchlines. If he can depend on their services, he does not position himself behind the blind-side scrum but deeper infield, approximately opposite the opposing centres, not his own. His position should never be in the middle of the pitch, as is so frequently seen nowadays. The attacking centres will indicate how the ball will be sent across the field, and it must be the full back's aim to be slightly ahead of the ball. His position in depth depends on many things. Against the wind he will be deeper. With the wind he will be shallower. With the sun in his eyes he will also be shallower in order to get the ball on his side. In rain he will be somewhat shallower because the ball is heavy and cannot travel far and also because he will be under constant pressure from high kicks and punts. The nearer he is to his own touch-in-goal line, the shallower he will be; the further away, the deeper. Experience will teach him what position in depth he must take up and the manner of play of the opponents will also dictate what he must do.

The full back must, on his way across the field, maintain the depth of his starting position, i.e. he must be the same distance in depth behind his back-line players. Thus he moves obliquely ahead, across the field and not backwards.

Mistakes made by defenders
1. As defenders, the backs go full tilt for their opponents instead of going up on the opponents' inside.
2. Their eyes are trained only on their opponents instead of looking at their team-mates to ensure that the defence line is straight.
3. They use the same formation in defence and attack.
4. Their position is too widely spaced.
5. The fly half does not come up and relies too much on his forwards.

6. They are too much concerned about the man carrying the ball instead of being concerned about the ball which is carried by the player. They must not only tackle the man but the ball with him. If a dive tackle is required, the ball must be "tackled" free.
7. They stop as soon as their opposing number has passed the ball. They should continue going forward for a short distance and then go across the field.
8. There is lack of understanding between the halves and between the halves and their loose forwards.

BROKEN PLAY, INCLUDING TACTICS

Here, once again, is the definition of broken play.

It is play which follows tight play and loose play when a back-line player departs from general attacking back-line play by not letting the ball out to the wing but breaking with it, and succeeds in doing this. This break can be an individual attempt, as when a back beats his opponent, or it can be a combined effort when one or other tactical movement succeeds.

If these attempts, whether individual or combined, are stopped or a handling mistake occurs, we have broken-down play which usually results in rucking.

How is a line broken, how is it dented, and what is to be done after breaking the line? It is impossible to describe every situation, but we will give a few tips which might be of use.

The problem is subdivided into two parts. But first a number of methods and when they are to be followed will be discussed; after which something will be said about what must happen if these methods succeed.

It has already been stated that general attacking back play enables the attackers to discover the defensive equipment of the opponents – the first aim of the attackers. Even if they should lose ground through this, it will pay them to do so. But little time can be given to making this discovery.

All the backs have a common and an individual task in broken play.

Study the starting position
The backs' common task is to study the starting position of their opponents. Are they lined up straight or obliquely to the rear? Are they close together? What position does the open-side wing take up: in line with the other backs or to the back of them, removed, or nearby? Where are the blind-side wing and the full back positioned? This can be determined at a single glance.

Study the general play
Now follow the individual tasks. This is when each player has his own specific job of keeping an eye on opponents when general play is already taking place. The scrum half will not be able to see when the loose forwards break up and what defensive measures they are applying, consequently it is advisable that another player keeps an eye on them, e.g. the blind-side wing. If it is a mid-field scrum, the wing to whose side the movement is not going is entrusted with the task. The same player will have the assignment of keeping an eye on the defensive

methods around the scrum: in what way does the fly half come up, what direction does the number eight follow, does he play ahead or to the rear? Do the flankers move forward? What does the scrum half do? It may take some time to study the defence around the central scrum. The fly half can see how the two centres come up while the wing and the full back can train their eyes on the opposing full back.

Summing-up and the plan of action
Now follows the third task: the backs make a combined summing-up. Each player shares his observations with his fellow-players. This combined observation, together with each player's own observation of his opponent, leads to a plan of action. Obviously players must know what to look for, and this requires a knowledge of back play. It is also a matter of course that the picture cannot be complete at the outset; yet there must be a picture, even if it is incomplete. After a time the full picture is bound to emerge.

Reaction to the conclusions made is now required. The player who co-ordinates everything is the captain, if he is a back-line player, or the leader of the backs. He makes the decision when all available information has been obtained. It can be that the distance between the defenders is wide, or that they are lined up straight and not at an angle to the rear, or that their fly half does not come up for defence. To all this there must be reaction. How is this achieved?

1. By deviating from the principles of general back play. Running, for instance, begins before the proper time in order to get closer to the opponents, who are to be tested. The ball is now passed – not back, but in line with the partner who is going to break; or the distance of the pass is adjusted to the gap to be taken.

Broken play therefore also means a discarding of the principles of general attacking back play. It is all very well if the attempt is successful, but it should not be used a second time because the victim will be on his guard. It is then that another attacker gets an opportunity – of course only if there are many flaws in the opponents' defence methods. It is an axiom that if an attempt is successful, uncertainty rears its head in the opposition camp and their eyes will be kept trained on the successful attacker. This may prove to have just the right effect, because another player can now come to the fore with an attempt based on the observations made. Studying the opponents is a continuous task, and changes in their actions bring about changes in the plans of the attackers.

2. It may be that all seems well in the opposing camp and that their formation will have to be broken or dented. Their method of play can be first-rate, according to your judgment, as it naturally should be in first-class Rugby. But now you use their methods, and your knowledge of these, for disrupting their style of play. In other words, you disrupt their general defensive play and the principles on which this is based. These would include delaying their coming up by making them hesitant about it, which would cause their line to buckle; or you cause them to stretch apart and make the gaps between them bigger; or you compel them to do things to which they are not accustomed by allowing them to come up much closer. Play here consists of passing, kicking, running, and tactics. To get them to alter their defensive methods, you do one of three

things, as you do in life when you encounter opposition, viz., you get "round" it, or you go "over" it, or you go "through" it. Rugby backs do likewise.

(a) *Circumvention*
(i) We have already seen that a threequarter line can remain stationary in general play and that this can be, as a change, a particularly effective method of attack if you have a strong outside and a good wing. The position taken up by the backs is a safe one because this is the passing line or safety line. This means that the opponents cannot bowl them over in possession. Apart from this advantage, it also means that the opposing backs must run much further than usual. Now it is only the opponent who is coming nearer and not you as well. This in itself can sow the seeds of uncertainty among opponents. This safety line serves as a starting point for a different kind of general play. Should we draw a hypothetical line running parallel with the goal-lines and through the place of safety of each back, we could also call them safety lines. A back can take up position at any place on that line, or if he runs, he can pass the ball out without any interference by opponents.

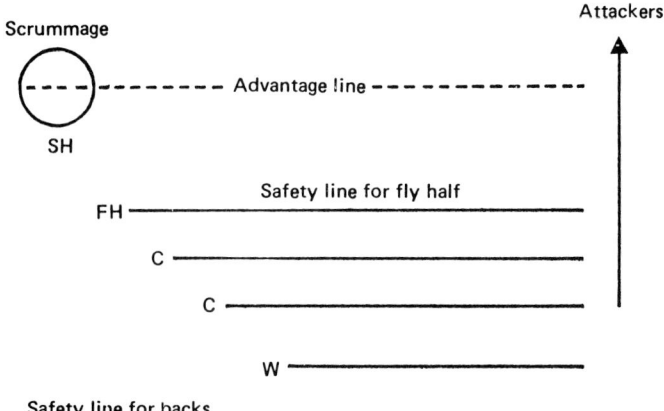

The threequarters now discard all the principles of general play. As soon as their hooker begins to strike the ball, they start running on their safety lines. They run further than usual, but they still give long passes. The outside centre inclines more to straight running and the wing contributes to making the line even straighter, and ten to one he will be able to get round his opposing number. After a few movements of this nature the opponent will start feeling the effects of running such a distance.

The same methods are followed from a centre scrum. (See diagram 1 on page 73.)

From a centre scrum both centres can move on the same side of the fly half and the aim is again "getting round" the opponents. These safety lines offer several possibilities, e.g. the fly half and the centre run far apart from each other from a side scrum, but the outside centre hangs back, and instead of the inside centre receiving the ball, it is given to the outside centre, who cuts through. (See diagram 2 on page 73.)

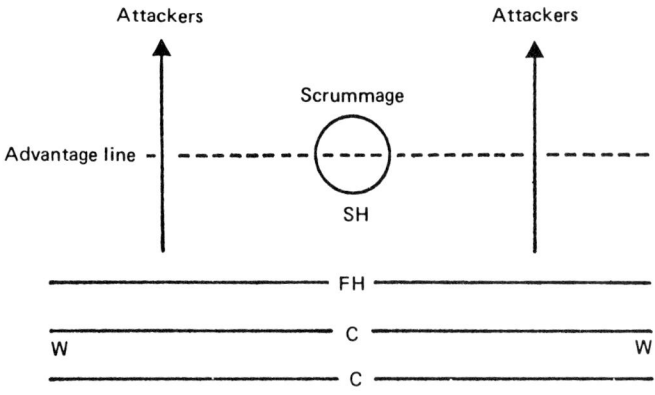

Diagram 1
Safety-lines at a centre scrum

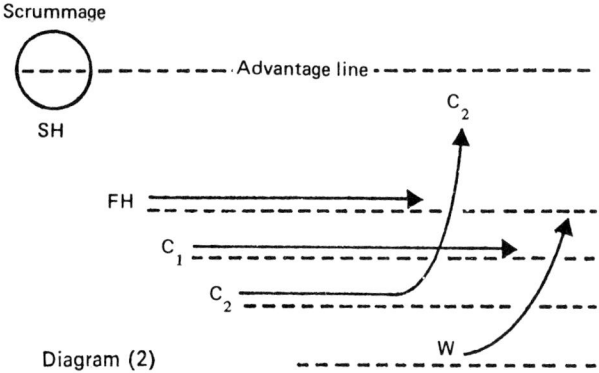

Diagram (2)

On another occasion (diagram 2) the wing hangs back and cuts in between his two centres. Another variation is that all the back-line players move out, but the full back cuts through.

(ii) Another method of circumventing is that of the "shift-pass". This consists of long "hidden" passes between the backs. We use the word "hidden" because this is what actually happens. The usual general back play takes place and the backs can stand even closer to one another than is their custom. The moment, however, the ball is sent on its way to a back, he "shifts" outwards and takes the ball a yard or three further away and in line with the travelling ball. If this is done by all the backs, the wing will have a passage taking him completely, or partially, round his opponent. (See diagram 3 on page 74.)

The inside centre is aligned, as for general play, far from his fly half, and the outside centre shifts out, even before the ball reaches him, by running diagonally across the field; otherwise he will not be able to continue the movement.

This movement offers the same possibilities as the previous one. The fly half and the inside centre, for instance, shift out as usual, but the outside centre does not; he cuts in next to the inside centre and on his outside. Another

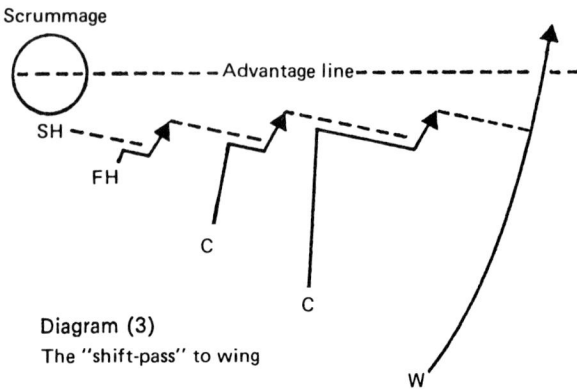

Diagram (3)
The "shift-pass" to wing

variation is when the outside centre shifts far out and then gives an inside pass to his wing. The secret of the "shift pass" is to straighten when receiving the ball, and this as a rule, leads to a pass from the opposite hip.

(iii) *The double pass.* The inside centre doubles round his outside centre immediately after has has passed the ball, taking it again on the outside of the outside centre. If he himself cannot cut through, he can send his wing round his opposing number.

By means of this movement an extra back is created. For this purpose, use can also be made of the blind-side wing, or of the full back, and even of the number eight. Again the object will be to "get round" if they themselves cannot cut through. "Getting round" usually works if a blind-side wing cuts through the first time and lets the ball out to the open-side wing. After the first penetration the opponents will expect another break and they will hesitate. The same applies to the full back when he cuts through the first time.

(iv) A long pass is given by the fly half – leaving out the inside centre – straight to the outside centre. This breaks the rhythm, the defenders "get behind schedule" and it gives the wing the opportunity of breaking.

(b) *"Over" the opponents*
This expression derives from the short punt over an opponent. The expression, however, applies to all kinds of short punts: the ground kick, the grubber kick, and even the knee kick over the opponent. Punts can be a powerful method of attack because they ensure that the ball gets behind the opponents' backs. Any ball in this area seldom spells danger to your own team, which is not the case when the ball is in front of your opponents, and especially when it is behind you. Another advantage of punts is that the attackers move ahead, whereas the defenders must turn back. Yet we see very few punts which are truly dangerous. Why?

(i) Players resort to punting in matches without having practised it a hundred times beforehand.
(ii) Players cannot use either foot for kicking.
(iii) The kick is advertised and lands in the wing's hands.

Punts must be preceded by a dummy because this causes the defenders to exert themselves, or it at least ensures that they do not start decreasing their speed.

Furthermore, one must run into an opponent before giving a grubber, or – after kicking the grubber – the opponent must be blocked. A final point to be remembered: one must create a gap for the grubber and again help to straighten by means of a sudden swerve to the side from which the grubber has been kicked.

Grubber kicks should preferably be placed in empty spaces and the aim should not be to "flatten" the opponent attempting to field the kick. In fact, the player kicking a grubber or a knee kick should place it so accurately that he himself can regain possession. Today, positional play has already been adapted for the corner kick, but if this is preceded by a dummy, it can sometimes still yield dividends. Players must be on the lookout for boxes if they want to attain success with corner kicks, hooked kicks, and certain types of grubber kicks. For this reason a punt need not always be in the same direction as that of the movement preceding it. If a blind-side wing is quick off the mark in starting to cover and the flank does not come in to deputise for the wing, a dummy infield, followed by a hooked kick, can do the trick.

(c) *The breakthrough*
If the methods of attack at your disposal do not achieve success because there are no gaps or these cannot be made, another plan for breaking the line must be devised – a scissors movement, in some form or other may be used. There are three types of scissors movement:
  (i) The player has the ball and runs in a certain direction. He passes the ball to a player who is running in another direction (the scissors movement).
  (ii) A player not in possession, draws attention to himself while the ball goes in another direction (the so-called "attention focus" scissors).
  (iii) A runner has the ball, and the impression is created that someone else is going to receive the ball and run in another direction, but this does not happen (the so-called "dummy scissors").

1. *The scissors movement:* This can be very effective. It can take place before or after success in broken play, but we confine ourselves to broken play, which has breaking as its aim. The scissors movement can be executed by any two backs, between the fly half and the inside centre, between the two centres, or between the outside centre and the wing. It can also be executed by two halves, or by the fly half and the blind-side wing on both the blind and open side. The best method is that of swinging the ball back with the furthermost arm (in terms of the direction from which the ball comes) and pressing it, as it were, into the stomach of the player who is breaking the stream.

2. *"Attention-focus" scissors:* In this movement the opponents' attention is drawn to a certain point by a player or players running in a certain direction, or running and shouting, or doing something to create the impression that he

or they are about to do something special. Then a surprise movement is launched and the ball goes in the opposite direction. Here are three examples: From a side-scrum the fly half comes up on the blind side to draw attention to himself. He does not receive the ball, however, but the ball is passed to the blind-side wing, who takes it on the open side, near the scrum and practically in line with it. The aim is to cut through the line. From a scrum in the centre of the field, the fly half runs to one side – if he wishes he can also shout while doing so – and the centre takes the ball on the other side, again also close to the scrum and in line with it. Again the primary aim is cutting the line. The scrum half crouches, feints to pick up the ball, and keeps running in the same direction. The number eight picks up the ball and breaks in the opposite direction.

3. *The "dummy scissors"*: Instead of the player in possession giving the ball to the player calling attention to breaking the stream, he keeps it himself. This movement can be very effective, especially if the ball is screened by the hip and if the player who dummies juggles with his hands as if he is having difficulty in getting a grip on the ball.

Broken forward play without and with the scrum half
Wheeling of the scrum. There is still another form of broken play to be mentioned: the wheeling of the scrum and what it entails. It was often said that fly halves should move with the wheel of the scrum. The reason for this was the presupposition that the loose forwards would move with the wheel.

Today all this has changed. When the loose-head can be on either side of the scrum, the scrum today veers only to the left and it is on this side that the scrum half puts the ball in. Wheeling the scrummage therefore no longer helps him. If, however, his forwards can win a tight-head and the scrum is wheeled, there's a golden opportunity created for breaking.

If a pack deliberately wheels and the movement does not come off, the ball must be hooked because it will be from a static ruck, which is grist to the scrum half's mill.

How does a scrummage wheel? The best formation for wheeling is 3-3-2. For this the loose-head flanker pushes straight ahead, and the tight-head flanker packs down between him and the loose-head lock. If the number eight is pushing in this position, the loose-head flanker goes down between the locks. In this position there are two additional pushing feet on the loose-head side and two fewer pushing feet on the tight-head side. Even if the pack should push straight ahead, the scrum would still wheel, and to expedite this the following should be done:

In the first place, the forwards must bear in mind that if they decide on wheeling, the wheel follows after scrumming. Consequently the scrum is not wheeled when the ball is put in, but only after the signal for wheeling has been given. This signal is not given before two things have happened: the ball must be in the back row, in front of the feet of the tight-head flanker or of the number eight.

In the second place, wheeling takes place only when superiority in pushing power has been established at that stage. Wheeling is impossible if a pack is pushed away or if it cannot hold its own. In fact, if a pack knows that the opponents are going to wheel, they push with all the strength at their disposal. And if this push is stronger than that of the opponents, wheeling is impossible. The reason why wheeling takes place after the upper hand has been gained is simply because displacement of feet is then possible, whereas feet struggling to cope with frontal power cannot change position. Because wheeling is a surprise move, it must be done at top speed as soon as the signal has been given.

What now happens is the following: the front row forms the axle and the pivot round which everything literally revolves. The loose-head prop, supported by the loose-head flanker, pushes towards the inside. In this way the prop "opens up", which helps the loose-head lock to get his head free. The hooker stands firm because he is the pivot of the whole operation. If he fails to do so, the wheel will be made difficult and the inside shoulder(s) of the lock (actually there is only one because the loose-head lock's shoulder is lodged in his partner's armpit) will "push through", impeding their task of breaking. The tight-head prop retracts his front foot. The locks push towards the loose-head side of the scrum and for this the left shoulder of the loose-head lock is already free. With the locks the number eight pushes with the flanker by his side. The combined pushing-power of these four helps the wheeling movement. The loose-head flanker sees to it that he gets out of the way, looking for shelter as it were, in or against the opening of the scrum.

The locks' angle of push is more acute than that of the back row whose players have to peel off from them.

Despite the angle of pushing and the swivelling movement taking place, the locks and the back row will still find difficulty in disengaging themselves. The loose-head lock and the tight-head flanker (or the number eight who is on the wheeling side) break from the scrum more easily and must consequently pull their team-mates free with their right arms.

The four extruding forwards remain in a crouching position for better control of the ball, which must be picked up as soon as possible. In former years the ball was dribbled, but today every forward is able to pick up the ball, and this is the advisable course of action.

If the ball is blocked on the ground because an opponent has fallen upon it, the ball can still be picked up as this action does not constitute a ruck. If this does not happen, the ball must be hooked immediately so that the scrum half can break from a static ruck or maul.

The wheel is a powerful attacking weapon and its lapse into disuse is to be regretted.

The "Willie-Away": The best position for this movement is either to the front of the line-out, not right up front, or as far back as possible, but not right at the back, i.e. at nos. 2 and 7. The surprise element is not so effective when either no. 1 or number eight is used as a pivot. This does not mean that they cannot be used for the movement. Usually they are used for other tactical moves such as no. 1 playing back to the wing and number eight deflecting the ball to the scrum half for breaking round the back of the line-out.

Like wheeling, the Willie Away revolving or churning must be done at top speed. One of the forwards is instructed to take the ball from deflection by nos. 2 or 7. To do this he requires a run-up to build up power. For this reason no. 5 is usually used for the Willie Away at the front of the line-out, and no. 3 for the same movement at the back. At the precise moment that the ball leaves the hand of the wing this forward is at the forefront and all the forwards behind and in front of him in the line-out follow him and link up with him except for the hooker. If the Willie Away takes place at the rear the movement is the same as that launched at the front. These two forwards both go straight ahead and link up with the movement if it succeeds.

The term "revolving wedge" is also used to describe the Willie Away to indicate what the forwards do: they "revolve" or "turn", trying to drive a wedge through the opponents. It can also be described as "purposeful milling around". The players turn and turn because they have to twist themselves free from opposition or must make progress against them. If the resistance is too strong, the movement enables the player carrying the ball to turn his back on the opposition and give the ball to a team-mate who continues the movement. Instead of turning, the player who starts the movement can run headlong in a crouching position, the remaining players following suit. In this way more power is generated and they are afforded a better opportunity of seeing the ball; in this way too the ball is also screened. Some forwards run in this position into their opponents, leading with the shoulder under which the ball is not held and keeping the ball under the furthermost arm, from which the next player can take it to carry on the movement. If a "churning wedge" movement is stopped, the ball must come back, and again we have a static ruck from which the scrum half can break. If the movement has been launched from the back of the line-out, the fly half can probe the blind-side.

Other kinds of broken forward-play with the scrum half. The scrum half will break when there is an opportunity, but he will also force breaks, for which he will need help supplied, especially by his loose forwards. If a scrum half can run into an opposing flanker – no difficult feat today – he must turn round and start a Willie Away movement for the number eight, who must be on the spot to take the ball from there. Even if the number eight takes a short pass from the scrum half, the latter must draw the flanker on the side of the movement, usually the opposition's loose-head flanker. He does this by compelling the flanker to crash-tackle him. The number eight is the scrum half's greatest ally for breaks round the scrum. Even if the scrum half applies the "turning break" on the side of the loose-head scrum, the number eight will be in attendance to do what is expected of him. As has been said before, the number eight withdraws his head from the scrum without withdrawing his arms, as soon as the hooker has struck the ball. Here is another reason for this: the scrum half must be able to depend on him in any form of breaking, or if he runs into trouble.

GOOD BALLS AND BAD BALLS

Good and bad balls are discussed here because they play such an important part in broken play. It is necessary that we distinguish between good balls and bad balls because they function in general attacking play and in broken set-pieces.

It is the accepted thing today in line-outs to spoil possession, so that if possession is gained by the opponents it will be bad possession. To achieve this, things legal and illegal are done to the arms of the line-out forwards. But we are not interested or concerned with illegalities. If a team gains possession in a line-out it has merely won the first phase of the struggle.

Now follows good possession: this entails getting the ball at the line-out without hindrance and letting it out when it suits, preferably when the line-out is still in progress, because the opposing backs must then remain 10 yards behind the line on which the ball is thrown. If the ball is passed out under these circumstances, quality possession has been gained. A team can, however, give itself bad possession if the ball is tapped back or if any kind of possession is won which, in effect, is more advantageous to the non-possessors than to the attacking team, e.g. a ball which drops on the ground in the line-out, causing a ruck and the consequent termination of the line-out.

Good ball from a scrum consists of the ball emerging quickly after being struck, but not so fast as to cause the scrum half to fall an easy prey to his counterpart and opposing loose forwards. If the ball gets stuck on its way out, the backs are caught flat-footed and any pre-planned moves or instant reactions to the situation are bound to be still-born.

The opponents' counter to possession is the creation of bad ball. They can achieve this by kicking the ball through to the opponents' side of the scrum so that it does not emerge from the usual place. The ball consequently comes out slowly because the feet are not prepared for such a contingency. These methods are deplorable however, because Rugby is a game in which skill is pitted against skill. If the skills of the opposing team are superior to the skills of your own team, it is a fact which simply has to be accepted. An athlete competing against others may not trip them up if they outstrip him. In Rugby the same code of conduct should be observed.

What a pack of forwards can do, however, when it loses possession is to keep on pushing. If this method is successful, the pack which has won possession will be forced to retreat, taking the ball with them. They will now have a scrum similar to one in which the ball is stuck. Unfortunately this method of pushing away opponents who have hooked the ball has died out.

A ball delayed in a ruck has the same disadvantageous effect on back play as has a scrum in which the ball is stationary; in fact, it has an even more detrimental effect, because the chances of scoring from a ruck are far better than from a set scrum. The defenders will infringe should they cause the ball to be retarded by falling over it when it is dribbled or booted ahead. Nowadays players hardly ever fall on a ball because the trend is to pick it up. Consequently a player lands on the other side of the ball today for only one reason: to indulge in an illegal practice. There is usually an outcry if a player bites another player's ear, and quite rightly so, but there are even worse examples of dirty play. What has been described above is a case in point, and should be publicly decried.

As is the case with the scrum, the ball can be delayed legally for the opponents by the forwards arriving first at the ball and then outpushing their opponents in a ruck. This, in fact, is the aim of Rugby. One of the aims of the forwards is the gaining of quality balls for their backs, and by legal means preventing their opponents from getting good balls. These, then, are the good balls and the bad balls from the scrum and the ruck for which the forwards are responsible. But there are others as well, of which the following are examples:

Any bad pass is a bad ball: a pass which is too high or too low; or one which is not in front but "into" the player receiving it, or on his hip, or behind him; or any pass which is too hard or too weak (a "fading" pass), depending on circumstances. A bad pass is one in which the ball gets to the receiver at the moment the opponent comes up to the receiver, and so are any passes which get the receiver into trouble.

Passes given when the opportunity leading to them has been lost are equally bad balls. Take a player who runs too far with the ball or does not accelerate his passing movement when he should. Practical examples are the following: a fly half or an inside centre who goes through an outside gap and keeps on running until he gets into trouble before attempting to pass the ball out. As soon as such a player takes the outside tap and his partner next to him is also through, he must pass the ball. It is not his function, but the outside centre's, to draw the full back.

If the inside gap is taken, the position can be different. His first attempt must be to go outside, but should this fail and his opponents have already turned round, as they often do under such circumstances, the player must run as fast and as straight as he can. By straight running he will gain the greatest advantage. The loose forwards also have sufficient opportunities to take his pass, because they are winning the race against opponents who have to turn before setting off in pursuit.

The same applies to a scrum half when slipping round a scrum. If the ball is passed too soon, the movement will peter out. Take, in this connection, an outside centre, with his wing next to him, coming down on the full back and passing before he has drawn the full back. Passes given to wrong players have caused many a team to lose a match, and so spoil a good game of Rugby.

This leads me to the dictum: "Outside passes are preferable to inside passes." All bad balls referred to so far have a bearing on handling, and in most cases the backs are involved. The importance of handling as a fundamental principle – *the* fundamental principle – needs no further emphasis. But if handling is neglected we get the sort of Rugby which is so frequently seen these days.

Apart from bad balls caused by handling errors, they are also caused by poor kicks: those punts which are kicked too far and are badly placed, and the kicks for touch which never cross the touchline. All these cause unnecessary running which merely dissipates a lot of energy.

How are bad balls treated? Before answering this question we must first of all discuss how quality balls are treated. The answer is simply this: "Attack."

A look at today's Rugby, however, will reveal the very opposite state of affairs. A good ball is often rendered valueless by kicking it away. No greater disservice can be done to Rugby. It is for this very reason that the game has lost its former prestige in South Africa and many other Rugby-playing countries. Quality balls are rare (fault of the forwards), and these are kicked away or turned into bad balls (fault of the backs).

Bennie Osler used to say: "Keep good balls good and kill off bad ones." Rather one should say: "Keep good balls good and kill off bad balls which defy being transformed into good balls." Some of the finest tries or movements in the annals of the game were the result of bad balls transformed into good ones. A movement which would otherwise have petered out gets infused with new life or a fresh start through such a transformation. In this way we may have two or three movements joined together, as it were, by means of good handling. The criterion of what is to be done depends on the time factor; this, in turn, is determined by the position taken up by the backs if something is to be achieved with a bad ball.

The time factor. Where are the opponents when a bad ball is received? Does their position allow the movement to be carried on further, as in the case of a good ball? If this is the situation, such a bad ball is never kicked. If the time factor is not entirely against the receiver, he can kick an attacking punt if he still has time at his disposal. The defenders will know only too well when it is a bad ball and will try to exploit the situation; their natural inclination will be to advance, never to fall back. For this reason a punt from a bad ball is often successful and is preferable to a desperate kick for clearance, which more often than not bounces off an opponent coming up for defence.

Another question which the recipient of a bad ball should ask himself, especially if the movement is already under way, is the following: is the field ahead open? If the backs, for instance, are moving with the ball and they pass it back to the number eight, who has to turn backwards to collect it, he has been given a bad ball. If he, in turn, kicks the ball into touch merely because it is a bad ball, and before even establishing the position of the opponents, he is guilty of a gross blunder. Very often there is sufficient time for turning a bad ball into a good ball, and again it is the position of the opponents which will indicate if there is enough time for doing so.

Bad ball from tight play is subjected to the same test, and the ball is not just kicked away. It is remarkable how often a player is forced to break, and succeeds in doing so. Perhaps he receives the ball with his opponents squarely in front of him. He must, as a rule, do anything but pass the ball, and so he decides to break with might and main. We are too much inclined to ignore the kind of break by which a player runs "through" an opponent. Yet this is a good preparation for breaks coupled with "down thrust" or, should the attempt fail, for forming the basis of a maul or a ruck.

Another example: the fly half aims for the blind-side and the opposing wing comes up quickly in defence; the fly half will not have time to take the ball – neither will he attempt to do so if he is a first-rate player – but will merely guide it on its way to his unmarked wing. For a good player like Bennie Osler, who sent Jack Slater over in the corner for the only try scored by South Africa in the first test against the All Blacks in 1928, it was a good ball. For a lesser player it would have been a bad ball. A characteristic of a good player is that he makes a difficult (bad) ball seem easy (good).

Postscript

What follows is a verbatim account of the system drawn up by myself for the Stellenbosch Maties which will indicate how the theory explained in the previous chapters can be put into practice. The word "tramlines" refers to the safety lines along which the backs can move diagonally across the field.

Attack from scrummages

The ball cannot reach the open-side wing in a back-line movement from a scrummage with opposing backs positioned in a shallow line. Only by means of tramlines, correctly executed, can this be achieved. But if tramlines fail, the attacking backs will be tackled behind their forwards and our opponents will already know about our tramlines ploy. *Consequently the way must be prepared for full tramlines.* How is this achieved? *By standing as near as possible to the advantage line.*

Our policy of tactics from a scrum will in the sequel be as follows:
1. *In our twenty-five* we kick for touch.
2. *In other areas*
(a) (i) We start with F 1, W 1 (side-scrum with blind-side). By F 1 we understand that the fly half will go blind-side, but that the right-hand wing will take the ball on the left-hand side of, and in line with, the scrum. W 1 means that the fly half also goes blind-side, but on this occasion the left-hand wing receives the ball on the right-hand side of, and in line with, the scrum. Then we have F 2 and W 2 (midfield scrummage). By F 2 we understand that the fly half goes to the right and the right-hand centre receives the ball on the left-hand side of, and in line with, the scrummage. W 2 supposes that the fly half goes to the left and that the left-hand side centre receives the ball on the right-hand side of, and in line with, the scrum. In all these instances the receiver of the ball attempts to break, even should he run into difficulties, because he will have crossed the advantage line and his forwards will be on hand for an inside pass or the forming of a ruck or a maul.

(ii) If the side-scrum has no blind-side, the inside centre gives a short punt (with dummy) *straight* over their heads and *slightly* towards the field-side wing.

(b) If we are in their territory and can start with F 1 and W 1 from a side-scrum, the second step is the tramline and the blind-side wing and the inside centre cut through the line. If the blind-side wing cuts through the line, our entire back line takes up a shallow position in order to support the wing.

(c) (i) After this our fly half goes round the blind-side and breaks, or:
(ii) the inside centre gives a short punt, for which purpose he positions himself deep, so that the opponents have to come up from far, and fast, and also so that the empty box behind them is the bigger, or:
(iii) the inside centre and the fly half do a scissors movement (with a tramline to get further away from the forwards).

(d) After this follows the complete tramline.

(e) Then comes cutting the line by the inside centre, the wing and the full back.

(Remember the inside centre must be at least 6–8 yards behind the fly half and the outside centre must be 6–8 yards behind the inside centre.

N.B.

(a) Our blind-side wing positions himself behind the scrum and not next to it, as would be the case for defence.

(b) The player cutting through the line receives the ball in line with the scrum or the player passing the ball, and his primary aim is breaking the line.

To summarise

Start with F 1 and W 1.
Follow up with tramline and blind-side wing and inside centre cutting through.
Fly half works the blind-side.
Punt by inside centre or scissors movement between him and fly half.
Full tramline.
Full tramline with the outside centre, wing and full back cutting through.

3. *Mid-field scrum*

(a) As stated, we start in their territory with F 2 and W 2.

(b) After this the fly half and the two centres line up behind one another and they all move in the same direction.

(c) Then we cut through with the full back on the side to which the fly half and two centres are *not* running. (For this the fly half and the two centres run *in front of* the full back in order to draw attention to themselves.)

(d) Then the fly half runs to the side on which the full back has cut through, but the two centres run to the opposite side where one of them will receive the ball.

(e) Our fly half punts ahead. (The reason for this will become clear when we study the defence drawn up for a mid-field scrum. More about this later.)

N.B.

(a) For all these "cutting movements" the scrum half gives a standing pass which is sent out as a "soft" (cushioned) ball. The exception is with a full tramline or tramlines in which the outside centre or open-side wing cuts through and in which the full back cuts through on the other side of the fly half; then the dive-pass (falling pass) is given.

(b) After the whole series of movements has been executed, we start at the beginning again.

4. *Line-outs*

(a) *Attacking from line-out:*

We change the formation of the line-outs for the following reason: we do not take up a deep position so that we are not too far from our opponents should they gain possession from our throw-in at the line-out. Our new formation is consequently as follows:

The fly half takes up his usual position and will run 2–3 yards for receiving the ball and passing it.

The inside centre stands 1–2 yards behind him and equally far from him for straightening the line.

The outside centre stands 1–2 yards behind him and equally far from him for keeping the line straight.

The open-side wing stands 1–2 yards behind the outside centre and somewhat further away from him in comparison with the distance between the two centres, so that he can straighten for inside breaks or outside breaks.

When do we start running? *Each player starts running when the ball is on its way to him.*

(b) *Method of attack*
  (i) Here our backs can break or make forced breaks (if they themselves create the gap by running straight and looking in another direction, holding the ball on the side towards which they are looking) or make opportunistic breaks (if the gap is there).
  (ii) Apart from individual breaks the following can be used:
  (a) The dummy scissors between the centres or between the outside centre and the open-side wing.
  (b) The dummy scissors with the full back cutting through.
  (c) Circumvention.
  (d) Passing "back" if we gain possession from their throw-in; i.e. the field-side wing runs a few yards to the inside and then passes the ball back to the inside centre, who continues the movement to the side of its commencement.
  (e) A punt given by the inside or the outside centre, preferably the latter.
  (f) Blind-side movement if we throw in deep, perform a Willie Away, and the ball emerges.

Defence, i.e. their ball
The scrum (side-scrum without blind-side)
Our starting position. Our *fly half* positions himself opposite the gap between their fly half and the scrum. *Our inside centre* takes up his stance opposite the gap between their fly half and inside centre. *Our outside centre* positions himself directly opposite the gap between their centres. *Our open-side wing* hangs back and far from his outside centre to enable him to get to all balls kicked to his side and over his backs.

How do we go up? For the first few yards we go straight ahead towards the inside gap and then swing outwards as soon as we see that we have their inside hips. The first few paces going straight ahead are taken at approximately three-quarter speed, and when we take the turn we are at full speed (regardless of whether our judgment is wrong or not; this is the point of no return).

The open-side wing runs at a moderate pace until their scrum half has passed the ball. By doing this he can turn back for their fly half's punts or diagonal kicks. As soon as the fly half passes, our wing increases his pace, but still not at full speed, so that he can still render harmless a short punt by their inside centre in his direction. As soon as their inside centre passes, he goes up at full speed.

Their outside centre should not receive the ball from a scrum. Should this happen, our inside players did not come up correctly and fast enough. Should their outside centre, however, get the ball and give a short punt, our number eight or our full back or our blind-side wing has to see to the ball. Our open-side wing consequently does not hesitate to come up at full speed if their inside centre has time to pass the ball.

Side-scrum with blind-side and mid-field scrum
The left-hand side of a scrum, irrespective of whether it is a side-scrum or a mid-field scrum, offers bigger problems with regard to defence than the right-hand side of the scrum. The reason for this is that our scrum half is positioned on the right-hand side of the scrum (on the side where the opponents put in the ball) and thus serves as an additional defender. For this reason the left-hand side of a scrummage requires a different approach (as far as defence is concerned) by comparison with the method adopted for defending the left-hand side. (Cf. again pp. 63-64.)

Side-scrum next to our left-hand touchline
1. If their fly half comes blind-side, *our left-hand flanker* (no. 6) still remains responsible for their scrum half. Only after the scrum half has passed the ball does the left-hand flanker go up on the inside of their fly half. Our number eight takes care of their fly half on the blind-side and is covered by his own fly half, who takes up his position opposite his opposing number in order to get up to him as soon as possible on either side of the scrum. Our blind-side wing stays as close as possible to the off-side line in order to nip in the bud all blind-side movements and to lend a hand with loose balls behind their scrum, or should their scrum half pass the ball to their full back near their goal-line.
2. Should their fly half work the open-side, our scrum half (who stands somewhat behind his opponent) sees to his opposite number as well as to their fly half. He goes up on his inside, supported on that side by our right-hand flanker (number 7) and covered by our number eight and fly half. Our fly half positions himself opposite his counterpart and somewhat deeper than our centres, who come up exactly as they would for a side-scrum without a blind-side. The same applies to our open-side wing. Our fly half aims for the outside gap of his opposite number so that he can cover if their fly half does not break. As soon as our blind-side wing sees that their fly half moves infield, he falls back diagonally in order to close the box behind his scrum. He starts covering as soon as their fly half passes out the ball.

Mid-field scrum (Cf. also pp. 63-64.)
As far as our loose forwards and scrum half are concerned, the defence on the left-hand side of a mid-field scrum is the same as that for a left-hand side of a side-scrum with a blind-side next to our left-hand touchline. Our fly half, however, aims for the outside gap of his opponent in an attempt to get to short punts by his counterpart and to cover.

Our centres take up positions directly opposite the inside gaps of our opponents and to the front of our fly half. *Our wings* take up their positions opposite the inside gap of the opposing wings.

Side-scrum with blind-side next to our right-hand touchline
The defence here is the same as for the left-hand side of a side-scrum next to our left-hand side touchline and the left-hand side of a mid-field scrum except that our fly half takes up a shallower position on the left-hand side of the scrum. He still covers the blind-side, however, and for this reason his position is slightly more shallow than the ones taken up by his two centres.

Conclusion
1. The left-hand side of all scrums (side-scrummages with blind-side and mid-field scrummages) is defended in the same way, and so too is the right-hand side of such scrums, except that our fly half takes up a shallower position next to our right-hand touchline and that our wings do not hang back too far in the case of a mid-field scrum. Thus our fly half has to close up the boxes behind our wings.
2. A punt by the attacking fly half from a mid-field scrum is dangerous owing to the fact that our wings cannot hang back too deep.
3. *Our number eight* always looks after the opposing fly half on the left-hand side of any scrum.

The line-out
The starting position of our back line is the same as that with a scrum, but the going up, as far as speed is concerned, is just the reverse. From a scrum it is first of all three-quarter pace and then full speed; from a line-out it is first of all full speed and then three-quarter pace or even slower.

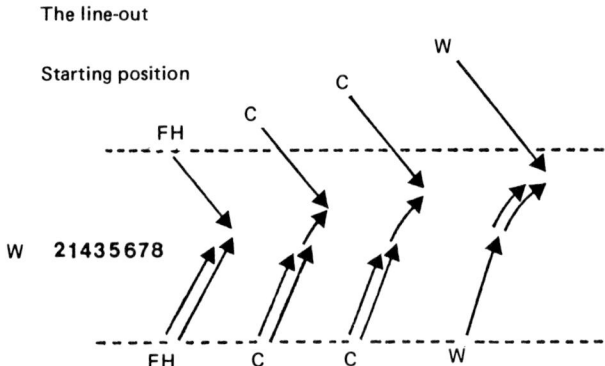

The double line indicates full speed. This is maintained until the inside hips of the opponents are attained. Then the speed is decreased so that the opponents can take only the outside gap, and so that we can fall back – and cover – if they use short punts.

Our fly half goes up at full tilt and straight for the opposing fly half. He will have forwards on his inside if his opponent beats him there.

Our blind-side wing stays in front of the line-out in case they play the ball back to the wing who throws it in. He also stays there in case there are loose balls at the back of the line-out and the scrum half is caught in possession there, and in case their scrum half passes the ball to the full back near their goal-line.

SPECIAL PLAY

The kick-off and the drop-out
The kick-off is taken from the centre of the half-way line. The drop-out is taken from the twenty-five yard line.
There are different ways of drawing up a team taking the kick, and the team receiving the kick. Here is the deployment we have found to be the best.
In order to facilitate the description, the following diagram is given, one which is suitable for both the kick-off and the drop-out. When a drop-out is taken the receiving team can, according to the rules, be closer to the player taking the kick, but the formation for both types of kicks remains the same.

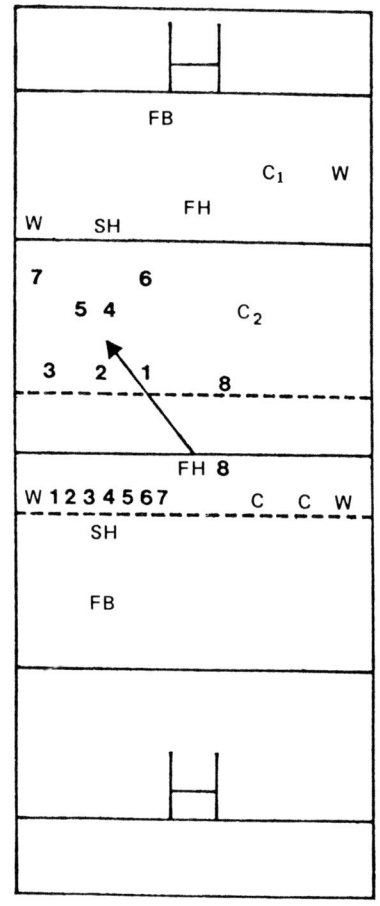

Explanation: the kick
The kick must be perfect, depending on the purpose. It must be high and deep enough for the forwards to get to the ball at full speed. It is thus an attacking kick which offers the same advantages as an attacking ruck. The receiving team

must, among other things, preferably fall back rather than come charging up for the ball. The kick creates the opportunities for an attacking maul or ruck if the side taking the kick fails to gain possession, which is their primary aim. Even a long, well-placed kick which has to be caught near the touchline can be tried so that the player catching it will not have much time for running infield in order to increase the angle of his kick.

The team taking the kick
As a rule the fly half takes the kicks. This is as it should be because he is the central link, as it were, between the forwards and the backs. With him is his number eight, who runs straight ahead in an attempt to smother any possible attack.

The remaining seven forwards line up in a row and behind the fly half. They move up step by step with him and are at speed when he kicks. They do not make a spurt from a stationary position. The wing on their side goes up with them except when he sees that the kick is too long for anyone to reach the ball. He then covers the touchline.

The two centres and the remaining wing are in line with the forwards and remain in this formation in order that possession may immediately be utilised or, if the opponents attempt to launch an attack with their backs, they can stop it up front. The full back is on the open-side flanks of his forwards, on the alert for the development of play to either side.

The team receiving the ball
The number eight is on the blind side of the player taking the kick so as to compel him to kick towards the side where his forwards are. The forwards maintain their scrum formation and are dispersed over a wide area. Behind them and next to the touchline is the right-hand wing. The scrum half is also on the open side, positioned behind his forwards in order to move to either side. The fly half is in his normal position in relation to his scrum half. The inside centre stands infield and deep while the outside is up front and shallow. The left wing is positioned deep and sufficiently close to the touchline to reach any long kick. The full back stands very deep and towards the centre of the field with the touchline on his right-hand side so that he can reach a long kick in that direction, or go across to the other side to render assistance if a long kick is aimed in that direction and where the left wing is, as it were, the full back.

If the kick is towards the right, the entire formation is reversed.

Penalty kicks
The so-called "short penalty" can be executed far more quickly than is usually the case. This penalty originated with a hooker who tapped or hooked the ball for the scrum half, who had to get away or pick it up, or the scrum half did both things.

Any player, regardless of the position in which he plays, and the first to be on hand, should be able to take the short penalty. If players cannot perform this task, they must practise it. The backs must see to it that they are immediately in line with the player taking the kick – in fact practically on the advantage line

—so that they can swing into attack at once. They convert the movement into general attacking back-line play, using it as a launching pad for broken play. The penalised team usually tries to cordon off the entire field to prevent a back-line movement. Near their own goal-line they tend to cluster round the kicker, thereby creating many boxes. Consequently the player taking the kick must exploit such a situation and he must be on the lookout for these even when he intends kicking quickly.

Chapter 3
The Skills and Sub-Skills

To repeat briefly: attention must be given to the following:
Skill building, which includes technique.
Rounding off of skills.
Application of skills.
Definition. Technique represents both the focal and satellite movements of a skill, but aims at letting full justice be done to the focal movement without neglecting the satellites.
Skill building. The principal aim is acquiring the technique of every skill and improving it. This is done, for instance, by putting a load on muscles which are concerned with certain skills, or by modifying the usual time, rhythm or space in which the skill is executed.
Rounding off of skills. The primary aim is the application of the satellite skills, where the individual merges into the team.
Application of skills. Of primary importance here are match situations and the players' reactions to them. These situations can be realistic only if two teams are opposed to each other, either in shadow play or in the game itself.

Exercises must be given to players for each of these skills. Although most of the players ought to be familiar with the technique, it will be found that this is exactly what they lack, and this leads to other defects in their game.

The coach will have to decide whether a player's technique (basic movements), or his rounding off of these (satellitic movements), or his application of them in situations is faulty, and will accordingly set about rectifying them.

Power and swinging-power must also be practised.

Various skills and sub-skills will be described in this chapter and definitions of each will be given. Inevitably the definition will be based on the basic movements, but the satellite movements will not be excluded.

Technique must therefore, in the first place, be mainly concerned with the execution of the focal movements. In other words, technique and focal movements become one.

THE SKILLS

Pushing in the scrum
Here we have two kinds of pushing movements – the thrust of the front row and, secondly, the shove of the third row. There is a world of difference between these two. The pushing of the front row depends on that of the other two rows, because if the latter's shoving is weak, the front row can only stand and will be unable to shove as well.

The front-row players also push with one leg, whereas the remaining rows should shove with both legs. The bodily position of the front row is totally different from that taken up by the other two rows, because the thrust is against both legs of each player in the front row. If they "lie too flat", as we say, the shoulders of the second row forwards will slip over their legs.

There is also thrusting against the inside thighs of the lock-forwards. This is merely a means of getting their legs completely straight after the shove. As soon as this has been achieved, shoving against them is no longer required. Pushing against the front row, however, remains imperative until the ball emerges from the scrum.

There is an additional difference between the shoving of the front row compared with the shoving of the third row: the front row pushes against a hard surface – shoulders – whereas the third row pushes against soft flesh. Woe betide the prop who has soft shoulders. (Pushing against a hard tree will help to overcome this deficiency.)

A final difference we must mention here concerns the loose-head prop who pushes with only one shoulder, a circumstance which can induce an outward curvature of his back if things become difficult for him. The flanker may experience this to a lesser degree. (By switching positions with the tight-head prop during practice, the entire back is strengthened for this task.)

Every scrum consists of three phases:
1. The pre-shoving or "cocking" phase, comparable with the cocking of a rifle.
2. The shoving phase, comparable with the pulling of the trigger.
3. The post-shoving phase, comparable with the recoil of a rifle.

1. *The "cocking" phase*

This is a most important phase because, apart from the fact that the scrum must constitute a unit, the leaning-power of the two packs must at least be equal. Often the pack with this advantage wins the initial shove. It is not permissible to push before the time, and the laws of the game stipulate that the scrum must be stationary. But a scrum can be stationary while one of the packs is struggling with might and main to contribute its share towards this state, while the other pack is "cocking" or bracing itself for the second phase. A pack which struggles with leaning power cannot brace itself. Leaning-power depends on how low the pack of forwards goes down, i.e. how much flexion they allow in their longitudinal axis. It also depends on their weight. A struggling pack will consequently curtail their flexions in order to hold their own, or they may abandon flexion entirely. But they do not push, because flexing, when straightened, supplies pushing power. This, then, is the first struggle in the scrum – that of leaning-power.

2. *Pulling the trigger*

As previously described, an explosion takes place here, one which – if not audible – is as powerful as that of the firing of a gun. The explosion comes from all the flexed joints which are straightened, either fully, as in the case of the second row and third row, or partially, as in the case of the front row. At the most the front-row forwards can straighten their pushing legs, but they cannot extend their hips. The hips are the most important focal point of pushing-power because the hips indicate how strong the front row is. Because the pushing foot of a front-row forward is not put far back, the power generated from it will not flow forward but upwards. In other words, the hip will lift. Now comes weight from up front. If this is more powerful than the weight from behind the front row, the hip will least of all be lowered forward, as happens when the weight from behind is more than that from up front, not forgetting that the front row is strong enough to withstand frontal and rear thrusts.

The hips of the front row which wins the "explosive" struggle go down and forward, and this is a continuous process. A distinctive feature of a good scrum is to be observed in the seats of all eight forwards: the buttocks of the front row go down and forward; those of the others go down until their bodies are fully straightened.

3. *The post-shoving phase*

If the bodies of the second-row players have been straightened, they have the assurance that, provided they remain a close-knit unit, their pushing power will be firmly lodged where it should be, i.e. where it has been brought by the shove – a gun will not recoil if well and closely held to the shoulder. If the two locks are straight as a post, and if the pushing legs of the front-row forwards are straight, they are assured that the opposing pack has wilted. And a beaten pack will be hard put to shove back its opponents.

With such a good scrum the flanks of the winning pack can break up sooner than their opposing numbers, who will be retreating and forced back on their heels. The ball may perhaps be hooked by the retreating pack, but it will obviously not emerge as quality possession. If the ball is held, it will in most cases be of little avail, because it is already a difficult task to push with the ball at your feet. To be pushed back with the ball at your feet is playing right into the hands of your opponents. It is good policy to force a pack which has hooked the ball into retreating because, when the ball eventually emerges, it is in most instances of no value to their backs. Moreover, each retreat is another nail in their coffin, and they will not be able to dictate the course of the match.

The ability to push better than your opponents entails so many advantages that a pack which neglects this aspect of the game does a great injustice to itself, to its backs and the Rugby game.

We may now venture a definition, and then say something more about basic movements.

Definition: Pushing means to lean forward, to make contact with the person against whom or with whom you are pushing, by means of shoulder strengthened by binding with the arms. After this a solid base is found for the feet in such a way that only slight movements occur in as few joints in the longitudinal axis as is required by the position taken up in the scrum. Now follows the quick straightening of all the flexed parts (second and third rows), or the straightening of these to the degree required by the position in the front row. The straightened joints are kept this way so that a forward pushing stream is created.

Which parts are straightened and how is this done?

As stated previously, forwards are concerned with leaning-power, and to cope with this they have to remove some flexions and decrease others in the longitudinal axis. The neck and back consist of vertebrae, or hinges, which can move. A great deal of flexion is found in the hips, the knees and the ankles. To resist leaning-power, the vertebrae of the neck and back are locked – the neck and the back are straight. If it were possible to keep them flexed and then straighten them simultaneously with the hips and the knees, more pushing-power would be generated. Unfortunately this is not possible; it is achieved to a certain extent with the front-row forwards who have to lower their heads in order to see the ball and who, by doing so, slightly bend their necks and backs. It would be better to lower only the head, without flexing the neck and the back. But this does not always happen. A slight bending is conducive to pushing-power if it is straightened. The flankers can perhaps also bend their backs and then straighten them with the shove.

As a rule the backs, however, are in a straight position before the shove. In addition to this a great deal of the flexing of the hip and also that of the knees is done away with. We maintain that it is better to flex the knees too little than too much. The aim is not to thrust far forward, but to assure that you do move ahead, however slight a distance. Your forward movement takes place at the expense of your opponents.

It has already been pointed out that the feet, and more specifically their front parts, are placed crosswise on the ground, and this also removes part of the flexing of the ankles.

Straightening thus actually means an action which takes place in the ankles, the knees and the hips. If all flexion, except that in the hips could be removed, one would be able to push by drawing the hips down. The muscles, however, cannot do this on their own, especially since they also have to resist leaning-power, and the first place from which leaning-power and pushing-power tend to escape is from the hips.

Pushing thus begins with the ankles, which are on the shoving base. But seeing that the ankles are the central point of the leaning-power, they will not be able to initiate the shove if the leaning-power from the front is too strong. Everything is thus determined by a pack's ability to control leaning-power. If leaning-power is controlled, the ankles can start the shove together with the knees and hips. These three joints operate simultaneously but in different directions. The ankles bend forward, the knees go up and the hips downwards. Here, then, is the focal movement – simultaneous straightening in different directions.

That it happens quickly is really subordinate; the faster it is, the more certain it is that you will be the first to set in motion the pushing-stream, against which the opponents will be powerless.

The focal movement in pushing can thus be defined as follows: the simultaneous straightening of ankles (forward), knees (upwards) and hips (downwards). In the case of the front row straightening is not complete in the ankles and in the hips, but in the case of the second row these joints are straightened to the full.

Jumping in the line-out
The steering-wheel of a stationary motorcar must be twisted very hard before the front wheels will be turned. The faster the car travels, however, the easier turning becomes. Why is this? Because movement makes the car "lighter". The faster the bird runs, the more easily it takes to the air. The same applies to aeroplanes.

The human being cannot fly, but jumping is a form of the same principle; one leaves the ground. The human being can jump from his tracks, but he will achieve more distance and greater height if he puts himself in motion, thus making himself "lighter". High-jumpers and long-jumpers achieve this more easily than line-out jumpers, because they have room in which to get into motion and make themselves "lighter". The line-out forward must do this from a stationary position or by means of a small hop or a short step, or both, or even by means of a rocking movement. His movements are therefore limited. By first bending his body forward and then straightening it while at the same time swinging up his arms, he makes himself even lighter, accumulating and increasing his jumping-power at the same time.

Jumping requires dynamic power whereas scrumming demands static power. A short step towards the front helps if a forward jump is taken because the run-up and the jump are in the same direction, whereas the short step and the hop restrict the jumper to an upright leap. If a player is accustomed to a short step and small hop, he will have to acquire the "one-step jump" or the rocking method, because this is what he will have to rely on if his opponents throw in the ball. He will not know where the ball is intended to land, but will have to wait and see, and then react immediately. Under these conditions there is no time for taking the small hop.

The short step, the rock, the small hop
A line-out forward has the following aids for putting himself in motion: the short step or the rock, which has the same effect, although it is basic whereas the short hop is additional. Another common feature of the short-step rocking hop and short-step rock is the stooping position of the body, which is forcefully jerked upright, and the upward strike of the arms. Everyone has a jumping foot, i.e. a foot with which he jumps better and with greater ease than with the other.

Whether a line-out jumper uses the rocking movement or takes the short step, the jumping leg does most of the work and the other is used merely as an aid. If the jumping leg is on the inside of the line-out, the player takes a short step in the direction of the line-out and obliquely forward to meet the ball. If the rocking method is used, the leg serving as aid can also help by guiding the leap in the desired direction. If the leg used for jumping is, however, on the outside of the line-out, the player will have to take a short step to the inside, and the rocking jump, also in that direction, will be taken by the leg used for jumping. Obviously a player should practise so that both legs can be used for jumping.

The vertical jumper (short-step and little-hop jumper) always steps out with the foot used for jumping and then takes the little hop. When his foot touches the ground again, the other foot is prepared to assist in the jump.

The vertical jump
Jumping vertically gives greater height than jumping forward. A tall no. 2 player who jumps vertically will always gain possession from a no. 3 player who jumps forward. To counteract a player who jumps forward at no. 3, his opponent takes up the no. 2 berth.

The function of the arms
The arms are flung upwards powerfully to make the jumper "lighter", and when the foot or the feet give the leap, the upper part of the body jerks upwards to straighten out. The chin is also flung up and the whole body is fully extended. The inside arm is flung upwards with great force because it is the shoulder-joint of this arm which has to be lifted higher than that of the outside arm. It is also the upward swing of this arm which facilitates the turn after possession has been won.

If both arms are stretched equally high for the jump, a few inches in reach will be forfeited. The inside hand is nearest to the ball and its function is to stop the ball. The other arm catches the ball. This technique also ensures less pushing and barging because when two forwards jump inwards, each trying to get both hands to the ball, they are bound to bump each other.

The stopping hand is thus higher than the other, which is ready for catching. Some forwards keep the auxiliary hand somewhat lower than the stopping hand, but this is not necessary. The higher it is, the better it is, provided it does not prevent the shoulder-joint of the stopping hand from attaining maximum height.

The jump
The jump itself, like the shove, occurs with the forward extension of the ankles and the backward stretching of the knee or knees. Unlike the shove, in jumping the hips are not brought forward but the back is brought backwards and upwards to come in line with the legs. This will retard the jumping-power as little as possible; indeed it will actually help it as much as possible in its upward movement.

Definition: Jumping means bending the joints in the longitudinal axis of the body, bringing the body into motion by means of a short step or rock, with or without a little hop, and making the movement explosive from a solid base, namely the ground, and stretching out fully so that the toes are the last to leave the ground. Simultaneously with the stretching, the arms, especially the inside arm, are stretched upwards vigorously and the entire body is extended upwards. This process happens in such a way that the extended outside arm attains maximum reach at the moment the hand touches the ball. At this precise point, as a continuation of the powerful flinging up of the inside arm, the back is turned on the opponents and the arms are forcibly struck downwards, and the player lands on the ground with legs outspread.

The focal movement consists of the explosive part, that part when maximum effort is made; in other words, the straightening of all flexions when the jump commences.

Pushing-in movement
In Rugby pushing is done with the shoulder(s), and to do so the body is bent forward. This forms the basis for pushing. Pushing also always assumes pushing away, which is its real aim. In a ruck it means pushing the opponents away and pushing open for the ball. These actions depend on each other.

Pushing in a ruck differs from pushing in a scrum in that the shove in a scrum is short, very short, whereas in the ruck it must be long. The deeper the ball is in a ruck, the longer the shoving process will continue. In a scrum the ball is hooked. In a ruck the ball, as a rule, is not hooked, because hooking is a waste of time and it entails the forfeiture of a leg for pushing. This is something no pack can afford, because every leg is necessary and every moment counts. It is the foremost foot that does the major share of work, because if the leg of that foot is not straightened, the rear foot cannot be moved forward. This forward positioning of the rear foot must go beyond the front foot. In other words, it must be a short step, and this can be taken only if the foremost leg is completely straightened. In this way it serves another purpose, in that it becomes an anchor which prevents the player from being pushed away. An anchor, again, assumes that the hips have also done their work jointly with the foremost foot. Pushing in the ruck is thus done step by step – hence the appellation "pushing-in movement". While pushing with the legs the hips are pulled downwards as far as possible to give power and to ensure that all the pushing power of the legs goes forward.

By binding with one hand or both a player ensures that a combined pushing-stream is created, that gaps which opponents may burst through are closed, and that the player secures more solidity for himself and his fellow-pushers in the team.

Definition: Pushing in a ruck means going in a bent position, getting yourself in motion, initially by means of short steps, pushing over the ball against all frontal opposition, and binding to friend and foe. All shoving-streams are thereby united in the creation of a joint shoving-stream.

Again the focal movement is the explosion: the straightening of the foremost leg and the downpull of the hips.

Catching and passing as skills in handling
The skill in the handling of a ball (the passed ball, the falling ball, the raking ball, and the picked up or scooped up ball) has the same underlying principle as the four types of balls to be caught, i.e. checking or stopping and then catching. (The word "catch" is here used with a special connotation.)

Types of caught ball
1. For a player receiving a ball which is passed out, it is a passed ball. Because a player first has to catch such a ball, it is called a "passed-on" ball. If he passes out the ball, it becomes a "passed-out" ball. These two actions are distinct from each other and will be treated as such.
2. A falling ball is a high ball which has lost its momentum and then plummets to earth. On touching the ground it usually bounces.
3. A raking ball travels lower than a falling ball and has not completely lost

its momentum when it has to be caught or taken. As a rule the ball rolls when it touches the ground.
4. A scooped ball lies stationary on the ground or rolls from fast to slow on the ground and bobs.

Common elements in catching
An element common to catching these four kinds of ball is that the direction in which the ball is travelling is checked by an action on the part of the receiver. The ball is thus stopped. Another common element is that the instrument used for checking (the hand or the body) must be relaxed and not tensed. Together with or shortly after the stopping of the ball, is the catch, made with the other hand, or with the body.
1. *The passed ball.* The passed-on ball is stopped with the hand furthest from the passer and it is caught with the hand nearest to him. The stopping hand is held vertically with the palm facing the ball. The palm of the catching hand points upwards because the ball comes to rest in it. The stopping hand is flexible and relaxed. The fingers are slightly flexed and act as shock-absorbers. The two hands here act simultaneously and they are therefore extended, in their respective positions, to the ball.

If the receiver gets the ball very close to, or on to, his body, both hands are used for stopping it and they are cupped for the purpose. They also catch the ball at the same time. Stopping and catching become one. If the furthest foot is in front, this method is used for getting at balls that are up against or behind the receiver.
2. *The falling or high dropping ball.* For the falling ball the hands are also extended. Both hands are flat and relaxed and on account of their being cupped and next to each other, the elbows are close to each other to form a "bowl" with the body. Not only do the hands break the fall of the ball, but they also give; and while doing so, the upper part of the body bends so so that the ball and body meet. Unlike the passed ball, catching takes place shortly after stopping the ball.
3. *The diagonal ball.* The diagonal ball must be stopped by the body. The body must also give, but the moment it stops the ball, the hands catch it and press it to the body. If the diagonal ball's flight is too high, a backward step is taken to provide a stopwall. If the flight of the ball is too low, a stopwall is provided by stepping forward. If no stopwall is provided, by stepping backward or forward, the cupped hands will have to stop and catch the ball. Stopping and catching thus become one, and all that one has to do is to allow the hands to give so that a flexible stopwall is formed.
4. *The scooped-up ball.* For a pick-up ball lying stationary, or practically stationary, one hand is used for scooping up the ball and the other hand catches it at the point where it is held in front of the ball. We prefer that the ball should be scooped up with both hands. The ball is collected and brought to a stationary position against the body. In other words, the body catches the ball. This can be done with any ball lying on the ground. A player must make sure when collecting the ball that his hands are low down. For this reason he places one foot past the ball and picks it up in the middle of the

step, as it were, at the point at which his arms are at their longest reach. The secret is to remain as low as possible for a bouncing ball because it is easier to come erect than to stoop.

Technique

Forwards who have gained possession in a line-out have a certain way of passing out a ball, and scrum halves have their own characteristic way of passing. There is, however, also a pass used in general and broken and loose play which is virtually always the same: the ball is passed out with both hands and travels more or less parallel with the ground.

What follows can be regarded as the most suitable for any kind of pass as far as distance and accuracy are concerned. It is basic, and from it all kinds of passes can be developed.

We often hear that a player should have one hand behind the ball when passing. We also see that players are wary of passing when the left hand is supposed to pass the ball.

A ball is passed with two hands, and these work in unison until the ball leaves them.

A passed-on ball is caught with both the stopping hand and the catching hand. For a falling ball both hands are behind the ball. Both hands are also behind a raking ball and a scooped-up ball. In the case of a passed-out ball both hands are behind the ball shortly after catching it. If, in the case of the other three kinds of ball, it should be "taken out" for a pass, the hand is simply lowered and both hands are again behind the ball.

It is not at this stage, however, that the one-hand story comes into the picture – it comes later in the passing-out process when the hands are already on their way, and in most cases while the player is running. This entails that the running is in one direction while the pass goes in another. If the upper part of the body is not turned away from the direction of running, the arms can follow only one course and that is sideways across the front of the body. The arm farthest from the direction of passing out will in this way lose contact with the ball sooner than the other arm. This is the reason why, as far as this arm is concerned, the pass comes to an end at that moment. It is then said that a player gives a one-handed pass.

By turning the upper part of the body towards the direction of passing, however, that arm becomes longer, attaining the same length as its counterpart. Both hands can then release the ball simultaneously.

This is the secret of passing. Moreover, if two hands are used for coping with a pass, their swing is sufficient in length for a long pass. If the pass is given with one arm, it causes the elbow of the "short" or "passing" arm to bend and, by its uncoiling, more power is given to the pass. One sees this every day.

Another secret concerning the technique of passing: the ball is swung with the arms and must leave the hands at some point. If this happens too soon, the ball will travel too low. If the ball is released too late, the ball will go too high. Obviously the ball must be released at the average height at which it has to travel, this being the point of the swing just before the arms start the upward curve. The player passing the ball stretches his arms towards that point. If a player stretches his hands in the direction in which the ball is passed, they will be at the furthermost point from him. Should he swing his arms beyond this, they will incline upwards.

Passing therefore means to let go of the ball at the point where the hands are farthest from the passer's body. Passing also means that a player stretches his arms if he wants to take out the slight bending of the elbows caused by his carrying the ball. This uncoiling and the turn of the farther shoulder take place at the same time in the direction of the passing side of the body. The ball is then pushed out to the height for passing.

Because both hands are behind the ball, passing-out entails that the hands are flat and still next to each other when the ball leaves them. The palms thus point as far as possible in the direction of the passing side and the fingers are pulled downwards. And when the arms have completed their work, their swing can terminate immediately at the end of their reach. In this way the margin of safety is lessened compared to what it would have been if the arms had continued their swing after the pass had been completed.

There is another principle involved in passing: if the body is turned, either foot can be in front. The old concept that a ball is passed from the farther foot or from the opposite hip is obsolete. A player should pass out the ball if he has drawn his opponent or the defensive stream, and this is but a fleeting moment. The foot which happens to be in front at this crucial moment is the one from which the pass is given.

Because the receiver of the ball never knows exactly where he will receive the ball, a distinction must be made between two kinds of passes:
1. In which the ball is received and must be passed out immediately.
2. In which the ball is carried and then, at a given moment determined by the player carrying it, is passed out.

As far as the first kind is concerned, if the catching point is too high, the hands must be lowered somewhat to the side of the direction of passing and the elbows must be slightly bent. From this point to the place of passing, the elbows are straightened, because it is this action which gives momentum to the ball. The focal movement of the pass thus begins when the arms are lowered and it ends when they are fully stretched.

This uncoiling is directed towards the point of passing, the point at which the two hands will be farthest from the body. The hands are practically pushed in that direction and the fingers are pulled down because they determine whether the ball will travel at the correct height. The arms merely assist with this by rendering momentum up to that point.

If the catching point is low, the ball is brought on the same plane to the passing side for the straightening of the elbows and the turn of the furthermost shoulder. In this instance the fingers are pulled just sufficiently down to send the ball on its way at the correct elevation.

For the carried pass, the ball is lowered for the pass as described above, regardless of whether the ball is being carried in two hands or tucked under an arm.

When it comes to passing or kicking, we are dealing with a different kind of power compared with that involved in pushing – swinging-power. Swinging the arms or the legs affords strength, but this is not everything: power from the arms and shoulders or from the legs must flow into the swing precisely and in correct measure.

What we have to bear in mind is that there are so-called focal points in the swing. The swings occur in a circular form and we have in both passing and kicking actually less than half a circle in which the proper task is to be performed. The focal movement, however, will be one which will keep itself as close as possible to the most important part of the circular arc, i.e. that part of the course in which the important focal points are situated. One of these is to be found in the very lowest point of the circle, so to speak. If this point is ignored, the swinging-power will suffer in consequence. A player brings his arms or the leg with which he kicks to that point, because this is where power is infused into the swing. The preceding motions also contribute to the swinging-power, but these serve the purpose of getting the arms or the kicking leg to that point.

Of additional interest is the point which is attained when the arms or the leg are fully extended, i.e. when their tasks have been completed. They then have to be straight, and this means that immediately afterwards they will move upwards. This is a specific point in a circle, and again it should not be ignored. The arms are fully extended, thus breaking the circle somewhat, as would be done when kicking through the ball to straighten the leg. Some players have a follow-through when passing, as when taking a kick, whereas others stop the movement as soon as the arms or leg have been straightened. Both have their advantages, but the fact remains that the action has been completed when the follow-through takes place. If the arms are already stretched to the full at the lowest point – and this is the best way – they will remain straight until the point of passing has been reached.

Passes by the scrum half
We differentiate between a pass given from a scrum, from a line-out, and from a ruck. At a scrum the scrum half follows the ball, which is on the ground. From a line-out the ball is let out into his hands – he is thus standing – and at a ruck he usually awaits the ball which is on the ground.

The sideways position in which the scrum half has to move or stand and wait for the ball is of the greatest importance. In his position he can make use of either the dive pass or the standing pass.

The dive pass
When a scrum half has put the ball into the scrum and his team hooks the ball, he must see to it that he goes close to the scrum after the ball or else his opposite number will fall on the ball between him and the scrum. If the ball has emerged from the scrum, it depends on how far the ball is out and on which foot the scrum half has placed behind it. If the ball is right up against the scrum, the scrum half will place the foot nearest to the scrum behind the ball. If the ball is somewhat further away, or quite a distance away, it is immaterial which foot is placed behind it. The scrum half's hands are flat and next to each other, with the palms turned towards the ball and as close to the ground as possible.

In this position of preparedness the scrum half is completely bent as far as his arms, his legs, his back, and his neck are concerned. These must be straightened as part of the process which is started when the foot is placed behind the ball or next to it. As a matter of fact, it is this leg which determines whether a dive or falling pass will be executed. The stretching of this leg thus launches the entire process of the pass at the same moment that the hands make contact with the ball. If the leg is stretched, the entire body is propelled forward, in the process of which the entire back and neck are first stretched, followed by the arms.

Observation plays an important part here. Before putting the ball into the scrum the scrum half must know where his fly half has taken up his position and consequently he first looks for his partner. When he next looks at the fly half, his legs, his arms, and his neck are straight, i.e. immediately before the arm movement takes place. This allows him to adapt the movement of his arms to the position taken up by the fly half. Because the leg is forcefully extended, the entire body is launched into the air, but forward and not upwards. The test, if the pass is correctly executed, is whether the back and neck and the arms are in line when the ball leaves the hands.

Another point that must be mentioned is that the scrum half must, as soon as he has landed on the ground, hoist himself up with his arms and get to his feet as soon as possible. Because his body moves forward he will have the palms of his hands under his shoulders for this action. This means that the arms first pass out the ball and then go quickly down to the ground for pressing up the body. The moving body thus goes over the arms, which cushion the body on the ground.

The dive pass from a line-out is given from a standing position, but even in this instance the scrum half will not be in an upright position but will take up a crouching stance. His legs will thus be slightly bent and his back will be somewhat rounded. There are three positions which the scrum half can take up:
1. He can be at right angles to the line-out.
2. He can be facing in the direction of the fly half.
3. His back can be turned to the fly half.

For the positions indicated in (1) and (2) above, his leg nearest to the fly half and furthermost from the line-out will be used for uncoiling, while the other leg will be used for jerking upwards in order to make rotation on the stretched leg possible. For the position indicated in (3), stretching takes place in the leg furthermost from the line-out while the other leg is flung up backwards to help rotation.

If there is a choice – which is not always the case – preference should be given to taking up a sideways position next to the line-out – position (3) – because this allows the scrum half to turn his back to the line-out so that his arms are kept away from forwards who are out to wrest the ball from him or get hold of his arms.

The dive pass should by preference not be given from a ruck, as the ball travels too hard for the fly half who, in the nature of things, will be nearer to his scrum half than in a line-out or scrum.

For the same reason, a standing pass is preferable when the fly half moves towards the blind side. The dive pass, however, is to be preferred if a foot can get to the ball before the scrum half can do so; if there are harassing forwards whom he has to keep off his back, and if a lengthy pass is to be given.

The standing pass (upright pass)
The approach to the ball is the same as that used for the dive pass, but in this instance the foot farthest from the fly half is turned crosswise and is placed not next to the ball but behind it. This means that the scrum half will be looking in the direction of the scrum, and that when his hands make contact with the ball his arms will have been turned in the direction of his fly half's position.

The rotation of the arms results in the inclination of the body being turned in that direction, and it serves as a preparation for the pass itself. As in the case of the dive pass, there must be no pauses between the different stages, but each movement must flow into the next. As soon as the hands have made contact with the ball, the arms swing out, and together with the swing a step is taken with the foot nearest to the fly half in the direction of his position. It is better to step out too far than too near because the swing of the arms must be comfortable, easy and complete. The toes of the foot used for stepping outwards point somewhat ahead of the fly half so that the swing of the arms does not impair the balance, as would happen if the toes were pointing at or behind the fly half.

In this instance the scrum half looks at the fly half when the ball rests safely against his (the scrum half's) hands, or even later when the pass has just begun.

A good tip here is that the chin should be kept down right through the motion because the tendency is to jerk the head, and as a result also the arms, before they have come to the end of the swing. Whereas the weight has been on the foot nearest to the ball at the start of the pass, it is transferred with the swing of the arms to the foremost foot. This displacement of weight is most important, and it is imperative that it should synchronise with the swing of the arms.

In both the stand-up pass and the dive pass there is, without stopping or interrupting the movements in any way, a distinct phase in the pass which must be considered as a separate aspect – getting safely hold of the ball. This does not mean that the ball must be picked up, or that there is a pause, but that this is the most important phase of the pass – that contact with the ball should be made correctly. The thumbs help in this by pressing the ball down as part of the contact of the hands with the ball. If the scrum half finds himself with his back towards the fly half, passing becomes difficult and this results in many a scrum-half overdoing kicking. In this situation he will move in a different direction to the one in which the pass is to be given. Two kinds of passes may be used:

1. Take a step past the ball with the foot nearest to the scrum – if the position of the ball allows for it – and place the hands over and on the ball and give a pass out, as it were, from under the arm furthermost from the scrum. As a rule the ball is first picked up, which is injudicious; yet this method has the advantage that the direction in which the scrum half moves or runs draws the attention away from the side to which the ball is going to travel. This is something which can stand the fly half in good stead.
2. The following method is preferable: the scrum half takes a step past the ball

with the foot nearest to the scrum and places his hands between his body and the ball so that the hands are next to and behind the ball (next to, in the sense that the side of the ball nearest to you becomes part of the grasp). His hands now swing in the direction of the fly half while his upper body jerks past the pick-up area, as it were, and rotates on the foremost foot so that he also faces in the direction of the fly half.

At the line-out
The pass given here is the same as that which is made from a scrum, regardless of the position in which the scrum half may find himself. Here, too, he passes the ball from the farthest foot while his other foot stretches far out, his chin is kept down, and the farthest shoulder is forcibly turned so that the arms can attain an equal stretch.

From a ruck
Here, too, the pass is the same as from a scrum, except that the scrum half usually waits for the ball; he must also take up a sideways stance so that, should he be compelled to step forward, he takes a short step and one which will be close to the farther side of the ball in relationship to his fly half. In this way it will not be necessary for him to rotate in order to give the pass, a movement so often seen nowadays. He must not turn his back to the fly half, but should this be necessary his method of passing is the same as that described above.

Throw-ins by the wing
The under-arm throw, the torpedo throw, and the "point over point" have become obsolete, but that does not mean that they should therefore be completely written off. If any of these should be a wing's most successful method for throwing in the ball, he should use it, especially if it suits one or both line-out specialists. The under-arm throw-in has the disadvantage of course that the forwards cannot see the ball. However, if the forwards know the signs, as they should, this is an advantage because they then know where the ball is to be thrown while their opponents will worry about not seeing the ball.

The over-arm bowling action may be a torpedo ball or a point-over-point ball. Whichever one is used depends on the line-out forward to whom the ball is thrown.

The secret of the point-over-point ball lies in the placing of the middle finger in the centre of the point of the ball and in the swing of the arm which is absolutely vertical in its swinging action past the head. The grip for the torpedo throw is also important. The ball is held crosswise in the hand and the stretched-out fingers are extended over one half of the ball so that the points of some of the fingers press down on a groove or seam. The point of the ball, indicating the direction of its flight, should be straight ahead when the bent arm propels it over the head and when the fingers underneath it pull through when the ball is released.

Definition: Catching is thus an action which stops a ball in its flight – or roll – with one hand (pass-on ball), or two hands (high-dropping ball and pick-up ball), or with the body (diagonal ball), or catching it a very short while afterwards with the body (high-dropping ball and pick-up ball). Passing is the straightening of the arms between two focal points and in the direction of, and up to, the level of passing. This action requires the swivelling of the farther shoulder which, together with the down-stretched fingers, determines the height at which the ball is to travel.

The focal movement of catching lies between the contact of the hands and the ball, i.e. stopping, and catching. That of passing extends from the infusion of power into the action to the point at which the arm is straightened.

Wet balls and windy conditions
The following few tips are worth remembering:

For catching a wet ball, the hands are more relaxed and pliable than for catching a dry ball.

A ball is caught against the body, passed only with the lower part of the arms, and travels in a lob. Scrum halves hardly ever use the dive pass. If the ball is very slippery it is seldom picked up, and in the wet there are consequently few picked-up balls. As for kicking a slippery ball, the kick should be straight through and no attempt should be made to "cut" the ball in order to get away a torpedo kick.

Because judgment becomes more difficult in windy weather, a player's eyes must be glued to the ball. It is advisable to remain on the spot where the ball is estimated to land for a longer period than would be the case in fine weather, as a player can adapt himself better to the whims of the ball from a stationary position.

When the ball is passed, it must travel absolutely parallel to the ground. If the ball's trajectory is low, the ball will be further depressed when being passed against the wind. Passing with the wind, however, will not affect the flight of the ball. If the ball travels too high, the wind will take it. The less power there is behind the ball the more readily it will be depressed or taken by the wind. If a player faces a head wind, his pass to a fellow-player will be thrown further ahead than usual. If playing with an exceptionally strong wind, the ball is passed directly at the receiver. If play is against the wind, the ball is kept low. For a kick into touch some players place one hand – the right hand for right-footed kickers – on top of the ball and press it down with the fingers to ensure that ball and foot meet at the correct point.

Against the wind the ball is placed at a more acute angle, whereas the ball is placed more upright with the wind. Kicks for touch with the wind are likewise lofted to allow the wind to carry the ball along.

If the wind is blowing diagonally across the field, the touchline is not made the target for touch kicks, but the ball is kicked straight, i.e. kicked parallel with the touchline or even more to the inside if the player is not too far infield. If he is deep infield, his kick will be somewhat in the direction of the touchline, but not aimed directly at it.

The push-off as a skill in attacking
Definition: The push-off – or leg-thrust – is a means of retarding the body in

its fast forward movement for a few paces, and then accelerating again and/or changing direction. This is done by the powerful stretching of the leg of the push-off foot at the moment that the full weight crosses over the base of the toes. This will let the body, as part of the stretching process, incline in the same direction as that in which the stretching occurs then to "catch up" the displaced bodily weight with the other foot and allowing the push-off feet either to repeat the push-off or take it further, the other foot being used merely as a method of transfer. The focal movement is once again the explosive part of the entire action.

A push-off is required for all methods of attack in which dynamic power – not brute force – plays a leading part.

The aim is to break through the defence or effect a break by means of weapons of attack and correct passing. These methods of attack usually include the following:

1. Straight running as part of the preliminary for the method of attack which is applied, e.g.
   (a) The swerve.
   (b) The sidestep.
   (c) The dummy.

   Each of the abovementioned actions begins at the starting point, which is where a player is just beyond reach of a defender (and his crash tackle). This controlled approach must decoy the defender or the defence into a different direction from that in which the runner intends breaking or passing, causing the defender or the defence to hesitate for a moment. This is done by running straight in the direction of the defender, looking at him at the same time, or looking in a direction different from that in which you intend breaking (or passing), or by inclining towards the side where the break will not take place, by selling a dummy, or even by leaning in that direction.

2. Concealment of speed, with which is coupled a certain decreasing of speed, in order to render strength to the legs in preparation for a method of attack. This means that a player must be ready to come to light with a sudden burst of speed in any method of attack.

3. Perfect balance, i.e. control over the force of gravity, regardless of the footwork and the change of direction involved.

4. Using the legs without using the arms which carry the ball.

The swerve

The steps are so arranged that the foot which the player requires for swerving, i.e. the foot which will determine the direction of the swerve, will be in front.

The swerve is given by pushing off with the front foot in the direction which suits the player. The foot used for pushing off propels him to one side while his other foot supports his weight. If this foot supports the entire weight, so that the foot used for the push-off can take a step straight forward, or diagonally forward, the result will be half a swerve. But if this foot acts as an obliquely forward transfer of the weight so that the foot used for the push-off passes in front of the other foot, supporting the weight itself on the other side and directing the course of running diagonally ahead, it is a swerve.

The side-step
For the side-step there is also down-thrust, but here the preparatory steps are shorter than those used for the swerve because the footwork is done more rapidly. Here too we have a deliberate slackening of speed which results in the foot not used for the push-off breaking off the last step leading up to the push-off, bisecting it as it were. By this the speed needed for perfect balance and maximum effect in the push-off as regards distance and direction is acquired.

The pace of the foremost foot is halved and the other foot is placed alongside it preparatory to the down-thrust.

In this instance too, the weight is supported, and if the player wants to advance after the first or second push-off, he can do so with the foot used for the push-off, as the weight is under complete control.

The dummy
The dummy is always coupled with a half-swerve, but the dummy goes in one direction and the swerve in another. Consequently a specific foot must be in front. The secret of a dummy is not so much in the push-off, but in the preparation for it, i.e. the arms swinging out as if they are going to release the ball – and the glance in the same direction. Everything is done as in the case of a pass, but as soon as the ball is to be released, it comes back with the arms while the push-off takes place at the same time. By its very nature the swerve cannot extend so very far, because the arms are in the opposite direction and the head is also turned in that direction because the eyes are looking that way. The swerve is thus coupled with a jerking movement by the arms and the head, the latter actually assisting in the movement.

Technique
At the precise moment that the entire weight is on the ball of the foot used for the push-off in its forward motion, the push-off must be made, i.e. the force of gravity is the same as when standing still. Thus the entire weight (weight-in-movement) is on the foot for the push-off. The leg used for the push-off is again straightened explosively, in the process of which it is given its course by the body, which inclines in the same direction as the push-off.

The push-off takes place with the big toe as its basis, or the pad under the toe. If the push-off is given too soon, this knob cannot function properly at this stage. If the action takes place too late, the toe, which is too weak for performing the function, is compelled to do so. In order to support the weight of the body, the leg which is flexed for receiving the strain is straightened, by means of which the weight is again brought "upright". If the weight is merely to be transferred further away, the leg remains bent. If a player wants to kick the ball, he does not do so at full speed, but adjusts it to the kick. The same applies to the push-off. Running at full speed, and then attempting a push-off as soon as the weight is on one of the feet, is mis-timing. For this reason speed is reduced in order to determine the exact moment for the push-off and for controlling the moving weight the better.

The underlying principle is a straight run-up, otherwise the movement is against the grain, and the distance of the push-off as well as its direction will suffer. This, in turn, can cause slipping of the foot used for the push-off. The more soggy the field, the more important is straight running, preferably with shorter steps.

The push-off may be used if a player is running diagonally across the field, but it can be carried out only in one direction. Suppose, for instance, that the running is directed diagonally across the field to the right-hand side. The push-off can then be done only to the left-hand side. Every player has a push-off area, i.e. the direction and distance of his push-off are in the same proportion to the direction of running and the place of pushing-off. If an opponent is past this area, a push-off with diagonal running may of course be effective, and should obviously be used. When speaking of straight running it is assumed that the opponent is not in the area where the push-off will occur.

Another principle holds good as part of the straightening process: there should not be any interchanging of feet, because this tends to break the speed, and the perfect balance required by the push-off is frittered away. If the point of impact cannot be reached by means of the usual paces, the paces are simply shortened. The push-off becomes, as it were, part of running another step and will, as a result of accumulated momentum, occur diagonally ahead.

Tackling as a skill in defence
Definition: Tackling means closing both arms around a player carrying the ball, clasping him against one so that he is not only stopped but also forced to his side or toppled to the ground. In this way he is put out of action. If the arms cannot reach him, a push-off is made and a dive tackle taken in order to reach the target.

The focal movement of the standing tackle is that part which brings the arms into action for pulling in the attacker. The focal movement of the dive tackle is the explosive part, the dive itself, and encirclement with the arms.

The standing tackle
Generally one gets hold of an opponent while one is running. When running, the arm opposite to the leg goes forward. This means that this pattern will be deviated from if a proper tackle is to be made. In other words, the arms no longer function as an integral part of running. Furthermore, the arm initiating the grab is usually the one which has to stop the opponent's direction of running. It embraces the body so that the body can be pulled. The other arm obviously comes into play, because pulling the body involves both arms.

The arms operate contrary to the direction of running. The chest can be used to make contact with the opponent, especially if the intention is to keep him on his feet and, in the process, keep yourself upright and prevent the ball from landing on the ground. The head is thus pulled backwards. If, at the same time, the intention is to put the player on to the ground by means of running into him or pushing him, the shoulder is used for making contact.

The dive tackle
Fundamentals for the dive tackle are:
1. The foot which is in front is used in the push-off for the dive. The leg of this

foot uncoils, and consequently there is no interchanging of paces.
2. Both feet leave the ground as the body is propelled from the toes and not from the entire foot.
3. The back is straightened – locked – and the head is held up so that the neck is straight as part of the back.
4. The eyes are fixed on the target.
5. The target is the player's middle – his hips. If the defender goes too low, his arms can be forced open by the action of the attacker's legs.
6. The head goes behind the opponent, not to prevent him from falling on the defender's head but to make sure that if the tackler's timing is somewhat out (as is often the case because the defender does not know when the attacker is going to stop short), his head will not strike the attacker's hard hip-bone.
7. The arms close more forcibly than a spring trap, because the tackler dives over his arms. If this is not done, the target is merely knocked away.

Kicking as a skill
Kicking as a skill always requires a target. For the kick itself the ball is shaped into a certain position in the hands and then released so that the position is retained when it touches the foot. In place-kicking the hands shape the ball on the ground.

Kicking is a controlled skill. Kicking-power is adjusted to the purpose that the kicker has in mind. Maximum power comprises the full swing of the leg used for kicking, and this swing is possible only if the necessary space is provided by a long step of the other leg.

Every kick has run-up steps and a kicking step. The run-up steps serve as preparation for the kicking step, which estimates the distance required for the full swing of the kicking leg. As soon as the leg used for the kick leaves the ground for the swing, the knee is first of all bent. The uncoiling of the leg supplies the power required for kicking. Thus the kick begins with the start of the uncoiling and concludes with the straightening of the leg. This should happen immediately after connection with the ball because at that point the final portion of the bend is uncoiled. The uncoiling is then also at its fastest, because momentum increases as the swing develops.

The kick is not completed when the ball is struck, but shortly afterwards, because part of the kick is the follow-through of the foot. (This follow-through must not be confused with the through kick.) In the case of some kicks the leg is not extended when connecting with the ball but is straightened shortly afterwards. This straightening after connection is the through kick: the player kicks "through" the ball, as it were, to straighten the leg. Then comes the follow-through, which is actually no longer a part of the kick but useful in that is is indicative of the correct execution of the kick. Some of the greatest kickert have no follow-through, but on completion of the through kick they bring the foot to a dead stop by jerking it back, as it were, resulting in the stab kick.

To give the kicker balance, the arm opposite to the kicking leg swings forward or sideways. In order that the swing, and especially the through kick, should not be cut short, the chin is kept down and is lifted simultaneously with the foot after the follow-through. If there is no follow-through, the chin may be lifted only with the recoil of the foot, i.e. after the through kick.

Types of kick
1. Kicks from the hands in which the hands give shape to the kick and the ball is struck before it touches the ground: (a) The kick for touch. (b) The high kick. (c) The punt. (d) The cross kick. (e) The hooked kick. (f) The corner kick. (g) One type of grubber kick.
2. The ball is struck a moment after touching the ground: (a) The drop kick. (b) The grubber kick. (c) The jab kick.
3. When the ball is kicked from the ground: (a) The place kick. (b) The dribble kick.

The grip for kicks from the hands before the ball touches the ground. The hands shape the position of the ball for kicks which are made before the ball reaches the ground as follows (for right-footed kickers):
1. The left hand is placed in front and along the left side of the ball with the right hand behind and along the right-hand side of the ball; or
2. The left hand is placed in front and along the left-hand side of the ball while the right hand is placed on top of the ball with the lace or the eyelets between the thumb and the forefinger. All fingers are turned towards the ground while the left hand is placed directly underneath the ball and is turned, i.e. the thumb points ahead while the remaining fingers are crosswise underneath the ball.

The ball struck before it reaches the ground
1. *Kick for touch*

The point of the ball is sufficiently lowered to "fit" the foot when the toes are pulled down to provide a hard surface for contact. The front point of the ball is turned somewhat in the direction of the kick so that the air pressure can push the ball in that direction.

The point of impact is in front of the non-kicking foot and at a height at which the uncoiling almost reaches its end, so that all the kicking-power goes into the ball at the end of uncoiling.

Consequently the ball is struck as low as possible. To achieve this the left arm is straightened, locked, and the right arm is then brought forward. The final phase of uncoiling takes place from the moment that the kicking foot passes some distance beyond the stationary foot. Thus the ball is struck at the point where the foot is almost furthest from the body and where it can kick "through" the ball. The foot therefore travels a short distance in the same direction as the ball before it is completely straight.

2. *The high kick*

For this kick the point of the ball is held straight to the front. The ball is not pulled down, as the foot strikes the ball considerably higher. The kick is also not "through" the ball. The higher the ball is struck, the straighter up is its trajectory; the lower the ball is struck, the further it is bound to travel.

3. *The punt*
For this type of kick the ball is held in the same manner as for the high kick. Because the toes are not pulled down the kicker requires a soft impact area. The execution of the kick is done gently, i.e. the uncoiling process does not run its entire course and is slowly executed. In other words, the first part of the uncoiling is delayed while the last part is dispensed with. The ball is consequently not released with extended arms.

4 & 5. *The centre kick and the hooked kick*
The point of the ball is turned in the direction of the kick to provide the kicking foot with a bigger surface, as the kick is usually taken at full speed. The ball is struck closer or nearer to the ground, depending on the height the ball is to reach.

6. *The corner kick*
The ball is held in a straight line, but the point is lowered because the toes are pulled down to supply a hard surface for accurate kicking. The uncoiling takes place slowly and can either be stopped at connection with the ball or the kick can go "through" the ball.

7. *The grubber kick*
For this kind of kick some players strike the ball before it reaches the ground. As such it becomes a kind of "mini" corner kick. The foot stops when it connects with the ball. Actually the foot is at the spot where it connects and the ball merely drops on to it.

Kicks from the hands, when the ball is struck immediately after making contact with the ground:

1. *The drop kick*
The point of the ball is dropped so that it is almost the same position as for an upright place kick. To fit the foot, the ball inclines somewhat backwards. In this position it is dropped in front of the non-kicking foot. The run-up is straight.

2. *The stab kick*
This is a miniature drop kick in which the ball, at the moment of touching the ground, is smothered, as it were, by preventing it from lifting from the ground. The ball is struck close to the kicker so that the point of his foot smothers it. Obviously there is no follow-through.

Another method of executing the jab kick is that of striking the ball before it touches the ground and then kicking it into the ground. For this method the ball is also dropped close to the kicker.

3. *The grubber kick*
The ball is held crosswise and is smothered with the ankle joint, as it were, so that it rolls slowly and only a few yards. Otherwise it is struck with the sole of a crossed foot. For this kind of kick the body stretches far forward.

Where the ball is kicked from the ground
1. *The place kick*
It has been proved that the upright ball travels farther than the ball placed at a slant, but whether it is more accurate still remains to be proved. For the long-range place kick, the ball is leant forward with the lace on the ground. For the upright place kick, the lace faces towards the posts. In both cases the lace of the ball should be higher than the point of contact, and for both types of kick the point of the non-kicking foot should be opposite the point of impact.

For both kinds of kick the mark made in the ground must be considered merely as a means of "shaping" the ball. The ball should not be "lodged" in the mark in such a way that it has to be dislodged or kicked out of it as this would cause the ball to spin too much and fritter away too much kicking-power. The leaning ball is not inside the hollow or mark but rests up against the small heap of soil. In the case of the upright ball the hollow should be made either shallow or open in front.

It is difficult to say exactly where the non-kicking foot should be placed in relation to the ball because a player's physique also has something to do with it. The toe is either in line with the rearmost point of the ball or just behind or beyond it. If the foot is placed too far back, the ball will be struck too high. If it is placed too far forward, the ball will be kicked into the ground. In any case, the variable difference in position of the point of the boot is certainly not more than 4 inches (100 mm) – 2 inches behind and 2 inches in front of the rearmost point of the ball. The foot used for the kick itself does not vary but maintains its natural position. The toes are thus not pulled down as in the case of a drop kick or a kick for touch.

The toes of the non-kicking foot must not only point straight ahead, but the foot itself must also be placed alongside the ball and as far from it as the kicker's physique can determine. If one should run on damp sea sand, for instance, one would see how far apart the feet are by drawing lines through the imprints of the left and right feet. The distance between these two lines is the distance which the non-kicking foot should be from the ball, and it is also the distance the kicker should keep his feet apart before the run-up. If this distance is not maintained, the kicker's balance will be upset from the start and further impaired by the non-kicking foot's first step, which has to be taken somewhat to the outside.

A kicker must see to it that his kicking foot, the ball, and his target are all in line for his run-up.

Kickers sometimes take their bodies and not their kicking feet as the starting point. The aiming-mark should not consist of the entire crossbar, but should be some smaller object behind the uprights and in the centre of the crossbar, e.g. a woman spectator in a red dress, the top of a tree, a chimney, a sparrow's nest – anything which will narrow down the aim.

Beginners
Before the right distance for the run-up can be estimated, it may be determined as follows:

Place the non-kicking foot where it should be, next to the ball, and take four paces of average length backwards, starting off with the non-kicking foot.

The kicker then adjusts himself to the run-up line and starts off by taking the first step with the left foot, followed by the right foot and then the so-called extended paces which will take the non-kicking foot to its correct position.

If four paces forward are required, take five paces backwards and start with the right foot. Starting the run-up with the right foot ensures more accurate aiming.

Even senior players struggle sometimes because they start with the right foot and then have only the so-called extended paces left for the kick. It is important to remember the following: start off with the left foot and you will require two paces before the extended pace; start off with the right foot and three paces are required.

Definition: The full swing of the kicking leg, from the moment it leaves the ground until it is straightened, or comes to the end of the swing, is made possible by the last step taken by the non-kicking foot, which is a "stretched" step. This type of kick is executed while maintaining perfect balance when running or walking up preparatory to the kick; and, by connecting with the ball at the right place in the swing of the kicking foot, this enabling the foot of the kicking leg to uncoil with increasing momentum, which is coupled with the infusion of power shortly before impact. This uncoiling sometimes takes place before connection, sometimes with, and sometimes after it, depending on the kind of kick. Sometimes it does not take place at all; sometimes it takes place slowly in special types of kicks, as in the case of certain punts.

The focal movement of hard kicks starts when power is infused into swinging-power, and it ends when the leg is straight; the focal movement of soft kicks is when the swinging-power is curtailed shortly before connecting, and it ends with connection.

Recapitulation on skills

Skill	Focal (*i.e. the nucleus*)	Satellitic (*the preparatory and supporting*)
Shoving	Straightening of ankles, legs and hips in so far as the position in the scrummage requires.	Solid base for diagonal front foot, straightening or keeping straight of back and neck: correct stance, packing down correctly, pulling with arms when this is required.
Jumping	Straightening of arms and back.	Rock or short step, or short step and hop; weight rolls over foremost foot, striking up with arms (harder with the inside arm), twisting of the body when hands and ball make contact; down strike of arms, straddled landing, body blocked.
Pushing-in movement	Quick straightening of foremost foot and pulling down of hips.	Eyes on ball; linking with team-mates and opponents, in crouching stance, remaining on feet.

Skill	Focal (i.e. the nucleus)	Satellitic (the preparatory and supporting)
Handling	*Catching:* Between contact with ball, thus stopping or checking in catching. *Passing:* Stretching of arm from the first focal point, at which power is "unleashed" to the second focal point.	Eyes on ball and correct placing of self for approaching ball, or for approaching the ball. Carrying of the ball to the first focal point; swivelling of the shoulders, follow-through if employed, balance.
Leg-thrust or push-off	Stretching of push-off leg at the moment that the weight is plumb on foremost foot.	Straightening; observing; leaning over of body; "catching up" or displacement of bodily weight after the push-off.
Tackling	Clasping pressure with arms (upright tackle); explosive stretching of down-thrust leg and body on their way to clasping the target (dive tackle).	Adjustment, pace variation; remaining on feet if not pressed for repossession, or getting the ball free if tackled.
Kicking	Infusion of power immediately before connection as part of the final straightening of the leg used for kicking; or controlling the swinging power by delaying it, as for the kicking of punts.	Correct adjustment with regard to the direction of the kick. Balanced walk on run-up and maintaining it until after the kick; follow-through or jerking back of the kicking leg, control of looking upwards.

IMPORTANCE OF SKILLS ACCORDING TO POSITIONS ON THE FIELD

To use the skill building exercises, quite a number of things must be seen in their true perspective, namely:

1. All the skills are not equally important for all positions on the field, and the importance of skills for each position must be graded and the time allocated to them must be determined accordingly.

2. The importance of skills required by forwards and backs makes it imperative that these players be separated for most of the skill practices.

3. This entails that different "areas" be arranged for forwards and backs so they can practise separately. But there will be a common "area" for rounding off speed, for instance, as in the case of body building, building up of speed, and building up of stamina.

4. With these facts at our disposal, we suggest a method of practice that can be used by both forwards and backs.

The seven skills of Rugby are not equally important for all players. Whereas there are seven skills in the game, there are only two sections in a team: the forwards and the backs. The forwards can be divided into four groups: the props, the hooker, the locks and the loose forwards. The backs can be divided into five groups: the scrum half, the fly half, the centres, the wings and the full back. For each group there are skills which are more important than others, and these must be selected.

In other words, the skills required by each group must be graded. This will assist us in determining the exercises for each group and assist the selectors in discovering the important skills of players in their respective positions. Selectors will therefore be guided in their choice of teams by the most important skills essential in a player's repertoire rather than by less important skills, even if these are complementary.

The following table is an attempt at grading the skills for each group. With the forwards the odd satellitic movements or duties are included.

Skills Graded According to the Positions of Players

(Expressed in terms of fundamental principles)

Props	Hooker	Locks	Loose forwards	Scrum half	Fly half	Centres	Wings	Full back
1. & 2. Stand and push in scrum and consolidate in line-out. 3. Shove-in movement. 4. Tackling. 5. Handling. 6. Leg-thrust. 7. Kicking.	1. Stand and push in scrum and strike (extra). 2. & 3. Tackling (line-out); pushing-in movement. 4. & 5. Handling; leg-thrust. 6. Jumping. 7. Kicking.	1. & 2. Jumping, pushing and catching in line-out (extra). 3. Shoving-in movement. 4. & 5. Tackling, handling. 6. Leg-thrust. 7. Kicking.	1., 2. & 3. Pushing; tackling; jumping, also consolidation. 4., 5. & 6. Shoving-in movement; handling; leg-thrust. 7. Kicking.	1. Handling. 2. Leg-thrust. 3. & 4. Kicking; tackling.	1. Handling. 2. & 3. Leg-thrust; kicking. 4. Tackling.	1. Handling. 2. & 3. Leg-thrust; tackling. 4. Kicking. (Attacking kicks.)	1. Handling (throw-in extra). 2. Attack and leg-thrust. 3. Tackling. 4. Kicking (Attacking kicks.)	1. & 2. Handling kicking. 3. & 4. Tackling; leg-thrust.

GRADING THE SUB-SKILLS

What has been done so far, however, is not enough. Each skill consists of several components. For instance, kicking as a skill includes the place kick, the drop kick, the kick for touch, the cross kick, the corner kick, the hooked kick, the high kick, the punt, the jab kick, and the grubber kick. All of these have kicking as their common element, but each one differs in its execution and in its importance for the different positions on the field. They are referred to as sub-skills, and they are of very great importance in other respects. All players do not require them to the same degree, and this means that players need not practise the sub-skills of the identical skill to the same degree. In fact, in some positions the practising of some of these is entirely omitted. There is no reason, for instance, why a hooker should practise place kicking or drop kicking. Should a wing, however, neglect centre kicks, should a centre neglect any punt, or should a full back neglect place kicking, an injustice is done by these players to themselves and to the game.

The following is an indication of the skills to which players must pay attention:

Importance of Skills and Sub-skills for Positions on the Field

(Calculated out of 5)

Skills and sub-skills	Props	Hooker	Locks	Loose forwards	Scrum half	Fly half	Centres	Wings	Full back
Pushing	5	5	5	5	–	–	–	–	–
Hooking	3	5	–	–	–	–	–	–	–
Jumping	3	3	5	4/5	–	–	–	–	–
Consolidation	5	5	5	5	–	–	–	–	–
Pushing-in movement	5	5	5	5	–	–	–	–	–
High-dropping ball	2/3	2/3	2/3	5	5	5	5	5	5
Diagonal ball	3	3	3	4	5	5	5	5	5
Scooped-up ball	3	4	3	5	5	5	5	5	5
Passed-on ball	3	4	3	5	5	5	5	5	5
Scrum half pass	–	–	–	–	5	–	–	–	–
Throw-in at line-outs	–	3	–	–	4	–	–	5	5
Swerving	1	1	1	3	5	5	5	5	5
Side-stepping	1	1	1	3	5	5	5	5	5
Dummy	3	3	3	5	5	5	5	5	5
Upright tackle	5	5	5	5	5	5	5	5	5
Dive tackle	3	3	3	5	5	5	5	5	5
Touch kick	1	1	1	4	5	5	5	5	5
High kick	1	1	1	3	3	5	5	4	3
Punting	–	–	–	2	4	5	5	4	–
Centre kick	–	–	–	3	2	4	3	5	3
Hooked kick	–	–	–	–	2	5	4	–	–
Corner kick	–	–	–	–	4	5	4	–	–
Grubber	–	–	–	2	2	5	5	3	–
Stab kick	–	–	–	–	2	5	5	–	–
Place kick	–	–	–	–	2	5	2	2	5
Drop kick	–	–	–	1	4	5	4	3	5

TIME REQUIRED FOR SKILLS ACCORDING TO POSITIONS

In order to do justice to the important skills in each position, we should have an approximate guide to the time that can be allocated to the skills of each position.

There are seven skills, and the following table is calculated on the basis that skill exercises must last at least 30 minutes.

In order to do this, several factors, of which the following are mentioned, must be taken into consideration:

1. The energy demanded by the skill. Experience has taught us that a spell of 3 minutes is sufficient for exercises in which strength plays a large part.
2. The practicality of such a roster, given the fact that forwards and backs work separately, and that the whistle is used when a changeover from one skill to another takes place. Thus the players could change from one skill to another when the whistle is blown, or the backs possibly change with every second whistle.
3. The time at a team's disposal. It is assumed that a team will make time for skill building and according to our experience the minimum time allocated should be 30 minutes.
4. Combination with physical exercises, the rounding off of skills or the application of skills. If only skill building is practised, the time can be increased, but a stage is reached when it must always be done alongside other exercises.

Time required for each skill in each positiion

Position	Pushing	Jumping (Consolidation)	Shoving-in movement	Handling	Down-thrust	Grab	Kick	Special Individual skills
Props	3–5	3–5	3–5	3	–	3	–	15–9*
Hooker	3–5	3–5	3–5	3	–	3	–	15–9
Locks	3–5	3–5	3–5	3	–	3	–	15–9
Loose forwards	3–5	3–5	3–5	3–5	–	3	–	15–9
Scrum half	–	–	–	3–5	3–5	3	6–8	15–9
Fly half	–	–	–	3–5	3–5	3	6–8	15–9
Centres	–	–	–	3–5	3–5	3	6–8	15–9
Wings	–	–	–	3–5	3–5	3	6–8	15–9
Full back	–	–	–	3–5	3–5	3	6–8	15–9

*15 is placed first because it is recommended that if pushing, jumping, and pushing-in movement each lasts 3 minutes, then 15 minutes are required for specific individual skills. If, however, 3 minutes are allocated to each skill, then only 9 minutes are required.

THE MEASURING OF SKILLS

As mentioned elsewhere, measuring is absolutely essential if a player wishes to see whether he is making progress. There is no greater incentive than progress. A player wants to know that he is making progress. If he is not making progress there must be a reason for this, and the reason must be discovered. As a rule practice methods will be to blame, and consequently these can be abandoned or modified or supplemented. If due to a lack of dedication, proven tests will reveal this.

A description follows of equipment and aids designed to test players.

1. *The shoving apparatus* (see diagram on p. 117)

   This apparatus is used for testing shoving power. Forwards can test their strength with regard to their positions, i.e. they can push as front-row forwards, as lock forwards or as loose forwards. As part of their pushing exercises is calculated to strengthen each leg, it is advisable that their pushing powers are tested with regard to the left leg and right leg respectively, and then in combination.

   As front-row forwards strengthen their legs by pushing like locks, they can also test themselves by pushing like a lock. In the same way locks and loose forwards can test themselves with regard to front-row pushing.

   Players must see to it that (a) they test only the first shove and not the shove following in the wake of the first one; and (b) that the first shove is given explosively.

2. *Jumping*

   Jumping power is measured by the height of the jump. The cross-bar of a high jump apparatus is struck with the head.

   In this exercise each leg's jumping power is registered separately and then in combination, and the results of both efforts are recorded on a form.

3. *Shoving-in movement*

   For this exercise no apparatus has been devised. The pushing apparatus, however, can be used until a more satisfactory one has been designed. If this is the case, the player pushes from his foremost foot by means of a short step against the pushing apparatus as if he intends putting it in motion.

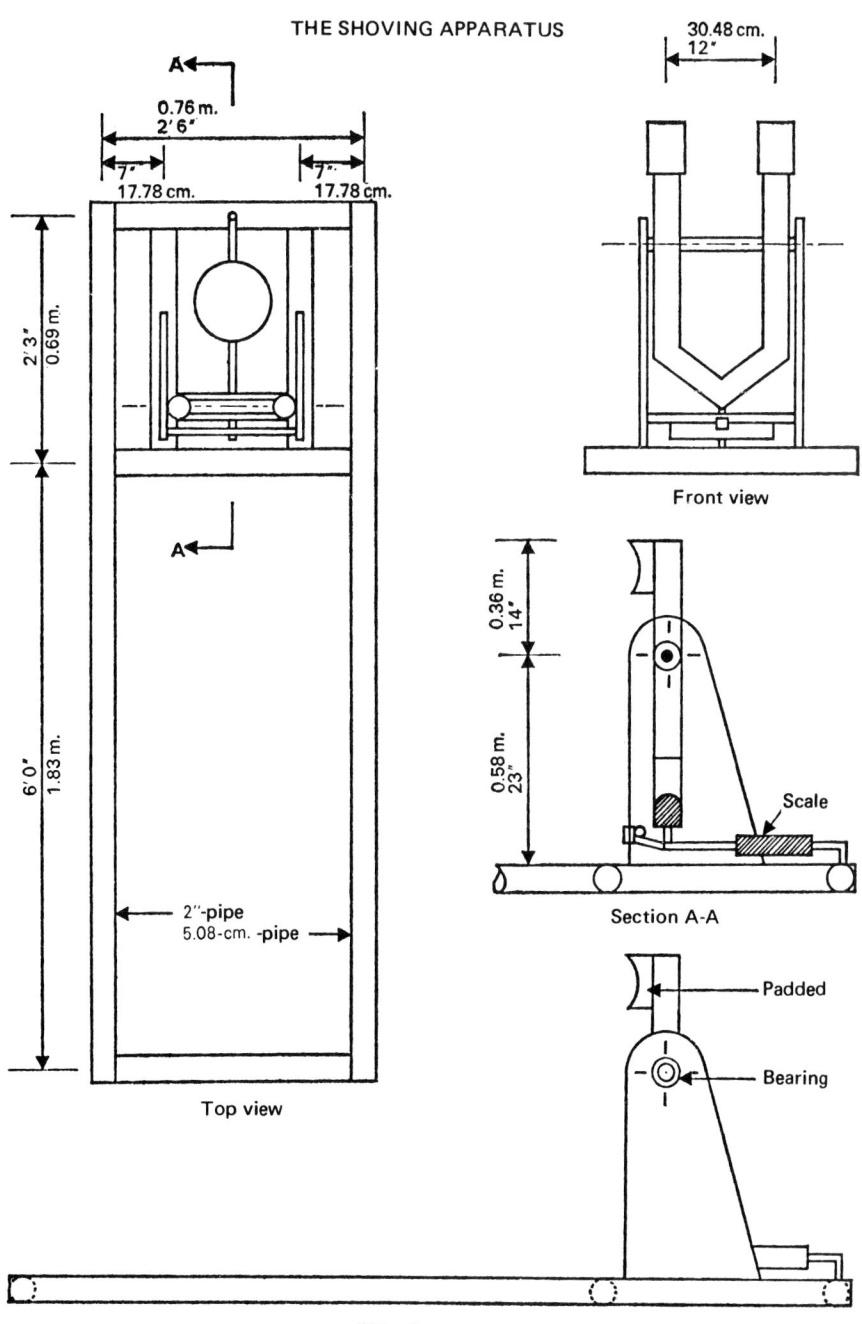

THE SHOVING APPARATUS

4. *Handling*
   (a) The player takes up a position between two nets (see diagram page 217) which are 5 yards apart and throws the ball to and fro against the nets. He passes 10 times against each net as rapidly as possible. Every miss or fumble is added to 20 and the total is divided by 20. The result is indicative of the player's ability. If no mistake is made, he is awarded 1. All additional points count against him.
   (b) The scrum half throws the ball against the net and flings out a pass aimed at any target 10 to 15 paces from the nets. He uses 4 types of passes, 5 times each: the upright pass without swivelling, the dive pass with and without swivelling. Twenty passes are given and only those which are successful are counted and recorded.
   (c) The wings throw in the ball from a position on one of three lines at the throw-in apparatus. The three lines represent the distance he is from the no. 3, the no. 5, and the no. 7 forward in the line-out. He throws in 5 balls from each line and uses two methods for doing so: the straight throw-in and the lob throw-in. This means that he puts in 10 balls from each line, giving him a total of 30 balls. Only those balls which are on target are counted and the result recorded.

5. *Push-off*
   A player runs along a line which has been marked out to provide for his start and his leg-thrust and the leg-thrust from the mark. From the spot at which his foot touches ground up to the "running line", measured directly, reflects the distance of leg-thrust. Two things are measured: the time from setting off to when the leg-thrust takes place, and the distance of the leg-thrust. The distance of the leg-thrust, calculated in yards or metres, is subtracted from the time taken in seconds of the duration of the run-up to the leg-thrust. The same track is used.

6. *Tackling*
   Provision for measuring can be made by using the pushing apparatus.

7. *Kicking*
   (a) *Kicks for touch.* The goal-line is used as starting point with the posts as target. The kicker (full back and fly half) takes up his position 5 paces from the corner flag on the touchline and uses the farthest foot from the goal-line for kicking a touch kick through the uprights.
   On the opposite side of the posts another player is tested in catching the ball kicked to him and he attempts to kick it through the uprights from 5 paces from the corner flag inside the in-goal area. Each player has 10 attempts, after which they exchange positions, and consequently feet, for kicking. The successful kicks are counted and registered. If one of the uprights is struck, it is taken as a successful attempt.
   (b) *Place kicks and drop kicks:* As above, but the ball is kicked 15 paces from the corner of the goal-line.

(c) *Punts:* An area is used for punts taken by the centres and the fly half. The area has 3 parallel lines 5 yards apart. The run-up commences at the furthermost line, the punt is given just before the centre line and possession of the ball is gained before the last line. Players also use these lines for dummying, kicking and catching. Five punts and 5 grubber kicks are given with each foot, i.e. 20 kicks. Balls caught or picked up faultlessly in front of the catching line are counted for each type of kick and the results are registered. At this stage we cannot supply the time for these types of kicks, but it is advisable that, as in the case of handling, there should be a time limit.

Testing of speed
The time for 25 yards is clocked.

EXERCISES FOR RUGBY II

Chapter 4

EXERCISE RECOMMENDATIONS

We have already become acquainted with the following:
There are different forms of fitness, and for these special exercises are undertaken.

Type of fitness	Aim	Means
Physical fitness	Building the body, speed, stamina.	Physical training, including exercises for building of strength, stamina and speed.
Fitness in skills	Building of skills in pushing, jumping, pushing-in movement, handling, leg-thrust, tackling and kicking.	Exercises for skill building with or without apparatus.
Fitness in fundamental principles	Rounding off of skills in sections before the fundamental principles are rounded off, especially in the scrum and in the line-out as preparation for the more involved situations already encountered.	Brushing up of the two sections – forwards and backs separately or combined without actually playing.
Fitness for play	All the moves are practised, either separately or in combination, i.e. tight play, general play and special play as the bases of the moves, plus broken play, broken down play and loose play (rounding off of skills). The situations during the practising of the moves are similar to the situations in a match.	Brushing up of the two sections together or of four sections, i.e. two teams.
Match fitness	Moves flow naturally into one another in play form, tactics are applied as part of tight play and the laws of the game are applied (application of skills). The situations are now like those in a game or in a match.	Brushing up of set pieces or practice match in which both teams play as in a match.

The foregoing are physical and skill exercises and include exercises for skill building, rounding off of skills, and the application of skills. Rounding off of skills, however, is absorbed by the brushing up of fundamental principles. The application of skill is again absorbed in the polishing of movements and in brushing up for matches. And yet these still form the basis of the game.

We are concerned with different age groups, with boys and adults. Obviously they cannot all do the same exercises, and for this reason we divide them into three groups:
1. Club players and secondary schoolboys.
2. Upper primary or intermediate schoolboys who are already playing in friendly matches.
3. Primary schoolboys who may be playing a type of Rugby but no senior matches.

The dividing line between the intermediate and primary schoolboys differs from club to club. In most cases, under eleven-year-old boys are the youngest to play in matches. Provision may be made for even younger boys, but age plays no real part here because the criterion involved is one of either playing or not playing matches. When speaking of higher primary schoolboys we mean boys who play friendly matches against other schools. We sincerely hope these will always be friendly matches because at this level Rugby should still be a great adventure. Their game should not be channelled, and tactics and patterns should be avoided. They are still in the process of development, and anything which can retard or stunt this should be avoided. Neither do we want to see them exposed to too much stress: there is enough tension in a match itself, and playing for trophies as if it were a matter of life and death may create far too many problems.

As stated, primary schoolboys or beginners play a "type" of Rugby. This simplified game aims at providing as much experience as possible of situations and movements, and in these they must not be curtailed. The more experience they gain the better are their chances of getting to the top later on in their Rugby careers. Today the youngsters do not have the same opportunities of activity that the older generation had, and consequently these opportunities should be given to them and created for them on the Rugby field. We are convinced that the diversified and regular activities in which they indulged as youngsters contributed to the making of the best Springbok players in the past. (This is still true in some instances today.) It has also been proved that the more active a boy is and the more diversified these activities are, the more opportunities for developing his skills are created so that it can be predicted with greater assurance that he is being well prepared for whatever awaits him on the road to Rugby.

So let the boys play; this is what they want to do. And let the game be enjoyable, adventuresome and natural. They do not want to be bothered with what they have to do and when they have to do it. Their minds must be free from everything except the business of the game as they themselves want to play it. For this reason the laws of the game should be simplified and, for what they may be worth, the laws that should be applied in the cases of both lower and higher primary schoolboys are supplied. These, obviously, do not conform to the official laws of the game and most probably will not meet with the approval of its legislators, but this cannot be helped.

In the practice programme no difference is made between club players and high-school boys because all these players play the game with more seriousness than primary schoolboys. After adolescence a boy wants to be a man and do

things like a man. Consequently a practice programme is supplied for these players, and to this programme that of the other two groups can be adjusted.
The season is divided into three sections for all three groups:
1. The pre-match period.
2. The mid-season period.
3. The end-of-season period.

Each period has its own features and consequently each is considered indispensable. One's approach to a season on hand is quite different from the approach to that part of the season when playing matches is practically routine. One becomes accustomed to playing matches and may even start wishing that the season will make way for the summer.

Primary-school teachers should study Part II of this book in its entirety because in it are many exercises for clubs and high schools which can be taken over for use in the primary schools. They should know best which exercises are suitable for their boys.

RUGBY FOR SCHOOLBOYS

We would like to explain why we are so keen that a boy should play some type of Rugby from the time he starts attending school.

1. The first reason is a selfish one, namely to promote Rugby. But our attitude is not selfish as regards Rugby exclusively, it is a selfishness which comprises all kinds of games. The more active a child is, the better are his chances of acquiring the skills of games and different kinds of sport in a natural way; the better, too, are his chances of gaining laurels for his country in later years. Rugby is inevitably a game teeming with activity and seeing that it is a contact game, it offers ample opportunities for knocking a player about and for brutality to come to the surface. And these are the very things we wish to curb.
2. Rugby can be used for educational purposes. With reference to what has been said above, Rugby lends itself *par excellence* to education, to the shaping of good habits in the process of developing a mature personality. The accent on playing Rugby must fall initially on its educational value rather than on whether a boy plays the game well, poorly, or even badly. Here follow a few examples.

Many a youngster already has the scars of a setback when putting in a first appearance on the Rugby field. Somewhere along the road he has been injured and has become frightened. Such a boy will hold himself aloof, imagining to himself that he is hiding; or he will look for sanctuary in the throng of players, but he will avoid touching the ball. Perhaps he will tackle an opponent, but usually he will render only token assistance. Such a boy must be helped and it must be done in a pleasant way. There are always "clusters" of players in the type of game they play, and these must be broken up as soon as possible by plucking the ball from the heap. When you once have the ball, you put it into the hands of one of these diffident youngsters, blocking unobtrusively any would-be tacklers so that he may run a few yards with the ball without being tackled. After this he may be brought down by a tackle. The first hurdle has been taken. To this, his whole attitude will usually testify to a realisation that it was not such a painful experience as he had expected. Sometimes such a youngster has to be assisted twice in the manner described, but I still have to learn of a case which required three treatments of this kind.

Sometimes a youngster loses his temper. It is natural for many of them to get angry if they are hurt or do not have things their own way. Avoid scolding the young culprit. If it is not serious, give him a friendly glance with raised eyebrows to make him realise that you have noticed his lapse. Should his anger be deep-rooted, you simply say: "Ah – a fighting player can't play Rugby." Never flare up yourself.

Some of the boys will start their own brand of game behind the posts; some will indulge in a wrestling game while others will be distributing sweets. If you pretend to chase them, they will start playing a game of their own invention with you, so that you can herd them towards the place where the real game is in progress and then quietly withdraw yourself from active participation.

These youngsters all want to score tries, which is natural. This is how our forefathers started playing the game. But like our forefathers these youngsters also realise that unity is strength. Do not encourage them at the start to pass out the ball. Running teaches them more than passing. It seems as if their game is subject to the process of evolution – they will get to a stage when passing, and also forming a scrum, comes naturally.

White lies are a feature of these "matches". The players seldom lose a match and each player has his own idea about what the final score is. They will even claim that they have "won" 0–6 or 4–4. Do not correct them. Like swearing, this has no meaning except that it is clearly a case of wishful thinking.

3. These youngsters go down hard, but they do not feel it because they are relaxed when falling. If they start late, in middle primary years, they may have lost the knack of taking a relaxed tumble. They have already acquired some sense of caution. I would like to see the relaxed way of falling that is natural to a boy under eight years and younger remain with him for the rest of his Rugby career.

4. They are not self-conscious, and this is another trait which I think they should try to retain. Their parents may come as spectators, but the boys blissfully ignore their or anyone else's presence.

5. They are extremely concerned about injuries to any player, and will flock to the youngster put out of action. This may be on account of curiosity, but this is immaterial. You should, however, guard against too much fussing or pandering to the injured youngster because it can be harmful, especially if the injury is a slight one. The incident can be dismissed by some or other remark such as: "Never mind. It's not too bad", or "This is how one becomes a man."

6. The most important point is that these youngsters want to play.

I want to conclude with a warning: see to it that there is water close by. They get very thirsty and one should give them the opportunity of quenching their thirst.

SCHOOL RUGBY POLICY

At a course for primary and high-school teachers held at Stellenbosch under the auspices of the South African Rugby Board, the place of Rugby in the broad framework of physical education and post-school sport was discussed. The delegates were unanimous that a game such as Rugby constitutes a single facet of a more important aspect of physical education – kinetic education, which helps the young boy towards attaining a mature personality in both the physical and spiritual spheres.

The following resolutions, as far as Rugby was concerned, were adopted by the delegates:

1. That children should take part, at a youthful age, in as many different kinds of activities as possible and consequently experience innumerable situations; and that this participation will improve their skills in games, in work, and whatever they undertake, and, under correct supervision, help in building their characters.
2. (a) That boys in primary schools, for the purpose of taking part in Rugby, be divided into three groups or stages:
    (i) Beginners (under 6–under 8 years).
    (ii) The pre-match stage – Lower primary (under 9 years–under 10 years).
    (iii) The match stage – Middle primary: (1) Under 11 years; (2) Senior group – under 12 and 13 years.
   (b) (i) That a variety of activities be arranged to take place during the physical education period, consisting of games including not only playing skills, but also the development of general skills which contain sufficient exercise value and, at the same time, create the diversity of situations which may serve as a basis for education.
    (ii) That something similar should be arranged for every type of sport.
   (c) That the beginner should take part in all these activities without stressing any particular skills; that the activities be continued in the pre-match stage, but that these be varied with specific skill development; and that in the match stage the general and the specific be continued.
   (d) With regard to the after-school programme, it is recommended that the beginners play but not be coached; that the laws of the game be modified – as will be set out later – so that the youngsters keep on moving and playing; that there be no specialisation in positions; that numbers will not play a part and that the field and the ball be suited to the boys; that in the pre-match stage these modified laws be made to conform gradually to the laws of the game, and that the laws be modified even in the match stage for making them more simple and giving fluidity to the game.

3. *High schools*
   (a) That secondary schoolboys be divided into two groups: (i) Lower secondary classes; (ii) Upper secondary classes.

(b) That the lower classes be considered a transition stage and that their exercises during the physical education period also be concentrated on the development of skill.
(c) (i) That the upper classes will do tables of physical exercises for fitness with a view to strength, stamina, speed and skill.
(ii) That these exercises be *general*, i.e. for the purpose of strengthening the muscles so that injuries are limited to the absolute minimum, and *specific*, i.e. drawn up for the different positions of the game which require more strength than is provided by general exercises for strength building. In this way achievements will be improved in these positions and, in addition, injuries will be minimised while pleasure will increase.
(d) (i) That the upper classes will also do exercises for rounding off skills, i.e. they will practise moves of the game in two sections – the forwards and backs respectively.
(ii) That they will also practise application of skills, by means of which they will develop anticipation (psycho-motor actions) and balance, coordination, reaction time, kinetic time, and judgment (neuro-muscular actions) to maximum capacity.
(e) That the rounding off of skills, and exercises for the application of skills, be continued in the afternoon programme.

Players' dress
1. The teachers present felt very strongly that the pupils in the primary school should all play barefooted. Even schools at which boys play in Rugby boots supported this motion. Injuries are almost entirely eliminated and expenses for the parents are far lower. If there are schools which prefer their players to play in boots, it is recommended that sandshoes or the hockey type of boot be used.
2. Jerseys without collars, and made of an elastic material are very popular with everyone. Unfortunately many primary schools have sets of jerseys and they might, owing to the expense, not switch over immediately to collarless jerseys.

Fields
Certain sizes are recommended for young boys, but if such fields are not available, the standard size field can be used by playing between the two twenty-five yard lines and the five-yard lines. Goal kicks can still be taken at the goalposts.

LAWS FOR PRIMARY SCHOOLS

Beginners (under 6–8 years).
The field: Half-size or even smaller.
Ball: Leather or plastic.
Teams: No definite number; 20–30 a side can play.
Duration of game: 10 minutes a side.

No coaching is done, for the youngsters must become conversant with the game in its simplest form. They play without laws because the accent is on running with the ball (attack and defence). If they form a "cluster", the teacher extracts the ball and pushes it into the hands of a youngster, usually one who is not keen on receiving it. If a player crosses the touchline with the ball, one of the players throws the ball in with both hands.

The youngsters must repeatedly be reminded what they are playing, because other minor games, such as wrestling, are bound to come up. See to it that the cautious ones, or those who prefer standing apart, or who wish to play full back, also get possession of the ball and that the others are unobtrusively herded away from them so that fear, which keeps them apart, can be shaken off.

Conversions are taken in front of the posts and are kicked from the hand.

Pre-match stage (approximately under 9–under 10 years).
The field: 80 yds × 50 yds (75 m × 45 m) (preferably not bigger).
Ball: Leather or plastic.
Teams: A side may have more than 8 forwards – 12 to 15 a side, but there should not be too many backs – 8 or 9 are sufficient. There must, however, not be specific positions; this means that a boy will play in any position.
Duration of game: 15 minutes a side.
Scrum: This group follows the same pattern of play adopted by beginners but they form a scrum if the ball is passed too far forward or if the ball is completely stuck. They like scrummaging. As long as they bind, the scrum is permitted. At first more than three can form the front row. The others merely tuck their heads in anywhere. A scrum half puts the ball in and the remaining players form the back-line.
Line-out: At a line-out they form two rows up against the touchline and one of the boys throws the ball in with both hands. The "line-out forwards" try to get the ball, but whether they succeed in this or not, the game goes on.
Handling: The youngsters must be encouraged to pass the ball out at the correct moment. In other words, selfishness must be curbed without stamping out individuality.
Conversions: They are still taken from the hand except in front of the posts, where the ball is placed.
Kick-offs: Kick-offs are taken by means of either a drop kick or a place kick, but dead ball touch-downs are discouraged. Should they occur, a 5-yard scrum is ordered.
Tackles: The boys must also be taught *not* to get hold of garments when going in for a tackle, but to go for the body itself.
Kicking: Kicking is forbidden.

Match Stage
1. *Junior group* (under 11 years).
The field: Not bigger than 80 yds × 50 yds (73 m × 45 m).
Ball: Of leather or plastic.
Teams: See to it that everybody plays. A player may not refrain from participating, even if there will be more than 8 forwards and 7 backs. In matches, of course, there are 15 players a side. See to it that the players exchange positions.

Duration of matches: 15 minutes a side. Matches should preferably be played during the week,

Referees: Should be suitably dressed in shorts and wearing either Rugby boots or sand-shoes.

Flags: Hosts should see to it that sufficient and distinct flags are planted.

(a) *Kick-off:* A drop kick, except at the start of a match or after half-time. Should a mistake occur, the kick is taken again. If the mistake is repeated, a scrum is ordered.

(b) *Drop-out:* Repeat the kick after a mistake, but a scrum is ordered should the mistake be repeated.

(c) *Knock-on:* Should the ball touch the ground, *an opponent must first of all play it* before the offender's team or the offender himself may play it again. If not, a scrum is ordered.

(d) *Tackle:* Players are not allowed to get hold of an opponent's jersey or arms except when an opponent has moved almost beyond reach, or if a tackle has been partially broken. If a player is tackled or is held and is brought down, he must release the ball *immediately*. Should such a player break the law, the opponents are allowed *a free passing movement* on the spot. The opponents move 10 paces back. It is illegal for a player to trip an opponent with the foot or hand. (See "Foul play".)

(e) *Lying on the ball:* Players may not lie on the ball or fall on the ball as a defensive measure. (Penalty: free passing movement.)

(f) *Penalty kick:* A player places the ball at the place of infringement and the offenders run 10 yards back. He may pick up the ball himself and run or start a passing movement – *thus no kick*. For foul play a penalty is also awarded. For repeated foul play the offender must remain on the sideline for 5 minutes. (This will seldom happen, but instances of repeated foul play may occur.)

(g) *Line-out:* Takes place 3 yards from the touchline. No option of taking a scrummage or a line-out. If the ball is not thrown in straight, the opponents are given the throw-in. If again it is not straight, a scrum is awarded. As soon as the ball is taken in the line-out, it is put on the ground and both packs of forwards pack down, all of them, on their respective sides, to push the ball free so that the backs can receive the ball. Should the forwards refrain from packing down and show an inclination for negative tactics, they should first be warned. A second similar infringement is penalised by awarding a free kick. The backs stand 5 yards back and not 10 yards as required by law.

(h) *Scrum*

(1) All the forwards remain in the scrum until the ball comes *out*. Should a forward get up or break away before that time, a second scrum is formed and the ball is put in by the non-offending team.

(2) The backs (except the scrum half) stand *5 yards back*.

(3) The player putting in the ball takes up a position directly opposite the centre of the scrum, one yard from it, holding the ball in both hands and halfway between his ankles and his knees. From this position he puts it in

straight along the centre line so that it touches the ground before the hooker may strike it. (Warning first and then a penalty – free passing movement.)
(i) *Kicking:* No kicks allowed except in own twenty-five or in the case of a kick-off, a drop-out, and a drop kick *in movements* near the posts.
(j) *General laws*
(1) No specialisation.
(2) No tactics in the beginning.
(3) Games may be played in physical education class for establishing certain skills and principles.
(4) Let the player try and outwit his opponents on the field by his own game.
(5) Cultivate the correct approach to the game for the boys by inspiring them with your own approach, so that each one is bound to become a Rugby enthusiast and to remain one for the rest of his life.

2. *Senior group* (under 12 and under 13 years)
The field: Not bigger than 80 yds × 50 yds (73 m × 45 m).
Ball: Leather or plastic.
Duration of matches: 20 minutes a side.
 (a) Matches are preferably played during the week.
 (b) *Referees:* Persons acting as referees should be suitably dressed in shorts and wearing either Rugby boots or sand-shoes.
 (c) *Flags:* Hosts should see to it that sufficient and distinct flags are put up on the field for the matches.

Laws
(a) *The kick-off:* Drop kick except at start of match and after interval. Should a mistake occur, the kick is taken again. If the mistake is repeated, a scrum is ordered.
(b) *Drop-out:* Repeat kick after mistake, after which a scrum is ordered if the same mistake occurs.
(c) *Knock-on:* Should the ball touch the ground, *an opponent must first of all play it* before the offender's team or the offender himself may play it again. If not, a scrum is ordered.
(d) (i) *Players may not get hold of an opponent's jersey or arms* except when an opponent has moved almost beyond reach, or if a tackle has been partially broken. If a player is tackled or held and brought down, the ball must be *released immediately.* Should such a player infringe, the opponents are awarded a *free passing movement* on the spot. The opponents move 10 paces back.
(ii) It is illegal for a player to trip an opponent with the foot or hand. (See "Foul play".)
(e) *Lying on the ball:* Players may not lie on the ball or fall on it as a defensive measure. (Penalty: free passing movement.)
(f) *Penalty kick*
(i) A player places the ball where the infringement occured and the offenders run 10 paces back. He can pick up the ball himself and run or start a passing movement – *thus no kick.*

(ii) For foul play a penalty, as stated above, is awarded. For repeated foul play the offender must remain 5 minutes on the sideline. (This will seldom happen, but instances of repeated foul play may occur.)
(g) *Line-out*
  (i) All the forwards must take part.
  (ii) They do not take up definite positions, such as no. 3 or no. 5, but must learn to do line-out work at any position.
  (iii) The ball is caught – *never tapped* – brought down and everyone consolidates before the ball is passed out or placed on the ground. All the forwards pack down. There are no hangers-on. If the ball is tapped, a scrum is ordered 15 yards from the touchline and the non-offending team puts the ball in.
  (iv) The backs stand 5 yards back.
(h) *The scrum*
  (i) Everybody remains in the scrum until the ball emerges. Should a forward get up or break away before then, the opponents put the ball in at the ensuing scrum.
  (ii) The backs (except the scrum half) stand 5 yards back.
  (iii) The player putting in the ball takes up a position directly opposite the centre of the scrum and one yard from it. He holds the ball in both hands, halfway between his ankles and knees. From this position he puts the ball in straight along the centre line so that it touches the ground before the hooker may strike it. (Warning first, then penalty – free passing movement.)
(i) *Kicks*
  (i) No kicks for touch are allowed except inside the twenty-five. Kick-offs, drop-outs, and drop kicks near the post are permissible.
  (ii) A grubber kick or a jab kick may be given, but only as exceptions.
(j) *General laws*
  (i) No specialisation.
  (ii) No tactics to start with.
  (iii) Games may be played in physical education classes so that certain skills and principles can be unobtrusively established.
  (iv) Allow the player to try to outwit his opponent by his own methods.
  (v) Cultivate the correct approach to the game in the boy by inspiring him with your own approach. Every boy is then bound to become a Rugby enthusiast and remain one for the rest of his life.

USING THE EXERCISES

1. What follows are physical education lessons, exercises for skill building, rounding off of skills, and application of skills. The exercises must be done correctly and we must know exactly how to set about them.
2. In this section we also give tips how the exercises are best used for the different age groups playing or preparing for Rugby. These groups are:
   (a) Beginners (under 6–under 8 years)
   (b) Lower primary
   (c) Middle primary

(d) Upper primary
(e) Lower and middle secondary
(f) Upper secondary
(g) Post school players.
3. The exercises can be done intramurally or extramurally. As far as physical education exercises are concerned, schools are in a fortunate position because the exercises can be done intramurally while the afternoon's extramural exercises can be devoted exclusively to other aspects of the game. Moreover, the schools can also give time to other aspects of the game as part of their intramural programme. In this way double opportunities are created and consequently every boy should be adequately equipped for Rugby when his schooldays are over.
4. The divisions above are given as a guide only.
5. The exercises have been tested, but there may be others. We sincerely hope that teachers and coaches will not only use these exercises but will also supply us with other exercises to be considered for inclusion in the next edition of this manual. In this way we shall all be contributing to the improvement of Rugby.
6. We strongly advise that as many high schools as possible acquire the apparatus recommended. All our exercises are conducted out of doors. Indoor facilities, even if it rains, are not required. What is required are cheap plastic balls and inexpensive apparatus for physical exercises and skill building. Diagrams of the equipment are to be found in the chapters dealing with physical exercises and skill building exercises. The apparatus can either be a do-it-yourself effort or can be made by a local carpenter.
7. It is pleasant to do the exercises on grass but any open ground is suitable.
8. The dress used is the usual garb for ordinary physical exercises. The boys may also be barefooted as this can only be beneficial to their feet.
9. Section work is recommended for skill building. There are as many sections as there are skills. Each section practises a different skill to which they devote one quarter (the beginners) or one half (other primary classes) of the period. At a signal or whistle the group moves on to another spot where the next skill is practised until all the skills have been completed. If the groups are too small for the exercise, two groups can work in unison. Adaptation may be required.
10. When it comes to rounding off of skills and the application of skills, the aim is that every boy should participate in every position. They are not being prepared for matches but for Rugby itself.
11. Usually a school has only two periods a week for physical education. We recommend that in the higher classes, special exercises are done for the torso and the neck. These exercises are also recommended at the start of the extramural programme. Strength must never be neglected. We take it that the legs will get sufficient exercise during speed and stamina exercises, but more difficult exercises should be given to the torso and neck.
12. A practice programme for senior players is given in the book and this could be used as a guide for high-school boys. We are far too inclined to underestimate these boys, and there is no reason why they should not use

the same practice programme. Boys and students must see to it that their general condition of fitness is maintained during their holiday periods so that on their return they can start with the exercises indicated on the programme for the last two weeks preceding the holidays. The best system is to test the skills of the pupils and the students before they leave on holiday, and then test them when they return. This will clearly indicate who the shirkers are. Times for road-work must also be clocked and be compared with times taken before the holidays. The same must be done for speed work etc.

BEGINNERS AND LOWER PRIMARY

Intramural
Nippers have a craving for movement and they must have as much of it as we can give them. The games they can play are divided into four groups: A, B, C and D, representing the seven skills in some or other form. For the lesson we suggest the following (see Chapter 5):
   2 games from group A.
   1 game from group B.
   3 games from group C.
   3 games from group D.

Many of these games are old familiar ones, if not for the younger generation, then for the older generation. They are the games played by the great Rugby players of the past and contributed in no slight measure to their success. If the old guard could achieve so much with fewer games, then the present generation, with more games at their disposal, should attain even more distinction. We claim this for another reason: children never tire of games which suit their nature. The games can therefore be played over and over again, and there is no need to draft a new lesson every day. If they have gone through all the games, new lessons with selected games can be drawn up.

If a ball is used it is – as a rule – a Rugby ball, and our recommendation is that schools acquire a sufficient number of plastic balls. They are cheap and can be used in all kinds of weather.

There may be a few schools which do not have the necessary facilities for these games. We are, however, going to suggest improvised methods and hope that a teacher will use his or her initiative before the game is dismissed. Yes, you have read correctly: female teachers can also help us by giving lessons. Moreover, they can also help with the extramural programme because the type of Rugby being played is, in many instances, less complicated.

Extramural programme:
The boys play the type of Rugby which has already been described.

MIDDLE PRIMARY

Intramural
This group is the bridge between the lower and upper classes of the primary school. The boys still do the game lessons, but in addition they do all the exercises which are used for acquiring the techniques of the skills. Performance

of the exercises can be left to the boys themselves – and this is what we recommend – or the techniques can be demonstrated and mistakes pointed out. We have nothing against the last-mentioned method, but experience has taught us that the boys must first be given a chance to try for themselves before they are helped. Only if they fail hopelessly and feel that they are inferior and compare unfavourably with others, should they be helped. Strength and other qualities are needed for skill exercises. Exercises for developing these qualities are given under the heading of Reinforcement for which there are three kinds of exercises:
1. Exercises for acquiring the technique of the skills.
2. Exercises for the further development of the technique.
3. Exercises which will strengthen the muscles or prepare them for the execution of the skills (with regard to tempo or speed, space, rhythm, etc.)

All three exercises must be conducted separately in detailed lessons.

Extramural
The kind of Rugby being played is no longer a "type" of Rugby but "simplified" Rugby. The boys become important and they do more than run and defend. Details of this have already been given.

MIDDLE TO UPPER PRIMARY

Intramural
Skill building exercises with special attention being paid to technique. Now and then a play lesson – consisting of selected games – can be given. We take it that every primary school will have a physical education teacher on its staff. He can include in the lesson specific strengthening exercises for the joints because the boys play the game far more seriously at this stage. The lesson including exercises with partners can be used for strengthening the joints. If apparatus is available, the suggested table of exercises can be followed.

Extramural
The youngsters now play Rugby in the same way as seniors do, but in certain instances the laws are not rigidly enforced, e.g. the knock-on law. Details of this have already been given. The boys can now practice the rounding off of skills.

UPPER PRIMARY

Intramural
Upper primary boys do physical exercises for strengthening the muscles of their joints and also skill building exercises.

Extramural
They will not be able to cope with exercises for speed and stamina as part of the intramural programme because this will sap the energy required for their work in the classroom. But speed and stamina must get attention after school. Strength exercises for the torso and the neck are also done and much attention is paid to the rounding off of skills. They play according to the laws of the game as already indicated.

LOWER AND MIDDLE SECONDARY
Intramural
Physical exercises are done first, followed by skill building and then rounding off of skills. If two periods a week are available, physical exercise and skill building can be done in the first period and selected physical exercises for the torso and neck – plus selected exercises for skill building and the rounding off of skills – can be done in the second period.

Extramural
Special physical exercises, stamina and speed building. Application of skills, if skill building receives sufficient attention in the course of the physical education lesson. Playing of Rugby under usual laws.

UPPER SECONDARY
Intramural
Physical exercises and skill building (special individual exercises) and rounding off of skills. Special physical exercises, preferably general exercises for strength and application of skills.

Extramural
Special physical exercises, stamina and speed building; general strength building exercises; rounding off and application of skills; and playing Rugby.

CLUBS
Here is a practice programme for clubs, one which can serve as a guide for all clubs and even for high school-boys.

THE PRACTICE PROGRAMME
The practice programme discussed here is exclusively for the Rugby season and not for the entire year, except for para. 1 following.
To have at one's disposal all the Rugby exercises is something entirely different from being able to use them correctly. Correct use depends on certain principles without which no justice can be done to them or to the game. Here are the most important exercises:

Training the whole year through
Physical exercises for strength, speed and stamina should be done three times a week in some form or other during the whole year. Plenty of attention should be given to this before the season and they must be maintained and even improved upon after the season.

When is a start made with physical exercises?
This is a difficult question, because we cling to old-established customs and are reluctant to discard them. We have become running-conscious however, and this in itself is some advance on the old concept that training starts only a week or two before the season begins. Today many players realise that they need

more than a month to prepare for the coming season. Those players, however, who really want to achieve something will have to realise that a season never ends. It simply does not pay to subject oneself every year to the process of breaking the body down and building it up again. Consequently it is advisable to differentiate between general physical fitness, which is not as difficult to maintain as a player might be led to believe, and specific physical fitness. As a guide, in terms of the three requirements for physical fitness, the following are suggested:

Division of the season
We use the following: Pre-season period.
Pre-match period.
Match period.
End-of-season period.

Pre-season period: General physical fitness must be seen to.
Pre-match period: All the other forms of fitness must also be seen to.
Match period: See to it that all aspects of fitness are maintained and are deliberately carried out.
End-of-season period: See to it that monotony neither impairs the acquired fitness nor destroys enthusiasm.

General fitness
This, in actual fact, is an attempt to maintain some of the specific fitness accumulated during the season, or to improve it, and this can be done by the following:
Stamina: Long-distance running three times a week.
Strength: At least three times a week, together with weights for building up stamina.
Speed: Can be practised as part of stamina building or even before the exercises for building strength. Actually this is the one component which is neglected during the summer.

With the beginning of the pre-match stage, the three component parts are used specifically. This means that they are used, in the main, as they would be in Rugby. Strength must be retained, while speed and stamina must be improved. One cannot build strength intensively while at the same time sharpening or polishing it up for Rugby.

The kinds of fitness
As stated previously, we divide fitness into subdivisions for the sake of convenience and by which we can follow a grading system and do the correct exercises step by step until match fitness – which is true fitness – has been attained. We repeat them once more:
1. (a) General physical fitness; (b) specific physical fitness: poised to start with skill building.
2. Skill fitness: The techniques of the seven skills have been brought as near to perfection as possible and a pitch of readiness for section work or basic principles has been attained.

3. Fitness in fundamentals: Rounding off of skills has reached such an advanced stage that the application of skills can now be given a place in the practice programme.
4. Game fitness: Readiness to tackle game situations in teams.
5. Match fitness: Readiness to play as in matches.

The time for exercises for fitness
General physical fitness: October, November, December, and part of January.
Specific fitness: January or middle February to October.
Skill fitness: At least three weeks before the first match.
Fitness in basic fundamentals: At least two weeks before the first match.
Game fitness: At least one or two weeks before the first match.
Match fitness: At least one week before the first match.

Division per week
Pre-match and match periods: We need to maintain or promote strength, speed, and stamina three times a week. Similarly we want to cultivate skill building and do rounding off of skills three times a week. The application of skills too should be practised three times a week.

How is it possible to practise all this three times a week? Actually there are four days needed – a day for physical exercises, a day for skill building and rounding off of skills, a day for application of skills, and a day for individual training.

Other facets find a place in the programme. *Strength* is allocated to the day for physical exercises, but strength also plays an important part in the execution of exercises on the day for skill building and rounding off of skills. On the day set aside for the application of skills, strength forms the basis for many facets of the game. Strength can even be assigned to the day for individual training.

Stamina is specifically practised – and obviously it plays a major part – on days assigned for physical exercises. But on the day for skill building and rounding off of skills it is not neglected, and especially not on the day for the application of skill. If too little attention is given to stamina in physical exercises, it must be incorporated in the exercises for the concluding days.

Speed is specifically practised on the days for physical exercises and obviously plays an important part on the day when skill application is practised. The backs will also use it on the days set aside for skill building and the rounding off of skills, but it may be advisable to conclude the day for them and for the forwards with speed training. On days for individual training, some players will practise speed again, giving them four speed-training sessions. Skill building has its day, and on the day set aside for the application of skill, speed is practised in another guise. On the day assigned for physical training the forwards will use the scrum apparatus as part of their exercises for strength, and all the players will, as part of their training for stamina, side-step through the posts, run through the tyres and practise on the tackling-bag. Individual exercise day is actually also a form of skill building. Rounding off of skills has its day together with skill building, and on the day set aside for application of skill, speed is afforded a major place. A third day must still be found, and therefore it is advisable to conclude physical exercises with speed training.

A day is set aside for skill application. This may be sufficient, but it may also be advisable to end off the day for skill building and the rounding off of skills, or the day used for physical exercises, with 5 or 10 minutes of skill application.

There is a day for individual exercises, but it is obvious that the individual player must see to it that he improves his game when skill building, rounding off of skills, and the application of skills are being practised. *Repetition* remains the basis of the strength, speed and stamina of fitness sought after. It should, furthermore, be remembered that the *intensity* of the exercise determines what kind of practice a player will get. Thus if daylight is not in a player's favour, he must not spare himself while the sun is shining and he must see to it that those things which are important for that kind of day are practised in light and the others in dusk or even in darkness, i.e. any form of running.

The match season and the end-of-season period
The end-of-season period is actually part of the match period, but we separate them for a very important reason: towards the end of a season most players are mentally tired of Rugby. For six or more months they have kept at practising and playing three to four times a week. Everything starts going against them, the knocks, the disappointments, etc. Their ideals and their clubs' ideals for the season have already been realised or lost. Only the cup winners and likely cup winners are still motivated. The others are merely playing in order not to finish too low in the points table.

It is difficult to say exactly when this period or reaction sets in, as all coaches will testify. A warning, however, should be sounded: some players imagine themselves to be tired, and the more they think this, the more tired they will become. Imagination, like monotony, is a sign that there is something wrong with the player and perhaps not with the game or with the exercises. Still, this is a normal reaction which one should be on one's guard against. In order to break the monotony, practice methods can be altered to stimulate fresh interest. These consist of other games such as speedball, touch Rugby, netball, volleyball, and soccer played with a Rugby ball, and they can change a player's mental condition by offering him some form of escape from himself. One can start the exercises with one of these games, and then leave homework till afterwards. After hard matches a practice day may be skipped; for instance, Monday. On Tuesday the players can do long-distance running at leisure and on Wednesday play a game and then do rounding off of skills, not skill application. Match practices are in effect responsible for players feeling sick and tired of Rugby.

Another remedy is to measure the players' progress in the skills every third or fourth week.

Although there is no reason why players cannot keep on improving in strength, speed, stamina, or skills, their spirit must be protected from wilting. Players who believe they are "stale" do not know what they are talking about. There is no such thing in a Rugby player who has been playing matches during only one season.

Another common fallacy, *rife outside South Africa*, is that players should have an occasional night out to prevent staleness. This remedy has no physiological or psychological backing, and it only demonstrates a player's own weakness, in that he has no mastery over himself and cannot escape from himself. It is accumulated tension which causes players to go for liquor and women; but instead of alleviating the mental strain, liquor and women encroach on fitness and trigger off another kind of tautness when conscience rears its head. The most relaxed people are those who have a clear conscience as their fellow-traveller.

Chapter 5
The Exercises

GAMES FOR THE PRIMARY SCHOOL

Group A
(*Pushing and pulling, jerking and tugging*)

1.
Circle pulling: The players are divided into groups or teams of 4 to 6 boys each. They lock arms or take hands and form a circle. In the centre of the circle a few balls or other objects are placed in the form of a triangle, or a few lines are drawn. The aim is to pull one another to the centre of the circle or to push one another so that one of the players is forced to touch a ball, an object, or one of the lines. One point is chalked up against a player who makes contact.

2.
Neck pulling: The boys are paired off. Each boy has his hands clasped round his companion's neck and they face each other. One leg is placed between the legs of the partner. Each boy pulls in an attempt to dislodge his partner or cause his neck to yield.

Group B
(*Jumping exercises*)

1.
Stick jumping: The teams line up in 2 rows with the boys 2 yards apart and the teams 5–10 paces apart. No. 1 has a staff or a longish stick and runs forward to a line 15 yards in front of the rows and back again. On coming back to his team he runs along the row, holding the staff or stick at one end, parallel to the ground, so that the other players must jump as high as possible (with outstretched arms) across it. In the jump they twist themselves completely round so that they are prepared to jump the stick on the return run. When this boy comes back to the front of his own line, he hands over the stick to no. 2, who repeats the action while no. 1 takes up his position at the rear end of his team. The race ends when each boy has had a chance of handling the stick and when each team is lined up in its original position.

2.
Rope jumping: The teacher stands in the centre of a circle of boys and swings a rope, to which is fastened some heavy object, and over which the boys jump while they extend their arms and twist their bodies round when the rope swings towards them.

Group C
(*Handling and kicking exercises*)

1.
Three-court Dodge Ball: The players form a circle in which a few "buck" players have to be "shot" with a Rugby ball. As soon as a buck has been shot, the player who has shot him takes his place. Players in the circle may pass the ball to one another. Specify the method of shooting – by means of one hand or both hands. Only underhand or only overhead throwing is allowed.
Variations
(a) The game can be played in teams in two circles with half the team in one circle acting as hunters and the other as buck. The aim is to see which team bags the largest number of buck.
(b) Bucks get a new life if they can catch the ball, but they are shot if they fail to do so.

2.
Circle Interception: The players form a circle with one or two players in the centre. The ball is passed to and fro by the circle players and the 2 players in the centre must try and intercept it. As soon as a player succeeds in doing so, he takes up the position of the player who has made the interception. A circle player may not pass the ball or give it to a player standing next to him.
Variations
(a) As a team game for 2 teams. Each team forms a separate circle with an interceptor from the other team in its circle. At a given sign the match begins. The aim is to see which team intercepts the fastest of the two. A mark is awarded for each interception.
(b) More than one ball can be used, especially if there are more than 2 interceptors.

Group D
(*Push-off and grabbing exercises*)

1.
Fish in the Net: 8 to 10 players take hands. They are the "fishing-net" and they try and catch the other players. As soon as the 2 end-players also join hands, and the "fish" inside have been caught, the game starts afresh.

2.
Chain-tag: This game can be played in a confined area. 2 players take hands and attempt to tag the others. Those who are tagged take hands and join the first two. The chain must be limited to 6 or 8 and only the 2 players at the extremities of the chain are permitted to tag. The game can be started with several couples. Those who form a chain of 6 or 8 players end as winners. The players may try to evade the catchers by means of dodging underneath their arms.

Group A
(*Pushing and pulling, jerking and tugging*)

3.
Dead Man: 10 or 12 players sit in a circle on the ground, facing inwards and with their feet almost touching. One of the players stands in the centre where there is just sufficient space left. He keeps his body perfectly rigid and allows it to fall. The players in the circle must see to it that he does not fall on to them. They do so by stretching out their hands and checking his body. They push him either to the left or right while he rotates with his feet as axis. All the players push the "dead" man so that he rolls round the circle. If a player fails to hold the weight of the dead man, or if the dead man falls on top of him, that player takes over as dead man.

4.
Indian Wrestling: 2 boys lie on their backs with their feet next to each other's heads while they take hold of each other's inside shoulders with their inside hands. Both say "Hook it", and they lift the inside legs. "Crook it", and they lift their outside legs. At "Have a go" they lift their inside legs quickly, hook them and attempt to throw each other. This is a good exercise for hookers, especially if the inside legs are the right legs.

5.
Pushing Across the Line: A row of boys stand 3 yards apart and 3 yards from a line in front of them. 10 yards behind each boy in the line stand a few more boys. At a signal, the boys in the rear split into couples and charge forward, packing down on both sides of the boy in front. They attempt to push him until he crosses the line. The couples themselves may not touch the line because they can then forfeit their push, even if they succeed in pushing the boy across.

Group B
(*Jumping exercises*)

3.
One-legged Football: A tennis ball can be used. The size of the playing area is approximately 20 yards by 12 yards (11 m × 18 m) for 20 to 30 players, or as large as would suit the number of players participating. The game is played as soccer except that players hop on one leg and kick the ball with the foot on which they are hopping. They are permitted frequently to interchange feet but must always have only one foot on the ground,
or
One-versus-one: A player defends an object or mark on the ground while hopping on one foot. Another player attempts to touch the object or mark with his foot while also hopping on one foot. They push each other and the attacker attempts to out-manoeuvre the defender. They are allowed to exchange feet, but may not have both feet on the ground simultaneously.

4.
Butting the Ball: The boys compete to see who can achieve the greatest height in butting either a tennis ball or a soccer ball with their foreheads.

5.
Jumps with Turns: The boys are drawn up in single file, widely spaced, and the teacher takes up a position to one side of them. At a signal, the boys jump in the air and make one turn so that they face him on landing. The teacher then takes up his position behind them and they must again jump and make 2 turns so that, on landing, they face him again. The teacher then takes up a position opposite to the first boy in the line and the boys must jump and make a 3 turn. If they can do this, the teacher stands in front of them and they must have made 4 turns after the jump.

Group C
(*Handling and kicking exercises*)

3.
Playing Concertina: The players form a circle and pass the ball to one another while each player jogs on the spot – a kind of quick marking-time. At a given signal the circle is decreased by moving towards the centre of it. The ball is continually passed from player to player. When the players are close up to one another, the ball is still passed and at a given signal the players move backwards so that long passes are given.

4.
Catching in Possession: All the players join to form a complete circle on the halfway line but the players of each team are on their side of the line. The ball is passed in one direction from player to player until the whistle is blown. The player who then has the ball has to run with it to his own 25 yard line, pursued by all players of the opposing team. If they succeed in touching him before he reaches the 25 they score one point.
Variation
(a) Instead of passing the ball it is rolled.
(b) Instead of passing the ball in one direction it is passed on to any player, or to an opponent. If a player knocks-on, he must pass the ball to one of his team-mates.
(c) If a player has to run with the ball, then his team-mates must also run with him. If he wants to avoid being touched, he can pass out the ball. In this case the player with the ball runs to the goal-line.

5.
The Moving Target: Players are divided into two teams and take up their positions in rows on each side of the medicine ball:

```
  X  X  X  X  X  X  X
                         Medicine ball
  O  O  O  O  O  O  O
```

The team winning the toss starts the game, the aim of which is to propel the medicine ball through the row of the opposing players by means of direct hits (throws) with a Rugby ball. More than one Rugby or medicine ball may be used.

Group D
(*Push-off and grabbing exercises*)

3.
Fox and Geese: The 2 teams line up in rows and hold on to each other around the waist. One player from each side (the fox) plays against the opposing team. At a given signal the foremost player in each row stretches his arms sideways to protect his geese and the entire team swings and wheels along with him in an attempt to prevent the fox in the opposing team from tagging the rearmost goose in the row. The team whose fox touches the rearmost goose first is declared the winner.

4.
Higgledy-piggledy Tag (All-in tag): Enough coloured ribbons must be placed on the ground to provide for the whole class. 1 or 2 players, wearing ribbons, are elected to start the game. When the signal is given, they run in among the others and try and tag as many as possible. As soon as a player is tagged, he puts on a ribbon and helps the others wearing ribbons to tag until everybody has been tagged. If there are no ribbons available, any boy who has been tagged must take hold of one of his ears and keep his hand there so that everybody knows who are the hunters.

5.
Release Tag: Several catchers are needed. If a catcher has tagged one of the players, the tagged player must sit down. If such a player is tagged by a non-catcher, he has been "released" and he can participate once more. The catchers must set about their task briskly because the purpose is to get players sitting down as quickly as possible.

Group A
(*Pushing and pulling, jerking and tugging*)

6.
Bull versus Bulls: A boy on all fours attempts breaking through 2 other boys also on all fours and close together. For this they can link to each other with their inside arms.

7.
Jibbing Horses: 2 boys represent harnessed jibbing horses by taking hold of each other. They "paw" the ground while a third boy dashes from behind, thrusting his head between them. While they are still pawing, he tries to push them into a wall.

Group B
(*Jumping exercises*)

6.
High jump: The boys compete with one another to see who can strike the highest mark jumping against a wall. A mark is made against the wall and is raised after every attempt. They are allowed only a single pace before jumping with either the left or right leg or with both legs. Each jump is a competition. For the first series with the left and right foot and with both feet, their right shoulders are towards the wall. Then they change to have their left shoulders towards the wall.

7.
Jumping up: One team takes up a position on a line. On both sides of the team the two halves of the opposing team are lined up. The latter use tennis balls for pitching them at the players on the line who have to jump to avoid being struck. A number of balls can be used and are thrown simultaneously at the player in direct line with the thrower. To get the boys to jump higher, the pitchers can aim 1 or 2 feet in front of the jumpers so that the ball bounces, or they can aim at the jumpers' knees or just below. The direct hits scored in a specific period are counted and then the teams change sides.

Group C
(*Handling and kicking exercises*)

6.
Swedish Blesbuck: The field – 24 feet by 12 feet (about 8 × 4 m) – is divided into 4 parallel squares. One team occupy squares 1 and 3, and the other squares 2 and 4. The duration of the match is fixed. The aim is to strike the players in squares 2 and 3 with a ball anywhere from the knee to the shoulder. If the players catch a ball aimed at them properly, it does not count as a direct hit. The players in each square keep their own score. At the conclusion of the game the score is then added. Players of each team must frequently switch to different squares.

7.
Ball-over-head and Rounders: Team A players stand in a row ready for taking turns to kick. Team B take up positions all over the field and they have to catch or stop the ball. After no. 1 of Team A kicks the ball, he runs round the perimeter of the field, which must be clearly marked out. At the spot where a player of Team B catches or stops the ball, he takes up a stationary position while the rest of his team come and stand in a row behind him. He then passes the ball over his head to the player behind him, and so on right down the line. As soon as the rearmost player receives the ball he shouts "finished".
The purpose of the game is to shout "finished" before no. 1 of Team A has completed his run round the field. If he fails to do so before the opposing team shouts "finished", Team A does not qualify as having completed a shift. The teams change over after each has had a session of kicking. After both teams have had a turn at kicking, the team with most shifts to its credit is declared the winner. The type of kick and the foot used for it must be determined beforehand and/or whether the ball should be thrown instead of kicked.

Group D
(*Push-off and grabbing exercises*)

6.
Catching Horses: One team comprises riders and the other horses. The riders have to corner the horses and each rider must catch a horse. The horses attempt to break through the line formed by the riders. 2 riders can join forces to get hold of a horse. If 2 riders succeed in catching a horse, it counts as a horse caught. Horses are not permitted to struggle once they have been caught, but they may try and break through the riders' arms before they are encircled and held.

7.
Tagging in Pairs: The catchers start as partners holding hands so that they are firmly linked. All the players tagged by them join hands in pairs and in turn become catchers. In this way the game continues until everybody has been tagged and all players are linked in pairs.

Group A
(*Pushing and pulling, jerking and tugging*)

8.
Clear the Circle: One of the teams is in the centre of the circle and the players of the other team set about pushing, pulling and bumping them from the circle. Not only are the players in the circle expected to offer resistance, but they push, bump or pull the attackers from the circle. After a fixed period of time the number of "casualties" is counted.

9.
Pushing Through: 4 or 6 boys form a circle, facing outwards. They take hold of one another tightly round the waist. In a fixed spot in the centre of the circle a boy holds a ball. His team-mates are on the outside of the circle and they try and reach him by penetrating the circle with their heads foremost. The defenders try and beat off the attacks by forming a moving circle as a shield. Only a single attacker at a time may attempt to break through the circle and the player inside may not move from his allotted spot. An attacker who succeeds in penetrating the circle and touches the ball – held out by the player in the centre – with his head, scores a point for his team.

Group B
(*Jumping exercises*)

8.
One Against Three: 2 teams of 3 boys stand close together in a line. The centre boy in one team has a ball which he throws into the air and jumps to catch again. His 2 team-mates catch him in the air at the moment his hands come in contact with the ball. At that moment, too, his opponent gets hold of his collar or his clothes and attempts pulling him over to his (opponent's) side without letting go of him, for he would then fall. The jumper's team-mates must see to it that he is not pulled through to the opponent's side. The boys take turns at being the jumper.

9.
Hop-scotch: A number of "courts" must be available so that some of the boys need not sit the game out. The length of the "court" is approximately 12 feet (about 4 m) and it is divided by lines into 10 squares of equal size. The player hops on one leg and pushes with that foot any object, even a stone, from square 1 through every square to square 10. He must not touch the lines with his foot. If he does, or kicks the object too hard so that it lands in the wrong square, or if it touches the lines, he has to start afresh.
N.B. The purpose of this game is to provide the boys with jumping exercise, not striking the object accurately. If kicking the object interferes with the jumping, the squares must be enlarged or the object must be replaced by a heavier one.

Group C
(*Handling and kicking exercises*)

8.
Tunnel Ball Passing Relay: The teams are in rows with the players lined up one behind the other with their legs astraddle, 2 to 3 yards apart. The positions taken by the foremost and rearmost players must be marked so that everyone has to run the same distance. The foremost player of each team holds a ball. At a given signal the player passes the ball through his legs to the player behind him and then runs round to the back to receive the ball from the rearmost player to send it on its way again until each player has handled the ball twice. If the ball should be dropped or if it should touch the ground, it must be handed forward to the player who has last handled it. When the rearmost player has received the ball for the second time, the players in the line do a right-about turn so that they face the opposite direction. The rearmost player starts off the back-passing movement which comes to an end with the team in its original position and with no. 1 having the ball.

9.
Tunnel Ball Rolling: In this game the same procedure is followed as in the tunnel ball passing relay, except that the ball is rolled through the tunnel. Every member of the team is required to handle the ball or the team will be disqualified. If the ball rolls outside the tunnel, the nearest player must catch it and set it rolling at the point where it left the tunnel.

Group D
(*Push-off and grabbing exercises*)

8.
Tagging by Couples: 2 players take hands and set about catching other players. As soon as one member of the couple succeeds in tagging a player, the former is "released" and the tagged player takes his place to form another tagging couple.

9.
Hunting players: Each team is equally divided and the players take up a position facing each other on parallel lines, approximately 10 yards (9 m) apart. A player from each team, the hunter, stands in the middle of his opponents' lines. Each team is given the name of an international side, and as soon as the teacher calls out one of them, the two sections of the team run and cross over to change places. While this exchange is taking place, the hunter tries to tag as many of them as possible. The team with the fewest tagged players is the winning team.

Group A
(*Pushing and pulling, jerking and tugging*)

Group B
(*Jumping exercises*)

10.
Tortoise Pulling: The players squat on all fours side by side in 2 rows facing away from each other. A rope with a loop on either end is used for each pair. Each player has one loop round his neck while the rest of the rope goes through his legs. From this position the two boys start pulling, each in the direction faced by him, and each attempts to reach a certain mark. If a rope is not available, the boys take hands through their legs and pull against each other.

11.
Pushing Away: The boys are divided into 2 groups consisting of 4–6 players.
One group takes up a position 5 yards in front of the other. A ball is placed approximately 5–10 yards in front of the foremost group. At a given signal both groups make a dash for the ball. The first group must move over it, holding on to one another, so that the ball is hidden, while the second group has to work the ball free by pushing the first group away in line with the spot from which they have set out. Allow the boys to push as they please and only later make them push with their shoulders. Also teach them that unity is strength. If a group succeeds in pushing away their opponents, let the teams change positions, but if they do not succeed, they must again be the rear group. Do not allow the contest to go on for long.
Give the group whose turn it is to push a time limit, to be signalled by a whistle.

Group C
(*Handling and kicking exercises*)

10.
Progressive Arch Ball: The teams are lined up in rows with the players 2 yards apart and each leader holding a ball. The ball is then passed or thrown overhead so that each member of the team handles it.
As soon as a player has passed the ball backwards he runs to the rear end of the line, where he positions himself for receiving the ball when it comes to him for sending away the second time. The team's no. 1 who, after two or three sessions, is again in his original position is declared the winner. Teams can also bring the ball back to the starting point by making a roundabout turn.

11.
Tunnel Ball Passing – Straddle Relay: The ball is passed backwards between the legs to the players 2 yards behind. As soon as he has passed the ball, the player has to lie down and curl himself up like a small hedgehog. When the ball comes to the rearmost player in this way, he runs straddle-wise over the curled-up players. The relay is completed when every player has had an opportunity of passing the ball out and running with it,
or
Arch Ball – Straddle Relay: The teams are drawn up in rows 2 yards apart with the players 2 yards behind one another. Each leader holds a ball. The ball is passed backwards and overhead from player to player until it reaches the rearmost player – A. The rest of the players curl up on the ground like hedgehogs while A runs straddle-wise over them to the front position. As soon as A has crossed over a player, the latter stands up. A then starts the ball-over-head movement afresh. When the ball reaches the rearmost player he, in turn, runs straddle-wise over the others to the front. This movement is repeated until each player has had a turn. The game ends when no. 1 has run back straddle-wise to his original position and holds the ball above his head.

Group D
(*Push-off and grabbing exercises*)

10.
Horse and Jockey: "Jockeys" are mounted on their "horses". At a given signal the jockeys try to unseat one another. The jockey who remains seated is the winner.

11.
Evade and Pursue: The players are paired off, either outside on a playing field or inside a gymnasium. One of them is the evader while the other is the pursuer. When the whistle is blown, the evader tries to escape from the pursuer, who tries to touch him with his hand. The evader may run about, jump aside and do everything within his power to avoid being trapped. Should he succeed, he is declared the winner; should he fail to do so, the pursuer is the winner. The players exchange roles and the game is continued.

Group A
(*Pushing and pulling, jerking and tugging*)

Group B
(*Jumping exercises*)

12.
Stick Tug-of-war: The boys work in pairs sitting on the ground facing each other with their feet pressed against one another. Both take hold of a stick held lengthwise above their feet. At a signal they start pulling, each attempting to pull the other over to his side. If sticks are not available, the boys take a double grip with their hands.

13.
Two Against One:
Two boys are on all fours with their knees not touching the ground. A third boy packs in between them from the rear, gets hold of them round their hips and tries to push them away. If the pair of boys should need assistance, another boy pushes against them from the front with his shoulders.

Group C
(*Handling and kicking exercises*)

12.
Stop: Each player is given a number. One of the players kicks the ball high in the air and calls out a number. The player whose number is called must catch the ball and immediately kick it up in the air, at the same time calling out a number. If a player misfields the ball, the other players dash away. As soon as he gains possession of the ball, he shouts "Stop!" as a signal that all those who have run away should stop in their tracks. He then picks out one of them as target and throws the ball at him. If he succeeds, the player who has been struck by the ball must get hold of it, kick it in the air and call out a number. If the stationary target is not hit, the player who has thrown the ball must fetch the ball himself and kick it into the air. To liven up the game the players must move in and out: in, whenever the ball is kicked in the air; and out, whenever they hear which number is being called. The area must be somewhat confined – it is best played in a circle – to prevent the target from being missed too frequently. The players may not run outside the circle. The kind of throw used for striking the target may be either underhand or overhead, with or without torpedo turn or point-over-point as in the kind of throw-in used for line-outs.

Variation:
Instead of kicking the ball, beginners may throw the ball into the air.

13.
Twist Pass Relay: This is played the same as tunnel ball passing relay, except that the players have their feet planted firmly on the ground while twisting their bodies to one side to pass the ball to the players behind them. If the ball is first passed down the left side, the ball must travel down the right side the next time, and so forth.

Group D
(*Push-off and grabbing exercises*)

12.
Partner Tag: All the players except 2 link arms or take hands in pairs. Of the 2 loose players one is the pursuer and the other is the runner. The runner escapes being caught by linking arms or taking hands with one or the other player of the different couples. If he does so, the third player of that group becomes the runner. If a runner is tagged before linking up with a couple, he becomes a pursuer. The couples keep on moving about in an attempt to prevent the runner from linking up with them.

13.
Progressive Over-the-legs Team Races: Players from each side sit in pairs facing each other with their legs a-straddle and their feet touching. At a given signal a pair of players at one end of the team get to their feet and run over the legs of the other players without touching them, after which they take up their position at the other end of the line. The second couple follow, and so the process is carried on.

Group A
(*Pushing and pulling, jerking and tugging*)

Group B
(*Jumping exercises*)

14.
Three Against Three: 3 boys bind like front-row forwards and attempt to push 3 other boys, similarly bound, across a line forming a circle. Winners push against winners until a winning team emerges. Losers compete against losers in other circles and the winning "loser" team is given a bout against the winners' champion team.

Group C
(Handling and kicking exercises)

14.
Progressive Rank Passing – Tunnel Ball Passing: The teams line up next to one another about 3 yards apart. A boy at one end of the row begins by passing the ball down the row in Rugby fashion. As soon as a player has passed the ball, he runs to the other end of the row where he takes up a position to receive the ball again. When the players are back in their original positions after 2 or 3 sessions, and when the last player has the ball, the movement is switched to "tunnel ball rolling" in the opposite direction with the players standing at least 3 yards apart. As soon as a player has rolled the ball through his legs to the player behind him, he runs to the rear end of the team where he takes up his position ready to catch the ball when it is rolled to him. When the no. 1 player of the team receives the ball at the end of the tunnel, he holds it aloft to indicate that his team has finished.

or

Progressive Rank Passing – Tunnel Ball Rolling: The teams are lined up in rows. The ball is passed down the line, but only no. 1 runs along the line to receive the ball at the other end. At the moment he receives the ball the whole team makes a round-about turn so that they face his way with their legs a-straddle. The ball is now rolled along the tunnel to no. 2, who fills the last position in the row. As soon as he receives the ball, the rest of the team take up the position for rank passing and no. 2 sends the ball on its way down the row while he himself runs to the other end (next to no. 1) in order to receive the ball at this point. This is followed by tunnel ball rolling the ball to no. 3, and so the game continues until every participant has had a turn at starting the passing movement and running to the other end, from where he starts the tunnel ball rolling movement in the opposite direction. The game ends as soon as no. 1 receives the ball, holding it aloft at the end of the tunnel.

Group D
(Push-off and grabbing exercises)

14.
Progressive Over-the-legs Team Race in a Circle: All teams form a single circle and the players are seated facing outwards with their legs stretched out. The player on the left-hand point of each team runs anti-clockwise round the circle, jumping across the legs of all the players until he gets back to his place, where he sits down as before. The next player then jumps across the legs of no. 1 and goes round the circle. The team whose last player goes round the circle first and is back in his original position is declared the winner. The game can be varied by making the right-hand end player start from the right, or the players may jump round the circle on one leg or with feet tied together.

Group AGroup B
*(Pushing and pulling, jerking and tugging)**(Jumping exercises)*

15.
"*Chop-chop*": 2 boys with their arms
clasped around each other's waists run
about while followed by their own team-
mates and two other "hostile" boys who
in turn are followed by their team-mates.
The foremost 2 determine the action.
As soon as they stop and lean forward,
the opponents take it as a signal for packing
against their thighs. It is also the signal
for their own team-mates to start packing
behind them and to attempt to shove
them away.

Group C
(*Handling and kicking exercises*)

15.
Goal Throwing Against Running Rounders:
A netball post, a Rugby ball, and 4 markers are required. The field is indicated by the markers. One of the teams is lined up outside the field of play behind their kicker. The opposing team's players are scattered about (inside and outside the field) and have to catch the ball when it is kicked. One of the players has to score goals by putting the ball into the net. Another player passes the ball to the no. 1, or kicker, standing outside the field, who has to execute a predetermined kick, e.g. a ground kick, a grubber kick, or a left-footed kick, after which he runs around the markers and back to his team. While he is running, the opposing team's players gain possession of the ball and throw or kick it towards their goal-thrower, who attempts to shoot as many goals as possible before the opposing team's no. 1 completes his run. The goal-thrower stops when the run is completed. The goals are added up after each player's sprint round the 4 markers. After all the team's players have completed circling the field, the teams change over. The team which has scored the most goals is the winner. In this game, as well as in the following 2 games, netball posts may not be available. In such cases a boy can be the goalpost. He will stand on a box, or a chair, or a bench, with his back turned towards the goal-thrower and with his arms raised to form a circle above his head. His head should be kept down.

Group D
(*Push-off and grabbing exercises*)

15.
Twirling: 2 boys take hands, cupped or with crossed arms, and then, with stretched arms, twirl quickly round. They take short steps to facilitate the movement.

Group A
(*Pushing and pulling, jerking and tugging*)

Group B
(*Jumping exercises*)

16.
Pushing Back to Back: The boys are paired off and stand back to back with their arms linked. One of them tries to push or pull the other away, or pull him over backwards by bending forward.

17.
Pulling Round the Bodies. The boys pull against one another in teams of 2, 3 or 4. The number depends on the strength of the foremost boy's double grip.

Group C
(*Handling and kicking exercises*)

16.
Netball Goal Scoring: A netball post and a ball for each team are needed. The teams are positioned in single-file formation with the players facing the posts. At a signal from the teacher the no. 1 player of each team runs towards his post and attempts to score a goal. Should no. 1 succeed, he passes the ball to no. 2, who in turn passes the ball to no. 3 after scoring, and so on. Each player in turn takes up his position at the back of the row after passing the ball to the next player. The team which is first back in its original position is the winner. It must be understood that the ball may not be passed to the next player before a goal has been scored.

17.
Goal Shooting Relay versus Zigzag Passing: For this game a single netball post and 2 balls are required. The players of Team A stand in single file with no. 1 on the starting line. The players of Team B line up in 2 rows and face each other. At a given signal no. 1 of Team A runs with the ball to the post and shoots a goal. After this he passes the ball to no. 2, who in turn scores a goal and passes the ball on to no. 3, and so on. As soon as no. 1 of Team A sets off, no. 1 of Team B starts a zigzag passing movement down the two rows. Team B counts the number of passes their players give. If the ball is dropped no pass is counted. The zigzag passing continues in this way until every player of Team A has scored a goal, when every player is back in position and when no. 1 holds the ball aloft. After this the teams change sides. The team which has scored most passes is the winner.

Group D
(*Push-off and grabbing exercises*)

16.
*Chase Him*1: All the players are scattered. The teacher points to one player and the others try and tag him. Before they can do this the teacher points out another player and the pursuit of the first boy is discontinued immediately and instead the new boy is chased. Quick switching of quarries is necessary to maintain a high tempo. The teacher must be quick and resourceful to keep the players continually on the move.

17.
Circle Chase: The players run round in a circle widely spaced from one another. At a given signal each player tries to tag the player in front of him. The teacher indicates when the direction of running has to be varied and sees to it that the direction is frequently changed.

Group C
(Handling and kicking exercises)

18.
Circle Passing versus Shuttle Relay Race:
One of the teams stands in a circle with the players facing outwards and with either the left or the right foot in front. One of them holds a Rugby ball. The members of the other team are divided into 2 equal groups arranged in pairs. They are positioned facing each other 10–15 yards apart. At a given signal the members of the circle team pass the ball in an anticlockwise direction, counting the number of passes given. If the ball is dropped, it must be returned to the player who has given the pass, and the same count is called when the pass is repeated. To ensure that the players also get practice in passing the ball clockwise, the direction of passing can be changed. At the given signal the other team starts its shuttle relay race. Each couple sets off passing the ball between them. When they reach the next couple, they in turn set off with the ball. The game continues in this way until every couple has handled the ball. As soon as the shuttle relay race has been repeated 3 to 5 times, the last pair to run shouts: "Done!" The other team in the circle then stops counting passes. The teams then exchange places. The team scoring most passes in the circle is declared the winner.

Group D
(Push-off and grabbing exercises)

18.
Neutrals are Safe: For this game quite a large playing field is required. Parallel squares of equal size are marked on the field. The first square is "guarded" by half the members of the defending team. The second square is neutral territory without defenders. The third square is guarded by the rest of the defending team, while the fourth square is again neutral territory. The attackers line up in battle formation in front of the first square. They must try and reach the first neutral square without the defenders clasping them. Those who are caught are "dead" and have to start all over again. From the first neutral square they must attempt to gain entry to the second neutral square without being clasped. Players are not permitted to run outside the field of play and defenders may not go beyond the lines of the squares. One point is allocated for every attacker who succeeds in reaching the last neutral square, otherwise 1 point can be awarded to the first to reach the neutral square, 2 points for the second square, 3 for the third, etc. More than 4 squares can be marked on the field. If there are 8, for example, the defending team will be divided into 4 groups, with neutral squares between them.

Group C
(*Handling and kicking exercises*)

19.
Passing in Threes: Each team is drawn up in a line with the players standing 3 abreast behind the starting line. The player to the left of the front row holds a ball.
With the other 2 players he sets off to a line 15 yards away and back to the starting line. While running, the ball is passed between them, 6 times on the way to the mark and 6 times on the way back.
After this the ball is handed to the player at the left of the next row. The first team to complete the course is the winner.

20.
Swerve Passing Relay: The game is the same as passing in threes except that markers are placed on the ground.
The players have to weave through them while running to the 15 yards mark and back.

21.
Running Circle Catch (*centre thrower*):
Each team is drawn up in a circle with the leader – who holds the ball – in the centre. The teams number to the right. At a given signal the players run to the left, keeping the circle intact, while the leader passes the ball to no. 1 and then to each player in turn. Each player, on the run, immediately passes it back to the leader. As a competitive game the aim is to see which team can complete 3 full circles first. After that the players may run in the opposite direction.

Group D
(*Push-off and grabbing exercises*)

19.
Giant Strides: The players stand in formation on one side of the field. At a given signal they start covering a certain distance by taking as few steps as possible, i.e. they run as if they were wearing "giant boots" or taking "giant steps". Instead of striding, the players may also jump from a standing position or hop on one leg.

20.
Zigzag Running (*weaving*): Each team is drawn up in a row with the players 2 feet apart standing behind each other. The first player runs with a Rugby ball, zigzagging his way through his team and back again, to a line in front of them. From here he kicks the ball to the second player in the line who, in turn, weaves through the players, after which he kicks the ball to no. 3. The player who has completed running with the ball goes to the back of the row and the other players move up one position.

21.
Zigzag Circle Relay: All the teams form a circle with the players sitting crosslegged and facing inwards. At a given signal the right-hand player in each team starts running anticlockwise and weaves in and out between players until he reaches his former position. As soon as no. 1 has seated himself, no. 2 sets off, and so on.

Group C
(*Handling and kicking exercises*)

22.
Running Circle Catch (*outside thrower*):
Each team forms a large circle. The leader stands 4 or 5 yards outside the circle between two parallel lines 5 yards apart. The leader holds a Rugby ball. At a given signal the team members start running in circle formation, quite widely spaced from each other. As soon as no. 1 comes to the first parallel line, the leader passes the ball to him, "counting the first sheep". Before reaching the second parallel line, no. 1 must pass the ball back to the leader. The leader then passes the ball to the rest of the players and they go through the same movements. The team to first complete the count is the winning team. Their leader immediately raises his hand on receiving the ball from the last player.

23.
Ball Chasing: The players form a circle facing outwards. Two balls are used. The idea is that one of the balls must catch up with the other while the players, with quick movements of their feet but with slow progress, increase or decrease the size of the circle while moving forward and backwards. The balls must be passed to both sides.

Group D
(*Push-off and grabbing exercises*)

22.
Tunnel Ball Rolling – Side-stepping Relay:
The players form teams by standing behind one another with their legs wide apart. The ball is then rolled along the tunnel. As soon as the rearmost player gets the ball he side-steps and swerves through his team-mates until he reaches the front of the tunnel, at which point he rolls the ball back. Alternatively the game ends when no. 1 has swerved to the front again and holds the ball aloft.

23.
Catch the Hare: An area is marked off into three or four squares. The attacking team stands on one side of the field and must attempt to reach the other side without being touched. The defenders stand on the lines of the squares and try to touch the attackers as they move from one square to another. The attackers are safe inside the squares as long as they are sufficiently far away from the defenders on the lines. The defenders appoint one of their players to act as a hare, and he is permitted to move along any of the lines except the 2 finishing lines. If a player is touched, he has to start afresh. Each team is given a set time as attackers, and at the end of the game the numbers of players who have got through the lines without being touched are compared.

Group C
(*Handling and kicking exercises*)

24.
Ten Passes: The players are divided into 2 teams who take up any formation on the field of play. One of the players throws the ball into the air and the player who catches it starts the game by passing to a team-mate. The aim is to get in 10 consecutive passes, thereby scoring 1 point. The opposing team naturally tries to gain possession of the ball to chalk up their 10 passes. Players should be encouraged to run about, but it could be advisable to confine the playing area.

25.
Passing Through the Gaps: The players stand in pairs 3 yards apart. The left-hand player of the foremost pair holds a ball. At the given signal the pair start running along the outside of the other players, passing the ball to each other through the gaps between the players in the row. They repeat this when returning to their original positions. The ball is then passed to the second pair and they repeat the exercise, followed in turn by the remaining pairs. As soon as one pair has completed the "course" they run to the back of their row while the rest move up a place.

Group D
(*Push-off and grabbing exercises*)

24.
Fly: The players draw lots and the player picked bends along a line. Each player selects another as his "fly", usually one who can jump exceptionally well, as it will depend on his jumping ability what length of time the picked player will have to remain bent. The fly jumps first over the bender and the latter moves up to the spot where the fly's feet have touched the ground. The fly now says "Fly", and the other players run up and step with both feet on the line and jump over the player who is bending down, as in "bucking". If the jumper fails to clear with one jump, or steps over the line, he has to bend down. When all the players have done the fly jump, the fly himself does it and the bender moves to the place where the fly's feet have come down. If he thinks that the distance is too long for a fly, he says: "One and a fly". The other players must then run, come down on one foot on the line, come down on both feet and from this position jump over the bending player. The fly can, however, make another fly if he thinks that it can be done in a single fly. Should he say: "One and a fly" and the bender challenges him to it, and one of the other players does it in a fly, he has to bend down. On the other hand, if he says: "Fly" and one of the players fails to do it but challenges him, he must do it in a fly or bend down. If he is challenged and succeeds in jumping over the bending player, the challenger must bend down. If nothing goes wrong, the player who bends down keeps on moving further away from the line after each jump or series of jumps. After the "One and a fly" follow "Two and a fly", "Three and a fly", "Four and a fly", etc.

25.
"Springbok": An area of approximately 30 yards by 15 yards is used. On one side of it make a "pen", in which one player stands. The other players – the springboks – run from one back-line to the other, and when they pass him, he attempts to catch one of them to take captive in the pen. Every caught player then becomes a catcher and helps in rounding up the remaining players for the pen. The springboks struggle and wrestle to avoid being taken to the pen.

Group C
(*Handling and kicking exercises*)

26.

"*Hurry*": The teams are drawn up in rows with the players standing side by side and 3 yards apart, with one of the players – the scrum half – 4 to 6 yards in front of the no. 1 player in the line. Next to him lies a ball which he passes off the ground to no. 1 at a given signal. No. 1 sends it along the line and the ball comes back to him the same way. The game proceeds in this way until each player has had a chance of playing scrum half. Each player takes up his position at the end of the line after being the scrum half.

27.

Time Ball (*Scotch Handball*): The teams are drawn up in rows, 2 yards apart and 2 yards behind one another with each leader 4 or 5 yards in front of his team and facing it. At a given signal each leader passes the ball off the ground to the foremost player, who runs with it round his team and passes it back to his leader, after which he kneels in his original position. While running, the player throws the ball over the head of every player in his team, catching it on the other side by making use of the gaps between the players. Each player takes the leader's place in turn and passes the ball to the other players in the team. The game is ended when the leader is back in his original position.

BIG OR BIGGISH GAMES

1. *Triangular competition*

There are three teams consisting of an equal number of players. The kicking team positions itself on the centre line and has as kicking area the entire half of the field in which the second team – the fielding team – takes up its position. The third team – the passing team – is drawn up on one touchline between the half-way line and twenty-five with players spaced out at a distance required of a long pass. Every member of the kicking team kicks the ball as far as he can and runs to the twenty-five yard line and back. In the meantime, the fielding side tries to catch the ball and then kick it to the passing team. One of the passing team's players has, in turn, to catch the ball and pass it to no. 1 in his line so that a passing movement can be set off right down to the last player in the line. Should this player get the ball before the runner of the kicking team is back at the half-way line, the kicking team scores no points. If the runner reaches the half-way line before the last player of the passing team receives the ball, the kicking team scores 5 points.

When each of the kickers has had his turn, they change over and become fielders; the fielders become passers, and the passers become kickers. If a player kicks the ball out directly from the field of play, his team forfeits the right of running. The passing team may go and collect the ball, but they must take up their normal positions when the passing begins. When each team has had a turn at kicking, the scores are compared to determine the winning team. If a player kicks the ball to the passing team and it is beyond the reach of a player for whom it is intended, another player in the line may catch the ball and pass it to him.

All kinds of kicks, except place kicks, are permitted.

2. *Kicking baseball*

The home base is the corner formed by the touchline and the half-way line. First base is the corner of the twenty-five yard line and the touchline and second base is 30 yards infield from that point. The third base is on the half-way line opposite second base. The pitcher's mound is 15 to 20 yards from home base, the distance depending on the players' ages and abilities.

There are two teams, comprising the "strikers" (kickers) and the fielders. The aim is to score runs within a stipulated number of "overs". If the team consists of 15 players, all 15 go in to "bat" in each over. The fielders have a catcher, a "pitcher", three base players, two short stops while the rest are out-fielders. The pitcher, from about 8 yards, throws the ball in as he would at a line-out to the kicker, who has to catch it and kick it immediately. The pitcher must throw accurately and must not attempt to bamboozle the catcher. He may, however, throw the ball as hard as he can.

The kicker uses either any kind of kick or a stipulated kick. If the ball lands in the field of play, the kicker makes a dash through the bases in an attempt to reach home base before being run out. The fielders can dismiss him if they get the ball to second base or home base before him. He need not be touched to be given out. The fielders, however, cannot dismiss him at home base before he has reached second base. A catch does not dismiss a player. A runner may not remain at a base but must try and get to home base. Fielders can pass or kick the ball to one another. More rules can be added if required.

3. *Gaining territory or "chasing on"*

Two teams take the field on either side of the half-way line and the players close all possible gaps. The team to win the toss kicks off from their 10-yard line with a kick from the hands. The object of the game is to chase the ball across the opponents' dead-ball line, in which a "try" is scored. The kicking must be quick and accurately placed in the "boxes". If the ball is kicked into touch, the game goes on nevertheless. The team to score most tries in the time stipulated is the winner.

Variations: (a) If a team can put over a drop kick, the kick is counted as a try and the game is restarted on the 10-yard line.
(b) Specify the kind of kick and indicate whether it should be to the left or to the right.

4. *Kicking for goal*

Two Rugby teams compete. The players take up their positions as indicated on the accompanying diagram. The aim is to kick drop goals from behind the goal posts. The players are opposed in pairs. One pair is behind each goal-line. One of these pairs is the team's goal kicker and plays towards his side. The other is the goal keeper and plays away from him. The rest of the players consist of three pairs in each area except for the section between the two 10-yard lines. Here there is one pair of players.

The game starts with the ball being thrown into the air between the two players positioned between the 10-yard lines. They try to gain possession of the ball and pass it to, or kick it towards, one of their team-mates, and so eventually get it to the goal kicker behind the posts, from where he attempts to drop a goal. The pairs are free to move about in their areas, but they are not allowed to cross over into other sections. Should they do so, a free kick is awarded against them. If the ball crosses the touchline, the goal-line, or the touch-in-goal line, the non-offending team is awarded a penalty on the spot. The ball may be dribbled but it must be picked up before it leaves a specific area. Players may also run with the ball but they may not cross into another area. If a player has possession of the ball, no player may interfere with his kick. Should this happen a penalty is awarded.

If the goal kicker receives the ball too far or too near the posts, he has a choice: he may either kick the ball back to a team-mate in the adjacent area and run closer to the posts for the return kick, or he may kick the ball and recover it himself. Whether the goal-kicker succeeds in kicking a drop goal or not, the game goes on and the match need not be started from the half-way line.

	OX	OX			XO	XO	
OX	OX	OX	OX	XO	XO		XO
	OX	OX			XO	XO	

EXERCISES FOR POWER, STAMINA, SPEED AND STRENGTHENING

These four components of fitness should be practised in summer so that they can be rounded off at the start of the so-called Rugby season. The sooner we realise that a "Rugby season" is a misconception, however, the better. The "season", in fact, embraces the whole year. The "Rugby season" is that part of the year when Rugby is actually being played, but the rest is also part of the season and serves to retain – even to improve – the strength, stamina and speed acquired during the period of actually playing the game. Any person can make himself stronger, and during summer a player must try to improve his strength. In this respect our track and field athletes are well ahead of our Rugby players. Our athletes use the winter season to prepare for the summer athletic season and they concentrate on the three aspects of speed, stamina and strength. In the summer itself they see to it that what they have gained is maintained and sharpened.

We do realise however that it will take considerable time before this idea is accepted throughout the country. It is a fact that most Rugby players, unlike athletes, are not unduly concerned whether they do well or not. They play the game because they enjoy it, and they do not want to go to a lot of trouble.

They play in order to get fit, and the more they play the fitter they become. We do not wish to change this kind of attitude. But what we do want to do however, is to advise the top players, or those who wish to get to the top, to follow a summer programme similar to that followed by athletes, and to be guided in this by athletic experts. Meanwhile, we must carry on in the old tradition and get our players fit in the time at our disposal. We must also give them exercises which will safeguard them from serious injuries. We can help them, too, to gain power to assist them in their Rugby tasks as well as speed and stamina to ensure that they will be able to play enjoyable Rugby. The exercises which follow should, however, be seen in true perspective.

Exercises for acquiring strength
In the old days many Rugby players had to carry bags of maize or wheat during the summer months. That kind of work, which helped to strengthen our players, must be cultivated today in an artificial way. This is what weight-lifting achieves. Athletes take their maximum push-up weight and push two-thirds or three-quarters of it up several times, with rest periods in between. After awhile they are able to push up a greater weight and "play" with it. In this way they increase their strength. They do these exercises 3 times a week for at least 3 months, skipping after each session. The strength they gain ensures that they will be able to push weights higher. In addition they increase their speed, for speed cannot be improved unless muscles are developed.

A warning must be sounded at this stage: weight-lifting or exercises for strength must, for physiological reasons, always be accompanied by exercises for stamina.

Before long we will be adopting athletic training programmes, but before such time we must concentrate on certain exercises for Rugby – such as those to minimise injuries, and exercises aimed at increasing Rugby skill. For these a number of general principles are given, which should be taken into consideration when the exercises are worked out.

PHYSICAL EXERCISES FOR BODY-BUILDING

A few principles
There are exercises for general strength, as when many muscles are involved in a task, and there are exercises for specific strengthening of specific parts of the body. We do these exercises to eliminate, as far as possible, injuries to joint muscles and to strengthen certain muscles for certain tasks, e.g. neck muscles for prop forwards, leg muscles for lock forwards, etc. We give lessons specifically designed for exercising the strength of the joint muscles and lessons for exercises to improve general strength. We also give examples of competitions and relays to be done as regularly as the lessons in physical exercises.

The flexing which can be brought about in the joints of the body consists, in most cases, of movements forward and backward and to either side. Further, some bodily parts can turn and rotate in the joints. There is a difference between turning and rotating. If I stand straight, I can hold my neck straight and turn

Stones and training equipment at Stellenbosch

my head to and fro. I can, however, also describe a circle as wide as possible with my chin. In the first instance the neck turns, whereas in the second instance circular movements are made.

If the force of gravity does not play a part, the following can be observed: front muscles are developed if forward bends are done, back muscles are developed if backward bends are done, lateral muscles are developed if sideways bending is done, and joint muscles are developed if circular movements are done.

Bending must be done to the full, except in the case of knees, when a half squat is sufficient.

By adding weight to the muscles which bend and straighten, the exercises can be done more quickly and more efficiently than if done by repetition and without added weight.

The weights can be any object, e.g. a stone or a beam, or the weight of a partner who offers resistance to the movement. The extra "load" can also be supplied by a resistance against which the muscles cannot be flexed. (Isometric exercises.)

The bigger the load, the fewer repetitions needed for the required strengthening, although quite a few repetitions are desirable.

For muscle stamina many repetitions are required and consequently the load is diminished.

The tempo of the exercises must be varied once the muscles have been attuned, and may sometimes be done as fast as possible. Repetitions should sometimes be done slowly and then as fast as possible.

Movements should be done to both sides of the body, be it arms or legs. Likewise, in exercises for pairs, each partner must be afforded the same opportunity even if the exercises are so designed that both participants do the same exercise.

The exercises must be done through the entire season.

As soon as the season begins, the exercises must be done continuously with one exercise running into the next to save time.

Lesson 1 – Physical exercises with stones

The weight of the stone is determined by the strength of the player and by the special joint muscles to be exercised, so it is advisable that stones of different weights should be available. Flat stones are preferable to round ones. In order to save time, exercises in which the same stone is needed can be linked together. It must be stressed once more that the heavier the stone, the fewer the repetitions required. However, the stone should not be so heavy that fewer than three repetitions can be done. As regards the table, it must be taken that the reference is to a stone or stones unless otherwise stipulated.

(a) Pull the toes downwards like a clenched fist and mark time slowly with a heavy stone balanced on the shoulders so that the feet take the full weight of the body and the stone alternatively.

(b) (i) Stand with the feet apart and on the toes. Turn the heels as widely as possible in a circle.

(ii) Feet a hip's width apart with toes turned slightly inwards. Stretch high up on toes and come down on heels with toes raised.

(iii) While the feet are flat on the ground flex the ankles first to the outside and then to the inside.

(iv) Stand astride and do circular movements with both knees, first to the outside and then to the inside.

(v) Stand astride with hands clasped behind the head. Flex the straight neck and back forward while keeping the legs stretched. When the hamstrings start pulling, stop the movement and keep the position. Then bend further down and stop the movement. Continue in this way until no further bending is possible.

(vi) Jump with both legs on to a low bench while holding a stone on the neck.

(c) (i) Lie on your back. Raise the legs up straight without lifting the coccygeal region. Lower the legs so that the heels are just above the ground and open and close the legs before they are again raised and lowered. Repeat a few times.

(ii) Lie on your back with legs apart. Raise the legs and describe small circular movements with each leg.

(iii) Lift the heels closely together slightly off the ground. Describe big circular movements with both legs extended and in unison. Do this to either side.

(iv) Lie on your back with hands clasped behind the neck. Raise flexed legs to perpendicular position and keep them in this position. Raise the trunk and try to touch the knees with the forehead. Repeat.

(v) Lie on your stomach with arms sideways. Raise legs and trunk as high as possible. Open arms and legs several times and lower.

(vi) Lie on your stomach with arms extended to the front and legs extended to the back so that the back is hollowed with only the stomach resting on the ground. Rock to one side and then the other while keeping the arms and legs fully extended. The shoulders, arms and legs may not touch the ground while rolling.

(vii) Stand with feet in wide straddle position and keep the legs straight. bend the neck and back (both straightened) as far to the front as possible with a stone placed on the nape of the neck, keeping the hips in the original position. Describe circles to either side with the trunk while the hips retain their position. Combine the circular movement with full turning of the back in the hips.

(d) While lying on your back with the knees strongly flexed, the toes are hooked under a beam or a low bench which is slightly raised above the ground, or a partner presses down the toes (not the foot). A stone is held on the chest and the trunk, and the stone is raised and lowered with or without turning the trunk.

(e) The same exercise as above is done, except lean backwards, pick up a stone and lower it while turning the back. The same exercise while lying on stomach (heels hooked). (See diagram for bench on page 171.)

(f) (i) Hold a stone with both hands in front of the body and raise it with extended arms above the head and as far back as possible. While the arms are fully stretched, circular movements are made with the shoulder joints. Then circle the stone with both hands in front of the body and lower it on the nape of the neck. Do a few push-ups from this position and then lower the stone with extended arms down in front of the body.

(ii) Now raise the stone only with the lower arms by pressing the elbows close to the sides and bending the lower arms in the elbows.

(iii) Hold the stone with the hands below against the buttocks and push it backwards as far as possible.

(iv) Lie on back with the arms along the sides and a stone next to each wrist. Push these stones with the palms of the hands and with flexed arms sideways and above the head without bending the arms at all except to adjust the stone. Then place the hands over the stones and push them back using the wrists.

(v) Heaving exercises on cross-beam.

(g) (i) Stand with a stone held against the back of the head and bend the trunk forward. Now move the neck forwards and backwards, turning it all the time while doing so. Also do circular movements to either side of the head.

(ii) To the sides: lean over to one side and place a stone against the side of the head. Now bend the neck up and down to the side of the shoulder joints. Place the stone over the other ear and repeat the exercise. N.B. While the backs are doing the above neck exercises the forwards do neck exercises with halters, stones or tree stumps.

(h) (i) A player kneels and clasps his hands behind his head with his elbows in line with his shoulders. Another player, stretched out on his stomach, presses his ankles down. The first player slowly lowers his trunk as far as possible without toppling forward and then comes up straight again. His partner does arm bending and flexing exercises.

(ii) Players stand on a low bench, each holding a stone in front of him. With backs straight and heads up, each player lowers the stone as far as possible, and when the stone is at the lowest point it is rocked up and down.

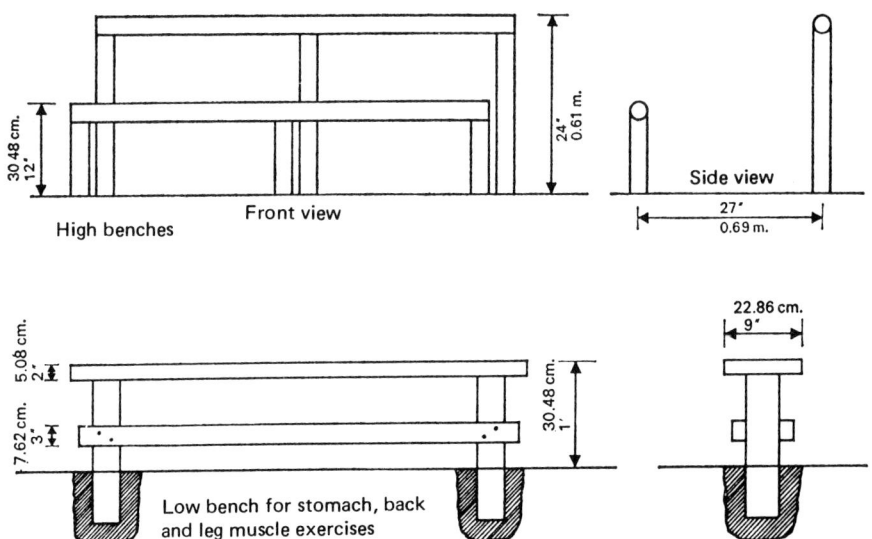

Lesson 2 – Exercises with partners
(a) (i) Front parallel standing. The players face each other and take hands. They bend the knees slightly with one partner's legs placed between those of his partner. They open and close the legs against resistance.
(ii) Back to back parallel standing with arms hooked and toes turned up. They squat and come upright, pushing down with their arms in the process while their backs are kept against each other. When they are in the squatting position their feet are kept flat on the ground. Their ankles are bent inwards and outwards while they press downwards with their arms.
(iii) Kneeling. A player holds a kneeler's feet so that he can bend as far as possible forward and backwards while keeping his back and thighs in a straight line without bending his hips. While he is doing this his partner bends and extends his arms from a front lying position with his hands clasping his heels.
(b) (i) "Crosswise back lying". Both players lie on their backs with the soles of the partner's feet offering resistance across the lower parts of the legs of the partner doing the exercise. He has to raise and lower the leg with the weight resting on it. Every leg is thus exercised. The partners change position of legs.
(ii) Both players lie on their backs, feet to feet. One of the players opens his legs against resistance while the other player closes his legs against resistance.

(iii) **In** the same position. While the heels are kept on the ground the feet are flexed outwards against resistance and the partner flexes them back inwards against resistance.

(c) Pushing from the knees in a scrum position. A player bends his back forward and then straightens it against resistance offered by his partner until the partner's back is completely arched. After this he straightens his back again. The player who straightens his back does so by turning it to and fro. For this exercise the players have to adjust their positions to suit themselves.

(d) The player lies with toes hooked under a beam or low bench slightly raised above the ground, or a partner presses the toes (not the foot) down. A stone is held on the chest and the trunk is raised and lowered with or without twisting the trunk.

(e) The same as above except lean backwards and pick up a stone. Lower it while turning the back. The same exercise with stomach-lying (heels hooked).

(f) (i) Front parallel standing with hands clasping each other's heads. Circular movements of the neck to either side against resistance of the partner's hands. The left hand is pressed against the right side of the head with the fingers parallel to the ground. The right hand is placed behind the head with the fingers splayed round the back of the head and parallel to the ground. Resistance can now easily be offered.

(ii) In the same position: circle the neck.

(g) (i) Back-to-back parallel standing. Take hold of hands. Lift arms sideways and upwards against resistance of one of the partners and press downwards against resistance of the other partner.

(ii) Front parallel standing and grasping arms. Lift arms forward against resistance to above the head. Move feet forwards and backwards. See to it that arms remain straight throughout. Lower again against resistance with the necessary foot movements. While doing this exercise, do shoulder joint circular movements in as wide an arc as possible, forward, upwards and backwards.

(iii) Heaving on parallel beam.

(h) (i) Front parallel standing. Take hold of hands. The elbows of one of the partners are strongly flexed and held against the body. Straighten elbows against resistance by pushing arms outwards and flexing the wrists forward when the arms are fully bent. Bend arms while resistance is offered, displacing feet if necessary. When the arms are fully bent the wrists are bent sideways and backwards against resistance.

(ii) Turn the arms against resistance before straightening them.

(i) Standing a-straddle with hands clasped behind the head, bend the straightened back and neck forward while keeping the legs straight. If the hamstrings start pulling, the action is stopped and the position held. Now bend further down and stop the movement. Continue in this way until it is impossible to bend further.

Lesson 3 – Isometric exercises

These exercises are done against a resistant object. A maximum effort is made against resistance while you count to six. Players can work out their own exercises, but the following are given because they reduce the risk of injury. These exercises provide variation, and they can be done with available equipment and by injured players who are able to do some of the exercises.

At high bench
(a) Head underneath the highest beam of the bench and neck completely bent forward; one leg in front of the other, the heel of the rearmost leg raised. *Exercise:* Try and lift the beam with the neck while pushing from the toes without bending the body at all. Do the same off the rear foot.
(b) Head underneath beam so that the latter is above the shoulders. Try to lift the beam with the back. (Feet are placed away from the beam.)
(c) The same exercise, but now the player crawls underneath the beam, and the knees are stretched. The ankles are brought over to the outside and then the inside. From this position start pushing against the beam.
(d) Kneel at one end of the bench and place the hands underneath in order to press upwards. Then place the hands on top of the beam in order to press downwards.
(e) Lie on your back at the end of the bench with the feet first placed underneath to press upwards. Then place the feet on top of the bench for pressing downwards.
(f) Stand on one side of a high beam with neck under the beam. Pull the beam over. (Do it for both sides.)
(g) Push the beam with straight arms forwards and backwards.
(h) Lift the beam with bent elbows.
(i) Try and turn the beam after taking a firm grip on it.

At low bench
(a) Lie on your back with feet underneath the bench. Raise bench with both legs.
(b) Lie on your back with knees raised and toes hooked under the lowest beam. A stone at arm's length is on the ground behind the head. Raise stone with straightened arms.
(c) Lie on your stomach with heels hooked under bench. Raise the bench with legs.
(d) With back to and heel underneath bench, try and raise the bench with the straightened lower leg.
(e) Take as long a stride as possible so that the heel of the foremost foot and the toes of the rearmost foot are on the ground. Attempt to close the legs with both working simultaneously. In order to maintain balance, one can stand next to an upright post, tree, or high bench.

Lesson 4 – Exercises for joint muscles for specific strength in limiting injuries
(a) Partners lie on their backs with feet towards each other. One has his foot between the feet of his partner and opens his leg against the resistance offered by his partner who, in turn, closes his legs against the resistance offered by his partner.
(b) Lie on your back with hands behind the head. Raise straightened legs to

perpendicular position and keep them there. Now raise the trunk and try to touch the knees with the forehead.
(c) Lying on your stomach with arms stretched above the head, raise the arms and legs, open them and close them and then roll over without letting the arms or legs touch the ground. Open and close the legs and arms again.
(d) Players stand next to the low benches and each holds a stone on his shoulders. They jump off both legs on and off the benches.
(e) Lying on their backs with bent knees, the players hook their toes underneath the bar below the low bench. Each player holds a stone on his chest. The exercises consist of the players raising their straightened trunks, placing the stone on the bench and then lowering their trunks in the same way in which they were raised.
(f) Heaving exercises on the cross-bar.
(g) With heavy beams on their shoulders, 2 to 4 players standing behind one another do circular movements with their knees, followed by circular movements with their ankles and ankle-bending to the sides, forwards and backwards. They also slowly jog on the spot with toes curled upwards.
(h) At the high bench, lie on your back with toes (not feet) hooked in. Backwards bend, pick up a stone and raise the body while turning it all the time.
(i) With halters fixed to the head, stones in wire gauze, or beams, the points of which are hooked into the halters, are used for stretching exercises to the side, forwards and backwards, with circling movements. Players can also press their foreheads on the ground while standing on their feet and with their arms behind their backs. The neck carries the body's weight so that neck exercises are done.
(j) Rope climbing.
(k) Standing with legs a-straddle with or without a stone held on hump. Bend the trunk slowly forward while keeping the legs straight. If the hamstrings start pulling, stop the movement and then continue in the same way until further bending is impossible.

General competitions in strength

These competitions are based on pulling and pushing, thus supplying general strength.

Beam pulling and pushing
1. (a) Two teams, facing each other on either side of a beam, push against each other. (b) back to back on either side of a beam, two teams push against each other.
2. (a) Two teams, facing each other and on either side of a beam, pull against each other. (b) Back to back on either side of a beam, two teams pull against each other.
3. Two teams on either side of a beam with faces or backs towards one another, pull or push against each other.
4. One team is between the two beams, the other divided into two sections on the outsides of the beam. The two sections pull the beams outwards while the inside team resists.

5. The members of both teams sit in rows facing each other, each player placing his feet against those of the player opposite while taking hold of the beam. Each member takes hold of the handles on the opponents' side of the beam when pulling against the other team.
6. Players lined up in threes or fours in the yokes attempt to pull one another away. They try to do the same when taking up the crab-walk position on all fours with their backs towards the ground and the beam resting on their necks with the rope underneath their arms.

The purpose of the beam apparatus is to increase strength. It can be used by two teams in different ways, as it has so many rope handles. The teams pull or push against each other either facing or looking away from each other. The pulling and pushing competitions can be conducted with the apparatus used in either its lateral or its longitudinal axis.

The same apparatus can be used for arm and shoulder exercises with two teams working at the same time to pick it up forwards, sideways, upwards and even backwards. In these circumstances the beam must obviously be lighter and adapted to the strength of the players. The weights used at Stellenbosch are as follows:

BEAM FOR PULLING AND PUNCHING

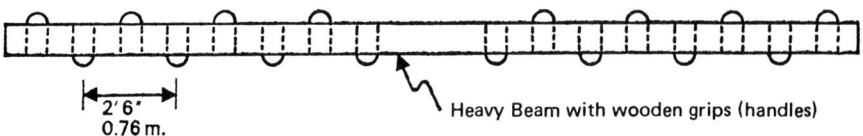

2'6"
0.76 m.

Heavy Beam with wooden grips (handles)

The beam used by forwards weighs 730 lb (331 kg) and the beam used by the backs weighs 200 lb (90 kg). Bluegum-tree beams are used for this purpose.

Clear the circle
One team is in the circle while the other team tries to push, pull or drag players out. The team in the circle itself attempts the same. At the end of the competition it is established whether any players have not been cleared from the circle.

Dead man lifting: One of the teams picks up the other and vice versa. The time is taken and compared. If a stopwatch is not available, a count is simply taken. The "dead man" lies on the ground and keeps his body as limp and slack as possible; his partner has to pick him up and sling him across his shoulder.
Horse and rider: Half the team rides pickaback on the rest of the team. The two teams attempt to dislodge the "riders" so they fall to the ground. When the match is over, the unseated riders are compared. Dislodged players take part in the game again.
Rope climbing: In twos, or with as many ropes as are available for competition.
General Strength Relays – with beams: We suggest that these relays take place between the half-way line and the twenty-five. Each team has a heavy beam.
Relay no. 1: The players are drawn up in flanked rows and carry the beam with

crooked arms in front of them. After this they carry it on their shoulders, first hopping on left foot, then hopping on right foot. Rest.

Relay no. 2: Beam is rolled forwards. Beam is rolled backwards. With the beam on their shoulders and in single file the players jump sideways. The same, but with the other leg in front.

Relay no. 3: Lined in a row and in squatting position, the teams frog-jump with the beams in their armpits. Rest.

Relay no. 4: Running on all fours, with knees not touching the ground, and the beam resting on their necks. Rest.

Relay no. 5: Crouched running with one hand clasped around the beam to keep it just above the ground.

Relay no. 6: Team members, standing in rows behind one another in a straddle position with the beam placed on the ground between their legs, move in line pushing the beam backwards along the ground. Rest.

Relay no. 7: Running up a slope while holding a stone or clasping a beam crosswise. This is done as often as required by the player's condition of fitness.

General strength relays – individual and with partners
1st relay

Hopping (left foot):	Goal-line to twenty-five.
Hopping (right foot):	Twenty-five to half-way line.
Running backwards:	Half-way line to twenty-five.
Giant strides:	Twenty-five to goal-line.

2nd relay

Hopping backwards (left foot):	Goal-line to twenty-five.
Hopping backwards (right foot):	Twenty-five to half-way line.
Hands dragging (front):	Half-way line to twenty-five.
Hands dragging (rear):	Twenty-five to goal-line.

3rd relay (partners)

Pickaback race:	Goal-line to twenty-five.
Pickaback race (exchange horses):	Twenty-five to half-way line.
Wheelbarrow pushing:	Half-way to twenty-five.
Wheelbarrow pushing (change partners):	Twenty-five to goal-line.

4th relay

Frog jumps:	Goal-line to twenty-five.
Crab walking:	Twenty-five to half-way line.
Running on all fours:	Half-way line to twenty-five.
Sideways jumping:	Twenty-five to goal-line.

STAMINA EXERCISES

First phase

On reporting to their coach at the start of the so-called Rugby season, players should already have sufficient stamina. This is more generally the case today than it was some time ago. Our players usually run right through the summer season, or they start running at the beginning of, or early in the new year. When players start on stamina building they must make running the basis. Their pulse-rate will increase rapidly, they become fatigued, and their throats will have a burning sensation.

At the onset of this unpleasant feeling, they should change to walking and take their pulse-rate (for this reason a wristwatch must be worn). The pulse-rate is counted for 10 seconds and multiplied by 6. The result should be more than 120 beats per minute. As soon as the pulse-rate is close to 120 the players start trotting again. In other words, they see to it that their pulse-rate is close to or more than 120 during 40–60 minutes of exercise.

How high the pulse-rate is while they are running is not important. If they later get over the unpleasant feeling of lassitude, they can run 40–60 minutes at a stretch because they know that their pulse-rate will be more than 120. If they can do this, they have already acquired a great deal of stamina. This is the stage at which stamina should be increased by increasing road work and when legs should be strengthened by running up slopes. At the outset, the players will walk after running up slopes – or even walk up them – until their pulse-rate has decreased sufficiently.

Second phase
When the slopes have been mastered, another form of loading can be included for the second stage – Rugby skills and sprinting. For the skills, for instance, the following are required:
1. Something to push against such as Rugby posts, which must be padded for this purpose. Push from either foot and from both feet. (For forwards only.)
2. A high beam, branch or wire to be touched by jumping from one foot and from both feet simultaneously. (For forwards only.)
3. At specific places, corners or bends in the road, the push-off can be practised, as well as side-stepping, swerving and selling dummies. (Especially for backs.)
4. Handling: This can be done with an imaginary ball for passing, falling ball and scooped-up balls. (Forwards and backs.)
5. Tackling: Posts or trees. (Forwards and backs.) For these, marks can be used along the road e.g.: whitewash spot on tree indicates pushing; whitewash spot on crossbar indicates jumping; whitewash spot on thin or thinnish tree indicates tackling and pressing; a single white stone on the side of the road indicates that a push-off should be practised; two white stones, one on each side of the road, indicate that a hypothetical ball must be scooped up and that the player must sprint with it to the next two stones approximately 15–20 yards ahead.

After each lap, players can walk again until their pulse rate is slightly more than 120 per minute before they start running back on the road. In this way they cover the laps until they can maintain it for 40–60 minutes.

Proposed long road and short road round the field of play
The long road: Players run round the field without cutting the corners at the goal-lines. The aim should be to run 40–60 minutes without stopping. As a

preparation for this it is recommended that players insert short sprints of 5–10 yards, say between one of the 10-yard lines and the half-way line on either side of the field and from one goalpost to the other.

The short road: If the long road no longer tires the players very much, they go over to the short road. Jogging is the basis of running round the field.

Sprints: The same as recommended above but 4 times each lap.

Stopping and making a complete turnabout: This occurs at the 4 corners of the touchlines and the goal-lines or touch-in-goal lines. The players stop in their tracks and turnabout. Then they jog on in the original direction.

Handling: Handling here is hypothetical. While jogging (passing the ball) and during sprints (scooped-up ball), see to the hands. They must be "ready" for catching and passing the ball.

Scooped-up balls are hypothetically gathered next to one of the uprights at the start of the sprint and players sprint while holding the "ball" until they reach the other upright.

Push-off: The corners of the touchlines and the parallel lines across the field are used for this purpose, and each foot is used for pushing off. In all there are 20 push-offs – 10 with the left foot and 10 with the right foot.

Tackling: As part of the sprints and scooping-up of the ball between the goal-posts, the player makes straight for the furthermost goalpost, stops in his tracks and gets hold of the post and tugs it several times before jogging on his way.

Pushing and jumping

Forwards: They change their activities somewhat, so make provision for this exercise. For instance, they grab the first goalpost, push against it as an isometric exercise, pick up the hypothetical ball and sprint with it past the second goalpost, make a turnabout, grab this goalpost and scrum against it. After this they attempt at least 2 jumps from either foot to reach the crossbar before they continue jogging.

After one lap, which ends at a goal-line, the players walk round the in-goal area until they come to the goal-line, at which point the first lap ends before the second is attempted. They must again run a sufficient number of laps to keep them busy for 40–60 minutes.

Here follows the short road through the apparatus used by us at Stellenbosch:

Backs: A sprint of 50 yards with the ball (two players work together). 20 throws (passes) between the handling screens. 3 times through the tackle-breaking apparatus (tyres) with dummy.

Flying tackle (2 bags); the ball is thrown ahead before the first back and picked up after the first tackle and then again thrown ahead before the second bag, where it is picked up once more after the tackle.

Through the tyres – with dummy – 3 times.

Through the side-step posts.

Sprint for 10 yards.

Walk back to the other end for the second round.

(This short road is 160 yards (146 m) in length. For the tackling apparatus and the tackle-breaking apparatus see pp. 214–15.

Forwards: At first the same as for the backs. Later they pull the yoke in fours to a line and back and then all 8 forwards push the scrummage sledge to the end of the circuit. Here they rest for as long as it takes the backs to walk back to the start of their circuit. The forwards then go back the same way for the second lap.

N.B. In all these exercises the time must be taken so that it can be improved. Times for completing the long road and the short road (every lap) must always be taken.

SPEED EXERCISES

First Phase

In the same way that a player competes against himself to increase his strength, he must also compete to improve his speed. For this he must clock his times over a given distance. Our suggestion is the length of the playing field of 110 yards (100 m), after which he walks back to the starting point and sets off for the second time. Ten repetitions are needed, of which the last nine must be done in the player's best time plus 20 per cent. As he improves he will reduce his time for the 9 repetitions.

To make this exercise more interesting it can be done in relays. In this way a player is also given the opportunity of a rest during the time it takes his other team-mates to run twice the length of the field.

For relays the teams are divided into pairs, some of them on one goal-line and the remainder on the other. Here is one method involving 3 pairs, or even groups who are approximately as fast as each other: the number of runners is divided into 3 equal groups or pairs, of which 2 stand behind each other on one of the goal-lines and the rest on the other. On reaching the opposite goal-line, the first group of 2 remain there and the next group runs to the goal-line where the race started. Here their fellow-players take over while they wait. The race proceeds in this way until repetitions become too much for the players.

Here is a list of exercises used by us for relays. An exercise can be repeated at least 10 times and last for at least 40 minutes:

Specific Speed Exercises
Quick off the mark
1. Trot from behind the twenty-five yard line, and when the right foot touches the line, sprint up to the 10-yard line and stop in your tracks. Turn back, rest for a short while and repeat, but push off from the left foot.
2. Walk and do the same as above.
3. Stand on the twenty-five and repeat.
4. Sit on the twenty-five, jump up and repeat.
5. Lie on your back, jump up and repeat.
6. Lie on your stomach, jump up and repeat.

N.B. For 1, 2 and 3 the time is taken from the moment the twenty-five yard line is touched to the moment that the first and last players are stationary on the 10-yard line. For 4, 5 and 6 the time is taken to the moment the players are sitting or lying down again. There are two times which must be bettered: the fastest time of an individual player, and the fastest time for the group or team. (The time is determined by the last player home.)

About-turn
1. Each player has a ball. A row is formed and the players run across the field. When they come to the 5-yard line, they kick the ball over their own heads, turn about and try and catch it before it lands on the ground. (It is advisable that the ball be held crosswise for the purpose.)
2. A row of players stand well spaced on the touchline with a ball each. In front of them is another row of players who run up to them. As soon as they reach the 5-yard line, the players on the touchline put in a short punt over the heads of the advancing players. They must then turn round and try and catch the ball. Make the advancing row run increasingly faster.
3. The row who does the kicking walks nearer and kicks when the other row is on the 5-yard line and they also try and get to the ball.
4. The same as 3, but a grubber is kicked through either the inside or outside gap.
5. Two rows, each given a name, start trotting towards each other in such a way that the players in one row can suddenly make a beeline for a gap between two players in the other row. The players must therefore be well spaced. As soon as the two rows merge, the coach or teacher calls out the name of one of the rows to turn round and sprint back while the other team tries to catch them. Let the players run faster and faster before giving the turnabout signal.
6. Same as 5, but now the two teams merge to run in the same row and in the same direction. On calling out of one of the names, both must turn round and the players of one of the teams try to catch players of the other.
7. Same as 6, but the players have their hands tucked into their shorts so that they have to run without arm action. The emphasis here is on increasing speed, which can be measured only by taking the time over a fixed distance. If the speed-building and other exercises serve their purpose, the times should show an improvement.

Passing
Take the time of a team running from one goal-line to the other. Now let the team pass the ball as quickly as possible while the players run at full speed from one goal-line to the other. Count the number of passes. Let the teams now compete against each other – against the time and the number of passes registered.

Second Phase
Speed building plus rounding off of skills
To develop speed as used in Rugby, exercises for speed and for the rounding off of skills will be practised during the season. Exercises for the rounding off skills

can be modified to suit the exercises for speed. The following is an example of such an adaptation:

Two back-lines are drawn up to face each other on either side of the half-way line. Each scrum half has a ball and when the whistle goes (and the stopwatch is started) he passes from a point where the 5-yard line intersects the half-way line to his back-line. If the open-side wings get the ball, they put it down on the half-way line at the point where it is intersected by the opposite 5-yard line. The backs all run to this spot and then take up their positions as fast as possible for the movement back again. When all the backs are on the spot with the wings, the competition is over and the time for the there-and-back handling movement is announced. The aim should be to equalise or improve on the time.

This exercise involves speed of handling, running and principles of back-line play, all of which are to be correctly executed. If the back-lines are not sufficiently "polished" in the principles of back-line play, the balls must be passed from the 10-yard lines at the point where they intersect the 5-yard lines.

LEG-MUSCLE STAMINA

To give special attention to this important aspect of the exercises, we use sand tracks or slopes. Running is practised up and down, up and down, with necessary rest periods. Exercises which provide energy, such as pushing the sledge or pulling the beam, are included in between.

TOUGHENING EXERCISES

In the soft age in which we are living it is imperative that our Rugby players are not only fit but tough. Fitness alone does not make Rugby players hard. Toughening-up before matches will prevent many injuries. The equipment mentioned earlier covered this, but here are a number of additional exercises. Coaches can work out other exercises which must involve physical contact.

1. (a) *Clear the circle:* A circle is drawn on the ground and a number of players take up positions inside it. An equal number attempt to push or bump them out of the circle. If a player is pushed or bumped out, or even dragged out, he goes back into the circle to undergo the same treatment. To make the competition interesting, the teams can change positions and the number of players forced out of the circle can be counted to find a winning team. If a complete pack of forwards takes part, the two props and two locks can, for instance, compete against the three loose forwards and the hooker. This, too, makes the competition more interesting. Backs can also be divided on the basis of their common interests. For instance, the two centres and wings can compete against the halves and full back, or the halves and centres can take on the wings and full back.
   (b) Instead of pushing, bumping and dragging players, backs hop on one leg with their arms crossed on their chests. In this manner they try and push one another from the circle. Players change the hopping leg.
2. (a) Two packs of forwards, each with a scrum half or number eight acting

as scrum halves, play against one another across the field between the twenty-five and the goal-line or between the twenty-five and the halfway line. They start with a scrum in the middle of the area and the scrum half who gets the ball must break with his own forwards helping him while the members of the other team must stop them and try and launch counterattacks. Rucks and mauls will form part and parcel of the game. If the ball goes dead, the game is restarted with a scrum. After a try a kick-off is taken from the centre. If the ball leaves the field, the match can be restarted either by a line-out or scrum. Seeing that a scrum in this particular game is the starting point of all the ploys, it will be advisable to order a scrum.

(b) The same as (a), but the match starts with a line-out in the centre and the team to gain possession starts "churning away" with it. If the ball is knocked on or passed forward, or cannot emerge from a ruck, a scrum is ordered.

(c) The match starts with a kick-off or a drop-out, and whenever there is an infringement – knock-on, forward pass, or if the ball fails to become dislodged in a ruck – it is restarted with a kick-off at the place of infringement.

(d) The game is played like an ordinary match; in other words, if a scrum has to be formed, a scrummage is ordered; if the ball is out, it is put in again – and the "churning away" movement follows: if a penalty kick is awarded, the tap-kick is given, and when a try has been scored it is followed by a kick-off.

3. Two back-lines play against each other. The two centres and the open-side wing of the attacking team each has a ball. Their scrum half takes up his position at the ball, which is placed on the half-way line. On the whistle he passes the ball to his fly half. When the fly half receives the ball the attackers set off and attempt to beat their opponents by picking identical gaps, either on the outside or inside. If some pick the inside gap and others pick the outside gap, they will run into one another and there will be collisions, which must be avoided. Consequently the attackers decide beforehand which particular gap is to be taken. Straightening is the basis of the methods of attack.

4. This competition is again one of attack versus defence. The defenders (backs and forwards), stand in a row at least 10 yards apart and 5 yards from the goal-line. The attackers are drawn up in a row on the twenty-five yard line, each facing a defender. The attackers have a ball each – if enough are available. At a given signal the attackers start sprinting and try and run through the defenders and touch down on or behind the goal-line. Instead of running through their opponents, the attackers can take the gap agreed to beforehand among themselves.

5. Three, 5 or 8 forwards play against one another. One of the teams has the ball and the players try to run through their opponents, who are 10–15 yards in front of them, by means of short passes. Forwards must learn to run into their opponents with their bodies hunched and to keep the ball under one arm. If the movement is stopped, another forward must come and take the

ball. If the movement is completely blocked, the ball carrier must turn and put the ball on the ground. If the ball is already on the ground, the forwards must push the ball free.
6. Exercises for rucking and mauling as previously described.
7. Running and falling. The back of the shoulder should take the fall and the arm of the shoulder be kept stiff by pressing it against the body. It is when players fall on their shoulders that injuries occur.

WARMING-UP EXERCISES

The following are recommended:
1. Every player should warm up before participating in exercises or matches.
2. Track suits should be worn while warming up and socks should be worn if there is a possibility of boots slipping on concrete floors. On wooden floors boots can be worn but they should not be tightly laced.
3. Warming-up should be directed towards the whole body and stretching the muscles, especially the muscles involving joints and thighs.
4. Players must have started sweating profusely to be considered warmed-up.
5. At least 12–15 minutes are required for this.
6. Bending and turning form the basis for the stretching of the ankles, knees, hips, shoulders, and neck. These exercises should first be done slowly and then the tempo gradually increased.
7. Slow running on the spot for a long period should be done first of all. Stretching exercises are done next and then running again (outside, if there is a place available) or running on the spot in the gymnasium followed by further stretching exercises, etc.

The following exercises serve as a guide:
1. Start with easy running on the spot, slowly at first, and then gradually faster, for at least 2 minutes.
2. (a) On toes with feet about 1 foot apart; turn heels.
   (b) With feet placed the same distance apart and toes turned slightly inwards, the ankles are bent to the outside so that the instep is lifted. The ankles are then bent to the inside.
3. (a) With feet flat on the ground and the same distance apart, the knees are rotated so that they come together when turned to the inside.
   (b) Do full knee bends and raise the body on toes when knees are stretched.
   (c) With feet widely spaced bend trunk forward, with hands placed on hips. Keep one leg stretched and bend the other leg until the seat is as close to the ground as possible, then stretch. Repeat in opposite direction.
4. (a) With feet widely spaced, bend trunk forward, with hands clasped behind head and elbows raised. Turn the trunk first to one side and then to the other, keeping the trunk straight throughout. The back is somewhat hollow and the head raised.
   (b) With feet widely spaced, clasp hands behind the neck. Bend sideways with trunk and move it forward, to the other side, round to the back and complete wide circles. Repeat several times in one direction and then in the other. Keep knees stretched and the feet firmly on the ground during the exercise.

(c) The same starting point: bend the straight trunk and hollow back slowly at intervals until it can go no further. Keep the legs straight. (This exercise must never be done quickly.)

5. (a) Front parallel standing. Describe circles with arms, first backwards and then forward and see to it that they are kept parallel throughout.
   (b) Stand with hands under chin and elbows raised in line with the shoulders. Swing the arms back as far as possible without lowering them or bending the trunk. Raise up on toes with every backward swing.
   (c) Standing a-straddle, with knees stretched, touch the left foot with the right hand while the left arm stretched upwards is swung back and the trunk and head turned in that direction, and vice versa. Do the exercise with a slight up-and-down pushing of the trunk between the swings.
6. Stand: roll the head in circles and to either side, keeping the shoulders rigid.
7. Stand and kick alternately with straight legs as high as possible, bending the leg not used in kicking as little as possible. Swing the opposite arm forward and try and kick the hand while it is lifted progressively higher.
8. Stand with hands on sides. Step far forward with one foot, bending the knee. Push slowly up and down on the leg while trying to get the seat as close to the ground as possible. Change legs and repeat. Keep the trunk up straight and the rear leg stretched. Change and repeat with the other knee.
9. Stand facing the bench with hands clasped behind the neck and with elbows raised. Place one foot on the bench and bend the straightened trunk slowly, pushing in between to get as far forward as possible. Keep the other leg perfectly straight. Change legs. (This exercise must never be done quickly.)
10. (a) Lie on your stomach with hands underneath the shoulders. Stretch and bend the arms and lift the legs alternately, straightening up with each flexing.
    (b) Lie on your stomach with hands outstretched. Lift straightened arms, trunk and flexed legs from ground, with the back as hollow as possible. Arms sideways and legs open, close and lower. Repeat.
11. (a) Lie on your back with hands clasped behind head. Do circular movements – and to either side – with the legs without their touching the ground.
    (b) Lie on your back, arms sideways, palms on floor. Raise stretched legs to perpendicular position. Lower stretched legs (feet together) sideways. Keep them rectangular to trunk, down to the ground, then slowly up to the other side.
    (c) Raise hips so that only the shoulders, the neck and the back of the head rest on the ground. Push hands on hips and bicycle-pedal.
    (d) Lie on your back, knees bent, feet apart and arms folded across chest.
    (e) Raise back, shoulders and hips. The stomach should be as high up as possible so that only the toes and back of the head act as supports.

Running on the spot
At approximately three-quarter speed. First normally, then lift legs up straight, then kick up backwards, then lift knees high and pump the arms – faster! Rest two to three minutes, lace up boots, take off track suit and go and play.

Chapter 6
Skill Building

AS PREVIOUSLY MENTIONED, skill building includes quite a variety of aspect. We repeat them briefly. First, acquiring technique involves taking a specific focal part from the entire action or movement and paying special attention to it so that it can be developed, and the muscles which execute the skill can be strengthened.

The focals are obviously executed by the muscles, and these muscles must satisfy certain demands. They must be strong enough for pushing, pushing-in-movement, and even for jumping and pushing-off (which is also part of the tackle). In addition, they must perform their tasks in top gear. Their kinetic time must be correct. They must react quickly.

But the muscles must also possess differentiated relaxation, for they work only to the extent they are made to work. This can be attained only by continual repetition. In other words, the voluntary action under control of the brain must become involuntary or automatic, so that the brain can be freed for satellitic actions, for summing-up, for judgments, etc.

The muscles must also be adaptable so that they can still perform in difficult conditions such as rain. To acquire all this, a variety of exercises is needed.

The question that now arises is whether we should teach the technique from the start, or whether boys should be given a chance to struggle with it themselves and acquire part of the technique in a hit-or-miss way.

According to the principles of academic or theoretical learning, everything must either be correctly learnt or acquired. Many also insist on this principle when it comes to Rugby skills. From my personal experience I find it advisable to give boys the opportunity of defining the skills for themselves, even if they do make mistakes. I say this for several reasons: if the boys have developed their own style and manner of executing the technique, it is easier to take what is wrong out of it. To iron out mistakes from the start is to eliminate mistakes altogether. The boy is still acquiring his own style of movement and he himself does not know why he selects a particular style. He must still develop a feeling for what is correct, and he is helped in this by certain centres in the joints and muscles. This is something he achieves through his own experience. Eliminate that which is wrong and the boy gets the feeling. This is something you will see on his face.

In the meantime he has acquired differentiated relaxation to some extent. He has also developed his reaction time, judgment, etc. and one does not have to start from the very beginning. For this reason we let the lower primary-school boys play with the skills and let the middle primary boys do the skill building exercises without acquiring particular techniques.

Principles of skill-building

A closer look at the skills will show that some of them cannot be performed without strength. These skills are measured and weighed against those of your opponent, and they must be better than his if you wish to play better than him and beat him in a match. Therefore you must be stronger than him in the skills in which strength is a feature, like pushing, pushing-in-motion, pushing-off, tackling, passing and kicking. Passing and kicking come into their own in the focal movements only as a result of repeated exercise. This means we assume that the strength which flows in passing and kicking will be obtained by other exercises.

In pushing, jumping and pushing-off the legs are involved. To put it differently: the entire movement is initiated by the foot, which is part of the leg. The leg, again, is dependent on the entire trunk, especially the back and the neck. For tackling, arm strength is needed, and the arms cannot be strong without the trunk. Thus the whole body must be strong, and this applies to both forwards and backs. But it means more. If the tempo of execution is the same, there is a similarity or connection between pushing, jumping and pushing-off. If the speed for exercising pushing, jumping and pushing-off is the same, exercises for any one of these will help the others. Jumping and pushing-off are always done quickly, supplementing each other. Slow pushing, however, has a detrimental effect on the other two skills. Consequently pushing should always be done as fast as the other two skills. All three should be done explosively.

The bending of the joints forms the basis of both physical and skill building exercises. The muscles must therefore be strong enough for the tasks they have to perform. If the muscles are strong they will also not be easily injured or damaged and will perform better against opponents.

In muscle exercises which involve straightening or partial straightening of the joints, an extra load is placed on the muscles. The more easily the muscles control this load, the more easily the skill will be mastered without it. If the load is bigger than that required in a game, the exercises will be worth while. In a scrum the legs, hips, back and neck are straightened against tremendous resistance. This should be borne in mind during exercises when a load is placed on muscles. If a load is used in a practice line-out, a player should jump higher without it. Another kind of load, however, is added during a match in the form of bumps and knocks. Provision for this should be made in exercises. In a ruck, opponents should be pushed out of the way in no uncertain manner. The load in doing these exercises should provide for this.

For the push-off exercises, a bigger load must be placed on the bent muscles than would be required in playing a match. A player should not look for ideal conditions but should practise push-offs in loose soil, in sand, or against a slope. Another kind of load consists of a player making himself heavier by carrying weights. Instead of carrying a ball, a load is carried – and what better load is there than a stone? Even space can act as a load. For example, a player will do more push-offs than required if his space is confined. Where he would normally do one he will do two.

A load can be placed on the muscles also for tackling where there is bending against resistance, which is the opposite to the other skills. The load added in tackling exercises must therefore strengthen the bending.

Exercises for strengthening muscles used in skills can be done with equipment especially designed for the purpose, which will add load to the muscles. If there is no apparatus available, exercises which will have a similar effect on the muscles are employed, and a load is thereby placed on the muscles. One way of doing this is to play someone in an unaccustomed position. For instance, a front-row forward pushes in the lock position. This will help the front-row forward to develop pushing power in his legs. If a lock is switched to the front row it will help him develop a strong neck and back. The loose-head prop sometimes packs down in the tight-head position so that both sections of his back are used simultaneously when pushing, instead of only one section. The tight-head prop can sometimes push on the loose-head where he will strengthen the right-hand side of his back and indirectly the left-hand side, which works in support of the right-hand side. The exchanging of positions must therefore be regarded as an indispensable exercise.

Another kind of loading is the transfer of work done by a specific foot to the other, or doing the work normally done by both feet with only one foot. Body positions are not changed, however. A loose-head prop can push by placing his inside foot forward, and a lock can alternately push with one foot forward. In jumping exercises a lock can jump off either foot.

The load placed on the muscles in handling is of a different nature, and involves adaptability and reaction time. It is achieved by catching the ball during practice at any speed and at any spot within reach. Another form of load is to cause the ball to spin excessively, to pass it out as fast as possible, or to use a smaller-sized or a wet ball.

As far as kicking is concerned we also have swinging-power and straightening of the knee joint. Whether it would help to kick a heavier ball is something we would not like to claim, because experience has taught us that if a player is accustomed to a heavier ball, he must check his strength when kicking a lighter ball because it is bound to "flutter". (This also holds good for passing.) Thus another kind of load for swinging-power should be found. Such a load should, to our mind, also aim at adaptability, as in the case of skill in passing, in which swinging-power also plays a part. Thus the run-up for whatever kick is taken should be shortened or lengthened, or the run up should be faster or slower than the speed accustomed to, and the balls should be kicked more quickly than usual.

To recapitulate with regard to loads:

Pushing: 1. Exchange of feet and using one leg instead of two.
2. Exchanging of scrum positions.
3. Greater pushing-power from the front. More opponents pushing than there are forwards on your side.
4. Weights (stones) on the necks or backs of the front-row forwards.

Jumping: 1. Exchange of feet.
2. Jumping with weights without using the arms.

Pushing-in-movement: 1. A heavier load to push away.
2. Quick repetitions of mauls and rucks.

Handling: 1. Time limits.
          2. Fast repetitions.
          3. Light and small ball, or wet ball.
Push-off: 1. Extra load on muscles.
          2. Rapid repetitions in small space.
          3. Push-off in loose soil or sand.
Tackling: 1. Rapid repetitions.
          2. Moving targets.
Kicking: 1. Shortening of run-up.
          2. Quick kicking.
          3. Repeated kicking, i.e. one kick after the other.

The full mobility of the muscles controlling the joints must be used in skill practices exactly as in physical exercises. For pushing in the front row the hips are not straightened, but if they can be completely straightened under a heavy load, they will be able to do the partial straightening better. In the line-out not only the legs are completely straightened but also the back, neck and arms. In the ruck the knees are mainly straightened while the hips are also straightened or sometimes kept in a partially-bent position. For the pass the elbows are straightened to make every use of the full swinging motion of the arms. There are players who cut short this movement and surprisingly they still deliver the goods, but we are not concerned with them because the result in this case counts more than the technique, and each player obviously has his own style or technique. For most of us, however, the straightening of the elbows is imperative when it comes to long passes. For the push-off, the straightening of the leg used for pushing off is essential, too – and, as is the case in jumping, the toes indicate correct execution. This means that the ankles also must be completely straightened. For tackling the opposite movement is required because the arms are in fact bent. For kicking the kicking leg is straightened entirely, and this takes place, in most kicks, after the ball has been struck. When the leg is straightened some players jerk the kicking leg back while others follow through. In both instances, however, the leg was completely straight and the task was completed.

Two further points should also be considered:
1. The "stepping out" foot is used by the scrum half to make provision for the full swinging movement of his arms. If his step is too short, his arm movements will be cut short and go up too soon. Therefore he should step out too far rather than not far enough. Should he make a dive pass, he creates a larger swinging zone for his arms than he would for a standing pass. The result is that he passes the ball harder and faster. In order to utilise the swinging zone to the full, the scrum half should not cut short or accelerate the dive without justification. Consequently he should propel himself away as far as possible with the push-off foot. In this way he has greater space for a full swinging movement of the arms.
2. The kicker must make the swinging movement of the kicking foot as wide as possible because greater power is accumulated this way. For this reason his last step is a "stretched step". If the step is too short, the kicking leg will go up too soon and the swinging power is less. It must be borne in mind

that if the field is wet the "stretched step" is not always possible, and as a result the walk-up actually becomes a run-up in order to shorten the final step.

To work out exercises for kicking and passing on the basis of a load, means, as stated previously, cutting short the swinging movements so that the swinging zone is short and the time for executing the task quickened. In this we deviate from the ideal, but at the same time we are doing something which often has to be done in a match. To do something quickly means that the full action is accelerated in a shorter zone. Consequently in passing and kicking we practise to cut short. This technique can also be usefully applied in exercises for push-off, in which the steps are shorter than for normal push-offs.

The cutting-short process, however, has no bearing on the satellitic movement of straightening for drawing an opponent before passing the ball. In fact, passing off one foot – the furthermost one – entails either not drawing the opponent by passing too soon, or sacrificing speed. Players must therefore learn to pass from either foot. This is an essential load for those not accustomed to it, the kind of load, like all loads, which becomes in fact an aid.

Exercises for skill building should be done in such a way that they serve a purpose. They should have transfer value, by assisting in the execution of the skill. For this reason they should be done as close as possible to the focal movements of the skills and should be similar, or contain more similar than dissimilar elements. If, for instance, I go in to tackle a tackling-bag, I should not make straight for it at all times, because in a match such a situation will occur less frequently than the so-called inside hip tackle. I should therefore come up to the tackling-bag from the side, or I should run straight up to it and then swerve to the inside.

These principles should always be borne in mind in skill building, and they have a place in the exercises we are going to give. Other special exercises or special equipment can be worked out.

The following is a series of exercises for each skill.

Schedule 1: Use of skill-building exercises

Positions	Lap 1	Lap 2	Lap 3	Lap 4	Lap 5	Lap 1	Lap 2	Lap 3 (*Specialisation*)
Lock forwards	Pushing	Push-in-movement, consolidation	Jumping	Hardening	Rucking	Tackling and breaking tackles	Handling	Line-out catching when wing throws ball in, or at apparatus
Props	Pushing	Push-in-movement, consolidation	Tackling and breaking tackles	Hardening	Rucking	Handling	Push-in-movement, consolidation (hooker)	Front-row: neck exercises with halter and yoke. Hooker: exercises for hooking.
Loose forwards	Pushing	Tackling and breaking tackles	Handling	Hardening	Rucking	Push-in-movement, consolidation	Jumping	Defend and attack with halves

Schedule 1: Use of skill-building exercises

Positions	Lap 1	Lap 2	Lap 3	Lap 4	Lap 5	Lap 1	Lap 2	Lap 3 (Specialisation)
Scrum halves	Tackling and breaking tackles	Handling	Push-off	Defensive kicks	Defensive kicks	Scrum half passes	Scrum half passes with fly half	Defend and attack with loose forwards
Fly halves and centres	Tackling and breaking tackles	Handling	Push-off	Short punts	Short punts	Fly half: drop kicks. Centres: push-off	Pass with scrum half	Fly half: Defend and attack with loose forwards
Wings	Tackling and breaking tackles	Handling	Push-off	Centre kicks	Centre kicks	Push-off	Throw-in (with wings)	Centres: Swerves, scissors, etc. Throw-in for line-out forwards
Full backs	Tackling and breaking tackles	Handling	Push-off	Kicks into touch	Kicks into touch	Handling of ground balls	Place kicks	Place kicks

EXERCISES TO ACQUIRE TECHNIQUE

Aim of lesson: To acquire the techniques of the seven skills, first in a natural way and later according to prescription. (Mainly for beginners.)

Pushing
1. *Aim:* To acquire the technique of pushing.
2. *Exercises*
   (a) *Players practise in pairs.* A player stands with his back to his partner and supports himself by propping one leg in front of the other, placing the weight on the foremost foot while leaning back. His partner takes up a position pushing against his thigh, and packs down against it. He straightens both legs explosively while lowering his seat. He does this with either shoulder and either foot. Partners exchange positions.
   (b) As soon as the technique has been perfected, the pusher intensifies his push by jumping after every shove with both feet forward to position himself for another shove, then straightening his legs, and getting into position for the next shove, etc.
3. *Mistakes*
   (a) Pushing is done too slowly.
   (b) The head is lowered instead of being raised.
   (c) The legs are straightened but not the hips.
   (d) One shoulder is lower than the other.
   (e) The arms fail to strengthen the contact with the partner's shoulder when pushing against him.

Jumping
1. *Aim:* To acquire the technique of jumping.
2. *Exercises*
   (a) Individual exercises. Feet slightly apart, the legs, hips, back and the

neck slightly bent and then straightened explosively while the arms are struck upwards.
(b) One foot in front of the other with the weight on the rearmost foot. Displace weight to the foremost foot and straighten the bent parts. Also jump from the other foot.
3. *Mistakes*
   (a) The entire body is not fully flexed and the chin is not lifted.
   (b) Flinging up the arms is begun by the elbows instead of by the hands.
   (c) The jumper looks down too soon to see where he is going to land.
   (d) The body tilts too far forward as the arms come down.

Pushing-in-movement
1. *Aim:* To acquire the technique of the pushing-in-movement.
2. *Exercises*
   (a) A player pushes with his shoulder against a partner's shoulder. The partner has his back turned. The player attempts to push him away by taking short steps while his partner resists.
   (b) The players are drawn up in two rows 10–15 yards apart. The players in the foremost row have their backs turned towards the second row. The teacher gives the signal to the rearmost row, whose members start practising the pushing-in-movement action against a partner in the front row. The teacher calls "Left, right, left, right, left, right" as the players approach their partners. When the players come up against their partners the teacher says "Stop". It does not signify that the boys have to stop, but only to push the better. The competition consists of determining how many boys are not pushed away and in comparing these numbers with those of the teams.
3. *Mistakes*
   (a) Players do not lift their heads high enough and as a result they topple forward should their partners give way.
   (b) The first two steps are stretched too far.
   (c) The checking movement is either too fast or too slow.

Handling
1. *Aim:* To acquire the technique of coping with (a) balls passed, (b) falling balls, (c) slanting balls and (d) scooped-up balls.
2. *Exercises*
   (a) Players – without using a ball – imitate the correct handling of the passed ball by taking the hypothetical ball from the right and then the left until the position of the hands is correct.
   (b) Next, passing is practised. The hands are held in the passing-out position so that the players can judge themselves if they have mastered the technique. The ball should be passed from the left or from the right and should be caught and passed in a single movement.
   (c) The boys are drawn up in rows or in a circle with their backs turned inwards. They pass the ball forward and back, pausing between stopping

and catching the ball. They pass first off the furthermost leg and then the nearest leg.

3. *Mistakes*
   (a) *Catching the ball:* (i) the players concertina and therefore keep the catching hand in the same position as the stopping hand instead of keeping it flat; (ii) the hands are too taut, with the result that the stopping hand cannot give. If the stopping hand is relaxed the fingers are slightly bent which helps cushion the ball; (iii) the ball is caught in front of the body instead of the hands going to the ball.
   (b) *Passing the ball:* (i) the elbow of the catching hand is bent while the elbow of the stopping hand is slightly stretched; (ii) the shoulder of the catching hand is not turned in the direction of the pass; (iii) the hands release the ball at different heights instead of just before they go upwards; (iv) the hands fly apart when the ball has been released or they are not parallel to each other, with the palms turned towards each other instead of turned upwards; (v) the ball is passed too hard instead of smoothly. The reason for this is that the swing rather than the focal points of the movement are used; (vi) passing from one foot, the furthermost foot.
   (c) *The high, dropping ball:* (i) the high, dropping ball is "caught" without a ball until the technique is correct. (ii) The coach shouts "There" and wherever he has pointed the players have to get underneath the hypothetical ball and take it. (iii) Players are drawn up in circles. A ball is in each circle and it is thrown up in turn so that the boys can catch it. To start with, the ball is thrown directly above the boy so that he need not move to take it.
   Mistakes: (i) Players do not get underneath the ball. Their judgment is at fault here; (ii) the hands do not go to meet the ball and the elbows are pressed into the sides; (iii) the hands are not flat and the elbows, as a result, are too far apart; (iv) the fall of the ball is not broken, or the arms bend faster than the trunk.
   (d) *Diagonal ball:* (i) Players catch a hypothetical ball. The coach's commands are: "On you", "In front of you" and "Behind you". At "On you" the players catch the ball from a standing position; at "In front" they take the ball sufficiently high to catch it against the body, and at "Behind" they make a high ball sufficiently low to catch against the body. (ii) The boys now draw up in two rows and throw balls to each other.
   Mistakes: (i) The hands are too late for catching; (ii) the stopping is unwieldy.
   (e) *Pick-up ball:* (i) A hypothetical ball is picked up. (ii) Each boy gets a chance to pick up a ball. If there is only one ball available, however, the boys form a single file and the ball is placed at the front of the row. The first boy walks towards the ball and as soon as he has picked it up he puts it down. In a later exercise he rolls it forward for the next player.
   Mistakes: (i) The player slackens his pace in order to wait for the ball to bounce to his liking; (ii) he fails to bend his knees sufficiently; (iii) he does not step past the ball, but tries to pick it up in front of his foremost foot; (iv) he snatches at a rolling ball instead of scooping it up.

Push-off
1. *Aim* To acquire the technique of the push-off.
2. *Exercises*
   (a) The players take a step forward and check themselves on their front foot in order to get a feeling of weight on the pad of the big toe.
   (b) The players walk – later they trot – and again check themselves on the front foot. When the balance has been restored, they lean with their bodies to the side they are going to make their push-off from. Then they transfer the weight to the other foot. As a rule the checking will be done by taking a small hop.
   (c) (i) A line is drawn where the push-off has to be done. Players approaching the line must fit their steps in so that the right foot comes down on it for the push-off. Judgment is essential and for this reason boys must first trot before they run. To make sure they push off at the correct moment, a person stands near the line to see that the player's weight does not go too far beyond the foremost foot before his push-off. (ii) Mark off the average steps taken in pushing off for the side-step and swerve. Once the boys can imitate the side-step and swerve they should try and pass or emulate the distance indicated by the marks representing the push-off.
3. *Mistakes:*
   (a) The push-off takes place too soon or too late.
   (b) The body is upright instead of being bent forward.
   (c) There is too much concentration on the "sideways" aspects of the push-off at the expense of the "forward" aspect.

Tackling
1. *Aim:* To acquire the technique of tackling.
2. *Exercises:* The tacklers are lined up in a row a yard apart. Their targets are lined up 10 yards in front of them with their backs turned. The teacher gives the command – to shorten the steps and get the body erect – of "left, right, left, right, left, right," etc. The tacklers advance in this manner and then grab the players in front of them, lifting them up and walking off with them.
3. *Mistakes:*
   (a) The eyes blink at making contact.
   (b) The opponent is not clasped tightly enough against the body.
   (c) Players stoop too low.

Kicking
1. *Aim:* To acquire the technique of kicking.
2. *Exercises:* Each player is given the opportunity to apply the holds for all the kicks; *and*, while taking a forward step, dropping the ball without causing it to wobble.
3. *Mistakes:*
   (a) The ball wobbles.
   (b) The ball is released too close to the body.

(c) The ball, when dropped on to the foot, does not have the same shape given to it by the hands.
(d) The eyes follow the ball too soon.
(e) The ball is sliced too much.
(f) Kicking is too hard.
(g) The ball is struck too high.

ADVANCED TECHNICAL EXERCISES

Pushing

Front rows versus front rows

Three players push against another three as would front-row forwards. One of the front-row forwards straightens only one leg while the opponents offer just enough resistance not to make it too easy for them. Should the opponents push too hard the shovers will have to use both feet and the purpose of the exercise will be lost. They exchange positions.

Locks against locks

Two players push against two others as would locks. One pair pack lower and push with both legs.

Front row against front row plus locks
1. Two players in the front row, supported by one lock, i.e. three players on each side, get sufficient chances for straightening the pushing legs.
2. Three players in the front row supported by 2 locks, i.e. 5 players on either side get the opportunity of straightening their pushing legs.

Loading
1. One player pushes against 2. They try to push him away while he tries to prevent this while also trying to separate his opponents by tossing and working his head about in between them, etc. Two rows of players can compete in this way.
2. Three players push against 3 – 2 props and 1 lock on either side.
3. Eight – the entire pack – against 5, i.e. a front row and 2 locks.
4. Ten against 8. The 10 pack down in a 3–4–3 formation.
   To make these exercises interesting, lines are drawn behind the "packs". The line is drawn progressively closer until it is eventually only a short distance from the feet of the rearmost player in the "scrum".
5. Eight push against 8. The forwards of one of the packs change position after every shove until every player has pushed in every position. The forwards in the other pack do not push too hard and offer only light resistance. Otherwise, players unaccustomed to the front-row position may be injured. It is advisable to follow a fixed pattern when exchanging the position of the players. For instance, the players change round to the left: the tight-head forward becomes the hooker, the hooker becomes the loose-head prop, the loose-head prop becomes the loose-head flanker, the loose-head flanker becomes the number eight, etc.

6. The forwards switch their pushing legs, or those who push with both legs alternate with one leg. The props and the hooker, for instance, switch their pushing legs and the remaining forwards push with their left legs. The team with the exchange players push against the "normal" pack.
7. Not only does one of the packs exchange positions but the players switch legs as well.
8. If available, pushing apparatus should be used for dynamic pushing. The apparatus should be moved and be kept moving. (See scrummage sledge p. 208.)

Jumping (and consolidation)
1. (a) Technique exercises are now done with a rocking movement. The body weight is taken on the heels, rolled to the ball of the feet and the body flung off the ground by stretching the knees.
   (b) The short step-hop-jump is practised, starting off from either foot.
   (c) Standing jumps are made with either leg extended.
2. Jumps – as in (a), (b) and (c) – are made but (i) forward jumping, (ii) upright jumping, (iii) sideways and (iv) while turning.

Exercises for jumping-power and consolidation
Loading
1. Giant strides are taken to see who can take the fewest paces over a given distance. (Be careful of slipping.)
2. The same as above but each stride is checked by the landing foot.
3. This time a short hop is taken by the checking foot.
4. Jumping off both feet to see who can cover a set distance in the fewest jumps.
5. Boys of the same height stand under a crossbar and see if they can strike off it with their foreheads. They should be spaced far enough apart to strike upwards with their hands, their arms coming up on either side of the crossbar. They jump first from the left foot and then from the right foot; later taking off from both feet and chalking up the winning foot/feet. Advanced boys or players do these exercises as individuals and compete against themselves. They can raise the crossbar considerably higher and attempt to dislodge it with both hands. This requires facilities for replacing the crossbar every time it is dislodged.
6. Three players arrange themselves as a "line-out" against one opponent who tries to disrupt them. The middle boy of the 3 is the jumper. He throws the ball above him and the moment he touches it in his leap, the opponent tries to pull him through to his side of the line-out, an action which his partners must prevent by correctly packing around him.

Pushing-in movement
1. The players stand in double-file formation facing in the same direction. At a given signal the players in the rear row run, as fast as possible, checking before lowering themselves and pushing the players of the front row on the move. The front-row players offer resistance and keep their backs straight – with heads raised – in order not to be pushed over. Before impact, the players

in the front row start moving slowly forward and the "pushers", on checking, adjust their speed accordingly.
2. One versus 2. A boy – the buffer – bends down, head lifted and with one foot in front of the other. This will brace him for the "attack" from two boys who are some distance away. At a given signal they rush at the player, pack down on either side of him and try and push him away. The player must attempt to remain standing. The two attackers must be taught not to run full tilt into the opponent – they might be injured this way – but they must in fact slacken their speed as they bend to pack around him. Vary the exercise by allowing the player to move about before he receives the impact.
3. Three versus 4 or 5. The same principle as above is applied, but now 4 or 5 players bear down on the buffer, who this time has two partners who assist him by packing down on either side of him. While the boys are learning this form of competition, the 2 partners should be so placed as to ensure they get first to their team-mate. Later on, the boys all stand in a line and it becomes a race as to who gets to the buffer first. Vary by allowing the buffer to move about.
4. As above but 3 buffers stand over a ball and the others have to push away without stepping on the ball or toppling over.
5. All the players line up in a row with a ball placed about 15 yards in front of them. They all converge upon the ball and the first player there picks it up and turns while 2 players pack down round him with the others joining in to push. The player with the ball releases it as soon as the movement starts forward.

Loading
1. (a) Two players are opposed and race in different directions towards a loose ball. The first player there picks up the ball and turns. The other player gets hold of him and tries to turn him back.
   (b) Should they arrive simultaneously at the ball they "fight it out" to step across the ball and to maintain that position.
2. Three compete against 3 and the winners of the ball either try to push themselves through the others (ruck) or they try to push the other 3 away (maul).
3. The groups are increased and divided into 2 sections with a ball between them. Three members of each team stand about 5 yards ahead of their team-mates and about 10 yards from the ball. The 3 foremost members of each team compete to pick up the ball first or to step across it. Their team-mates help them to hang on to the advantage gained.

Handling
Passed balls
1. Players pass the ball to one another while standing in a circle and looking outwards. There is a pause between catching and passing to ensure that catching is done correctly. The ball is passed to either side, first 6 times to the left and then to the right. See to it that when the ball is passed to the left

that the right foot is placed in front 3 times and 3 times behind. The same applies when the ball is passed to the right.
2. The same as above but one hand is used to catch the ball. The other hand comes into action only to make the pass.
3. The circle moves in one direction, and without the players breaking up their formation or leaving their positions, some of them run forward, take sideways jumps or run back. This will teach them to handle under difficult circumstances.
4. The players turn inwards. They move back to give long passes and forward to give short passes.
5. The players run in rows consisting of 3 or 4 players and pass the ball to one another. They begin by trotting, and as their handling improves increase their speed until they are running flat out.

Passes for scrum halves
1. (a) Players take up the positions of a back-line, standing obliquely. Each player, however, takes on the function of a scrum half. The first player gives a standing pass to the player next in line. He places the ball on the ground and passes it to the third player . . . and so the ball is passed down the line. The last player who catches the ball places it on the ground, and starts the movement again. In the meantime, the players have naturally fallen back so there can be no forward passes. More than one ball can be used.
  (b) If a player is unable to handle, he not only puts the ball down, but rolls it a short distance, first to his passing side, then forward, then backwards, and finally in the opposite direction of his pass so that he has to turn round in order to pass.
2. Same as above, but the ball is dive-passed.

Throwing in the ball at a line-out
1. Two wings stand on either side of the goalposts, and try and hit one of the uprights with the ball. They must therefore learn to throw straight – how high or how low they throw does not matter. If they are satisfied that they can throw accurately from any distance, they then concentrate on throwing at different heights, which can be marked on the upright. Not only does this exercise involve target competition but it can also include competition between the two players. The crossbar or netball posts can be used as well.
2. Four players – 2 line-out forwards, a wing and a scrum half – can practise among themselves. The wing throws the ball for the forward who passes to the scrum half, who relays it back to the wing.

The high, dropping ball
The players are drawn up in circles. A ball is thrown up in turn for the players in each circle to catch.

Slanting ball
The players are divided into groups of 4 or 5, approximately 10 yards apart.

Working together they throw the ball to and fro over their heads.

Pick-up balls
Several balls are placed in a large circle. As soon as one player has run in and picked up, he puts the ball down for the next player.

Loaded exercises for handling
Passing
1. The players space themselves in a circle. The ball is deliberately passed badly between them – high and low, soft and hard balls. If it is a soft pass, the players must reach to get it.
2. The players pass as above but on the run.
3. This time 2 balls are used, one chasing the other. The players – facing outwards – start the exercise standing still but later pass on the run.
4. The players face inwards. One or 2 players inside the circle intercept the ball. Selling dummies is permissible. If a player intercepts the ball, he takes the place of the player who has passed the ball. Ensure that all players get a turn inside the circle even though their passes may not have been intercepted.
5. Three or 4 players run in a line with the ball. The ball is passed from no. 1 to no. 4 down the line. No. 1, following up his pass, takes the return on the outside of no. 4. The ball then goes back to no. 2 who passes and follows up in the same way.

Variation: the same as above, but the player who follows up from behind plays scrum half and places the ball on the ground when he receives it. He then passes it off the ground.

6. *Bouncing ball passing:* Three or 4 players run and pass the ball to one another, but on receiving the ball each player bounces it on the ground in front of him and catches it again.
7. One of the players above is the leader and takes up a position behind the others. From there he calls out the name of a player who has to pass the ball to him. He shifts his position continuously so that the others do not know where he is.
8. The players stand in single file. No. 1 runs as fast as he can away from no. 2. No. 1 holds the ball with one hand behind his back ready for no. 2 to take. As soon as no. 2 has the ball he runs past no. 1 to give the same pass to no. 3, etc.

Variation: Instead of holding the ball behind the back, the player flips the ball up or turns and gives a short pass.

9. The players line up behind each other. No. 1 runs and falls with the ball, but turns in the fall to allow no. 2 to get hold of it. In this way the players move down the length of the field so that every player can fall, turn, and pass.
10. A number of players are widely spaced in single-file formation along the twenty-five, approximately 8–10 yards from the angle which the line forms with the touchline. The foremost player has a ball. At a given signal he runs as fast as he can and when he comes to the corner, he pulls up sharply,

turns round and passes the ball to no. 2, who repeats what no. 1 has done. Every player gets a chance, and when he has passed the ball he falls in at the back of the line. Players must pass off either foot.

11. The players jog in rows. The ball is passed – soft, hard, high, low – in front of and at the receiver, who has to adapt himself to taking a hard ball (swing-out) or a soft ball (swing-in). The pace is increased until it can be done at top speed.

12. *Racing:* Any race for which handling forms the basis can be used to correspond with match conditions. Two teams, for instance, are divided into 2 sections with one section on the half-way line and the other on the twenty-five. The section on the half-way line has the ball. At a given signal they sprint – passing the ball at the same time – to their team-mates on the twenty-five. The ball is then given to this section and they have to continue the race back to the half-way line. The section to arrive there first wins. If a player runs more than 2 yards without passing, his team is disqualified.

13. *Ten passes:* The players are divided into 2 teams and they take up positions anywhere on the field. One of the players throws the ball up in the air and the player who gets hold of it starts the game by passing to one of his team-mates in an attempt to chalk up 10 unbroken passes in order to score 1 point. The opposing team naturally tries to gain possession of the ball and give 10 passes. When the ball is dropped or intercepted the counting starts afresh. Players should be encouraged to run about, but it could be advisable to confine the playing area.

14. *Simplified netball:* For this a Rugby ball and the area between the goal-line and the twenty-five yard line are required. Play takes place across the field. The size of the team is determined by the size of the field, but for 2 full-strength Rugby sides the area suggested is sufficient. The positioning of team pairs can be haphazard, but it is advisable to have a fixed arrangement.

After being thrown up between 2 players in the centre, the ball is passed in any manner from team-mate to team-mate until it reaches the goal-thrower, who has to pass it into the hands of his team-mate behind the goal-line to score a goal. Only the goal scorer and goal defender may move about behind the line. The goal scorer may not knock the ball on.

If the ball is held by 2 players at the same time, the referee restarts play by bouncing the ball between them. If the ball goes out of play it is thrown in in any fashion. For an infringement a free pass is awarded.

Scrum half pass

1. Players line out obliquely in back-line formation, each player taking on the role of a scrum half. (See acquiring of technique.) In this exercise, however, there are 2 lines of players, one line behind the other. The players make a race of passing – whether it be standing passes or dive-passes – the ball through the line.

2. The wing throws the ball to a line-out forward who is covered by another forward. From there the scrum half feeds the fly half, who gives a long pass to the wing. The fly half can also put in a short punt for the forwards who

gather the ball, turn and feed the scrum half. He once more passes to his fly half.

Throw-in at line-outs and scrum half passes
In order to give several players the opportunity of playing scrum half and wing, the following "game" can be practised: the wing throws the ball to a forward who feeds the scrum half who, in turn, passes to the fly half. The fly half then runs to the wing position to throw in the ball while the wing becomes the forward, the forward becomes the scrum half and the scrum half becomes the fly half etc. The same method can be followed with the forward forming a scrum instead of a line-out.

Pick-up ball
1. The same as for the improvement of technique, but when the player has picked the ball up and put it down for the player following, he makes sure that he puts it with one hand placed on the middle of it.
2. Two players – A and B – stand in front of a line of players. The ball is rolled by A to the first player in the line, who picks it up and passes immediately to B. He rolls the ball across to A, who rolls it to the next player in the line. B can even kick the ball along the ground – preferably with the inside of the foot – to get the ball back to A. After a player has picked up and passed the ball, he falls in at the back of the line. Exchange A and B with players in the line and let these players also take up their position on the left-hand side of the "roller".
3. *Loading. Relays:* Players are drawn up in single file on the twenty-five yard line. At a given signal each player rolls a ball in front of him, gathers it, comes upright and then rolls the ball ahead again to pick up. The distance between the twenty-five yard line and the half-way line is 30 yards and players are allowed 3 yards for gathering the ball, which means they have to pick the ball up 10 times.
4. *Ground handball:* Two teams – consisting of either all backs or all forwards – play across the field between the twenty-five and the half-way line. The aim is to score goals by striking the ball with the open hand – not scooping it up – and putting it across the touchlines between twenty-five and half-way. In other words, the function of the game is to dribble the ball with the hands. A player may pick up and pass the ball but the player taking the pass must immediately place the ball on the ground and start dribbling it. If the ball is tied up, play is restarted by throwing the ball in the air. If it goes out of play, it is put in again by striking it with the hand off the ground. A free strike is awarded for any infringement.

High, dropping ball
1. Six to 8 players take part. One of the players has a ball and the other players are all numbered. The player with the ball throws it as high and as straight as possible in the air. At the same time he calls out the number of one of the players, who has to catch the ball and throw it in the air for another player to catch. All players must be close to the player catching the ball so that

they have to run out in any direction to catch the ball when it is their turn. This makes the game more lively.
2. The same as 1 but the ball is kicked into the air. The kickers hold the ball by its ends to make the kick more accurate.
3. *Chasing:* Two full-strength teams take up position on either side of the half-way line, closing all the gaps. The team winning the toss kicks off – not a place or drop kick – from their 10-yard line. The aim is to chase the ball across the opponents' dead-ball line, in which case a goal is scored. The kicking should be fast and accurate. If a player knocks on, he must retreat 5 yards before he can kick. If the ball touches the ground before a player gathers it, he must also retreat 5 yards. If a ball is kicked into touch, the other team is awarded a kick 10 yards out from where the ball has gone into touch. The side scoring most goals in a time stipulated is the winner.

Variations: (a) A drop goal is counted as a goal and the game is restarted on the 10-yard line. (b) Specify the kind of kick, whether it is to be to the left or to the right.

Oblique ball
1. The players are drawn up in 2 rows facing each other and the aim is to roll or throw the ball through between the players in one of the rows. If they succeed, the team scores 3 points. A knock-on counts as 1 point against. All kinds of throws – under-arm, overhead, and torpedo – can be used.
2. If the players have acquired the skill of kicking, grubbers, punts and low touch kicks are used.

Push-off
1. The players run in file about 3 yards apart from each other around the perimeter of the field and practise the push-off to one side of the touchline and back. Players can then see how far they can push off and with which leg they can do it best. The exercise should also be done with the dummy, with the full swerve and with the double side-step. The corners of the field can also serve as "opponents" to be beaten.
2. Use flags or markers to represent opponents. The players are drawn up in 2 rows so that push-offs can be practised with the left and right foot alternately. *First step:* The distance between the rows and the distance between them and the flags must be made to suit the players. *Second step:* The positioning of the flags is arranged so as not to suit the players. The rows, which need not be straight, are brought close to each other. *Third step:* Make use of the double push-off with regard to side-stepping, swerving and the dummy. This can be done by tagging the markers with notices, indicating whether a side-step, swerve, etc. is to be done.

A maze constructed of latticework or several markers is placed in the ground in a haphazard fashion through which players must weave.
3. The players form up in two lines and, in this formation, run towards each other. When they start running the teacher shouts out: "Side-step", "Swerve", or "Dummy", followed by "Left" or "Right". This means that every player makes a push-off to the left or to the right. The players will not collide but

by way of precaution this exercise should be done while jogging. If all 3 kinds of push-off can be done satisfactorily, the gaps between them are narrowed so that the boys can just manage to get through.
4. One player leads out doing push-offs while the others follow, imitating him. The leader should run about 10 yards ahead of them while they follow in pairs about 5 yards apart. If he slackens speed, pulls up suddenly, swerves, side steps or sells a dummy, they follow suit.
5. Players are drawn up in 2 rows. Two players side-step or swerve through the players in the lines and fall in at the rear. As soon as they have passed the first player in the line he goes forward to do his turn of side-stepping and swerving.

Loading: The players in the line walk forward while their 2 team-mates are side stepping and swerving between them. Once the players are well versed in the exercise the players in the line lift their arms halfway and then in line with their shoulders.

Tackling
1. The players are divided into 3 rows standing 3–5 yards apart facing one another. Each player in one row has a ball and they walk towards the opponents. The other row advances at a jog. The attackers, those with the ball, take a step to the left or right (as previously arranged) and at that moment are taken in standing tackles.
2. Same as above, but the defenders also try to rob them of the ball.
3. Same as above, but now both rows run slowly towards each other.
4. Same as above, but attackers turn their bodies to avoid the danger of injury.
5. Make use of the tackle apparatus, which is absolutely indispensable for any school or club. (See p. 215.)
6. *Mistakes in using the apparatus:*
   (a) The tackler varies his steps in order to use a specific foot for the push-off.
   (b) He takes off from both feet.
   (c) He lowers his head and consequently humps his back.
   (d) He closes his eyes or blinks.
   (e) His arms do not close like a spring-trap.

Loading: (Attack and Defence)
1. One player is positioned on the goal-line, another on the twenty-five, one on the 10-yard line, one on the half-way line, another on the next 10-yard line, one on the other twenty-five, and another on the other goal-line. The attacker starts running from the dead-ball line with a ball tucked under his arm. He tries to beat the first defender who, whether successful or not, moves to the dead-ball line while the rest of the players move forward a position. The original attacker moves down the field, tackled in turn by the other players, then takes up a position as the last defender. The first defender then becomes attacker, and so on. Four of these lines can be used at once, 2 on the touch-lines and 2 between them.
2. *Tackle breaking and tackling:* The players are drawn up in 2 rows 15 yards apart with the players at least 10 yards apart. Every player in one row has a ball and he tries to run through the player in front of him. The defender may

move forward or backwards. The attacker tries to keep the ball alive in the tackle, and the defender tries to smother him, ball and all.
3. *"Churning":* One team is drawn up in single file with the foremost player holding the ball. Their opponents are drawn up in front of them in a row with 5 yards between each player. No. 1 of the team with the ball runs into no. 1 of the opposing side, holding the ball when checked at the ready for his no. 2. No. 2 runs into the opponents' no. 2 and when checked, he holds the ball for no. 3 to try and beat his opponent. After checking an attacker, a defender goes to his team-mates' assistance. If an attacker beats a defender, the next defender has to take him on.
4. One team tries to "churn" its way through the other team. Not only do the defenders check them, but they must try to rob them of possession and start churning away themselves.

Kicking
Touch kick: The players are drawn up in rows facing each other and kick the ball to one another.
Grubber kick or short punt: The kicker picks up the ball on the touchline and kicks a grubber or a short punt. He pursues his kick and tries to catch the ball before it crosses the 5-yard line. He then turns and kicks from the 5-yard line back towards the touchline, trying to catch the ball before it crosses the line.
Place kicks and drop kicks
1. Players work in pairs, one in front of the posts and the other behind, kicking either place kicks or drop kicks to each other.
2. Several balls are placed ready on the twenty-five and in front of the posts for the kicker to place kick at goal. He kicks the balls as fast as he can. Players behind the goalposts catch the balls and place them either on or behind the dead-ball line. For drop kicks the balls can be passed in rapid succession to the kicker.

Cross or centre kicks. Pairs: Two players start on the goal-line – one from the posts and the other from the corner flag. They run the length of the field cross kicking to each other. They vary the distance between them for longer kicks

Loading: touch kicking
1. The players form a big, widely spaced circle and kick the ball to one another. The catcher turns his back to the others and kicks "round-the-corner" as he would when kicking defensively. Both feet are used.
2. In pairs, using the touchline, to the left and to the right.
3. *Groups:* As many balls as possible are used and are placed in a row on the twenty-five approximately 15 yards from touch. A kicker must pick them up, one after the other and kick, as fast as he can, in the direction of the opposite twenty-five. There players catch the balls and place them on their twenty-five for the next kicker.

Instead of the kicker picking up the balls, they are passed to him in rapid succession, first to suit him and then not to suit him, as this will improve his handling ability. Later, the kicker must run to pick up the balls so that he can acquire the habit of retarding his speed sufficiently before kicking. The balls can also be passed over his head, so that he must turn and catch it before kicking.

Short punt or grubber kick: Two players, each with a ball, run towards each other and when they are close they kick a short punt or a grubber which they field themselves. Care must be taken that they do not collide and they must agree beforehand that one of them will run on the outside and the other on the inside of his partner after the kick. Both feet are used.

EXERCISES WITHOUT EQUIPMENT

Scrummaging exercises
1. Five tight forwards push against 8 (heave followed by pushing away).
2. Eight push against 10 who are in a 3–4–3 formation.
3. (a) One pack pushes against another and after every scrum the positions in both packs are changed.
   (b) One pack pushes against another and only one pack exchanges position. The exchange takes place to the left, e.g. loose-head prop becomes loose-head flanker, loose-head flanker becomes number eight, etc.
4. Two packs push against each other, one using the "wrong" feet. For instance, all forwards push off their left feet and then with their right feet.
5. Two packs push with flat feet. This way their seats will be higher than usual. Both packs push by pulling their hips down and lifting their heads.
6. Two packs push against each other and the 2 flankers try to pull the 2 locks apart.
7. Two packs push against each other and the 2 props try to swing out.
8. Two packs push against each other and the props of one of the packs push inwards.
9. Two packs push against each other while the hookers hang on to the props.
10. Two packs push against each other and one pack straightens all pushing legs.
11. *Using 3 packs:* Each pack has a specific place on the field; for instance, one in the corner of the twenty-five yard line and the touchline, the second on the opposite side of the field at the corner of the half-way line and the touchline, and the third on the same side as the first pack in the corner of the other twenty-five and touchline.

    The first and second packs pack down in no. 1's position. At the whistle they break up and run to the no. 2's position and pack down again.

    At the whistle no. 1 returns to its position while no. 2 runs to where no. 3 is positioned to pack down another scrum. At the whistle no. 2 returns to its position and no. 3 forms a scrum against no. 1, after which the packs return to their original positions and the cycle is started again.
12. *Using 4 packs:* Each pack is again allocated a position on the field. no. 1 runs first to no. 2 and a scrum is formed, then to no. 3 and finally to no. 4. No. 2 then starts its round, and on completion no. 3 sets off. To speed the exercise up, no. 2 can start its round as soon as no. 1 has completed scrummaging against no. 3, etc.

Line-out exercises
Individual jumping exercises: Players wear heavy boots or jump with weights tied to their bodies. Heavy belts or even lead jackets can be worn. The purpose is to place a load on the muscles used for jumping. Players should also have a jumping target which can be adjusted. They can, for instance, use high-jumping equipment as used for track and field athletics, or the crossbar of a Rugby post. It should be remembered that the legs should be used alternately so that each leg is strengthened. Players must jump as they would in a line-out, i.e. take, at the most, one short step and not two or three. Sometimes they must also jump off both feet, applying only the rocking movement before the jump.

Combined practice (for consolidation): Two packs work against each other, one of them trying to catch the ball while the other tries to prevent all their attempts at catching and consolidation. This exercise is actually part of the rounding off of skills, but because it is such an important aspect of the game it can never be done enough.

Rucking exercises
Attacking rucks: Balls are strung out in a line in front of a pack positioned on the goal-line. One of the balls lies on the twenty-five, one on the half-way, one on the other twenty-five, and one on the other goal-line. At the whistle the forwards run to the first ball and as soon as it has been worked clear, they go on to the next ball.

Defensive rucks: As above, but defensive rucks are practised.

Loading: The balls are arranged differently this time. The first is in the corner of the twenty-five and the touchline; the second on the opposite side of the field, on the half-way line; the third on the other side on the twenty-five; and the fourth ball is on the opposite side of the field in the corner of the goal-line and touchline.

Neutral rucks: Two balls are used and they are placed on a line some distance apart. Rucks take place on the line or a short distance in front of or behind it. The forwards run to and fro for the exercise.

Mauls: The same exercise as above, but the ball is picked up by the player first to it.

Exercises for handling, pushing-off, tackling and kicking: See exercises under loading for acquiring technique.

Exercises with equipment
Skill building can be attained by using equipment. This has the following benefits:
(a) Players need not have a partner, but may use the apparatus as a partner or opponent.
(b) The player can repeat exercises more readily than he ever would in a practice match.
(c) If a player is weak in a certain skill, he can practise it whenever he has time.
(d) Apparatus always offers sound variations on usual practice methods.

(e) If the apparatus serves its purpose, it will offer more strenuous exercises than the game itself.
(f) The player can gauge his own achievement, even if it is only to count how many times he can perform a skill.
(g) The player can work against the clock more easily.
(h) If a club does not have many members, the players can still do all the exercises in the world to prepare themselves for their matches.
(i) The equipment puts a load on the muscles which can be controlled according to a player's strength.

EXERCISES WITH EQUIPMENT AND INDIVIDUAL EXERCISES

Two points are vital in considering these exercises:
1. Exercises which are complementary to the usual programme must be provided.
2. Exercises must be worked out according to the players' positions.

Forwards
They can never possess too much strength.
(a) *Combined*
    (i) Dragging a beam, first with the legs straight and backs humped and then with the back straight but the legs bent.
    (ii) Pushing the scrum sledge. (p. 208)
    (iii) First heave at heaving apparatus. (p. 209)
(b) *Separate*

Locks
(a) Jumping against rubber tyres between two posts.
(b) Hitting a hanging tennis ball with the head.
(c) Grabbing a hanging ball by jumping up and jerking it downwards – apparatus. (p. 211 & p. 212)
(d) A wing throws in balls for one of the locks.
(e) A wing throws in for a lock opposed by two other locks.

Props
(a) Picking up beams or stones by means of halters.
(b) Two props push and hook against each other. Scrum halves and fly halves join them.

Hookers
Push and hook with front-row.

Loose forwards
Working in teams of 3 against one another, they take up their positions as they would for a scrummage. A ball is placed near one of the teams. At a given signal the loose trio races to the ball to gather it and to get it free by rolling it out.

Binding (linking), pushing and depriving the possessor of the ball are part of the competition.

Backs
Combined
(a) Skipping with the jumping foot and moving it forwards, backwards and to either side.
(b) (i) Picking up balls (select the fastest and most difficult from the exercises).
(ii) Running in 3s and 4s and passing badly, e.g. too low, too high, to the hip, to the shoulder, too hard, twisting balls.
(iii) One of the players is bombarded with all kinds of passes thrown by the others, who are drawn up in a semicircle around him. The players and the catcher run on the spot during the game. The semicircle starts at the catcher's side so that he can catch the balls on his shoulder and on his hips. the length of the passes is varied, but should never be made easy for him. The catcher returns the ball to the player who has passed. As soon as the ball leaves the catcher's hand, the next player passes. The passes must come from every side, and for this the players, who each have a ball, agree among themselves whose turn it is to pass. To make the exercise more effective, the catcher has to stop the ball with one hand before catching it, except when the balls are aimed at his middle, his shoulder and hips. These cannot be caught unless both hands are used.
(c) Push-off exercises coupled with defence.

Scrum halves
(a) Players work in pairs passing through an opening in a net made specially for the purpose. The nets are moved further away for longer passes and the scrum halves see how many passes per minute they can give.
(b) Putting the ball in between front rows.

Scrum halves and fly halves
Practise passing – as from scrums, line-outs and rucks – to a fly half who takes the ball while in a stationary position. The fly half is opposed by his opposite number as he would be in a match.

Fly halves and centres
They work together and against one another, taking up their positions as they would at a scrum or line-out. Each has a ball and practises short punts and grubber kicks.

Centres
Practise shift passes, short passes, scissors and dummy scissors in pairs, plus any tactical movement with which they are concerned.

Wings
(a) Practise throwing in at the throw-in equipment.
(b) Throwing balls in for lock-forwards.

Full backs
A player in front of the posts and another behind, practise place kicks and drop kicks. By using the touchline they practise kicking for touch, to the left and to the right.

Forwards and backs
Exercises for shortening the steps before getting to the scene of action, which should be the main aim of every player. There are 3 steps to be taken: getting there, preparing yourself, and acting. The first involves speed, the second step-variation – decreasing or shortening the steps – and the third either tackling, climbing in at a ruck, picking up the ball, taking off etc.
(a) The players are lined up on the twenty-five, 5 yards apart from each other. On the half-way line, in front of each player, is a ball. The players sprint beyond the 10-yard line and then shorten their steps as much as possible without losing speed. When they have adjusted themselves correctly they shoot forward and gather the ball. This exercise is repeated a few times.
(b) The same sprint on the same part of the field, but when the players cross the 10-yard line they shorten their steps and look around before taking off.
(c) Two rows of players form up in pairs and sprint towards each other, one row as defenders, the other as attackers. The attackers try to pass their opponents on the same side. The defenders bear down on their opposites, adjust themselves and tackle. Attackers and defenders exchange positions and then the opposite side of the defenders is tested.

The scrum sledge
The scrum sledge is used to develop strength for pushing in a scrum and to give forwards the opportunity of pushing in different positions.
 The best use of the sledge is as follows: a pack starts off with a heave, and then tries, by taking short steps, to push the sledge away. As the sledge can be pushed to and fro, it can be used in a small space. It can also be taken to the field when a full team is practising. The

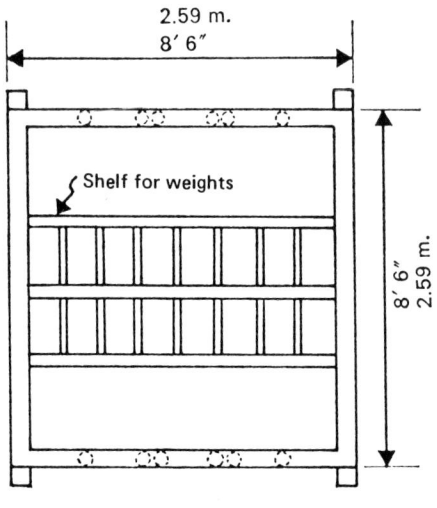

TOP VIEW

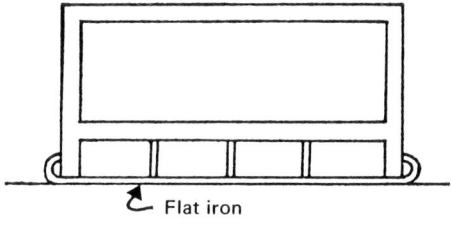

SIDE VIEW

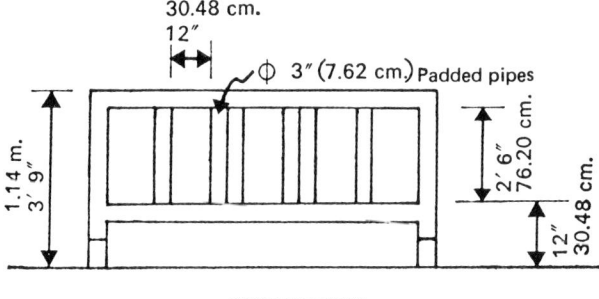

FRONT VIEW

SCRUM SLEDGE

forwards pack down against the sledge, the ball is put in and it is hooked and either passed out immediately or after the sledge has been pushed some distance. The scrum half passes the ball to his three-quarters and the forwards take part in the movement. Rucks or mauls can be brought in if players place the ball on the ground, or if they keep it and turn their backs. At the conclusion of each movement the forwards return to the sledge.

Weight: The metal apparatus used by us weighs 930 lb (421 kg). Cement blocks are placed on the platform to increase the weight. The blocks weigh 390 lb (176 kg) each, and we use 6 of them for the first and second teams. Obviously other weights such as stones, beams, or sandbags can also be used.

The heaving apparatus

This equipment is used with or without the ball, to perfect the heave given by a pack of forwards. The heave is measured with a line marked off in inches along the topmost pipe. Because it is square, the apparatus can be lifted out of its pipes and the direction for heaving changed, if the soil has been churned up. The springs can be increased or decreased to accommodate the strength of the pack.

The springs used are like those used in the wings of a windmill. The old type of spring – which, by the way, are hard to come by – are longer and wider than the modern variety. The length of the springs determines the width of that part of the apparatus against which the forwards push.

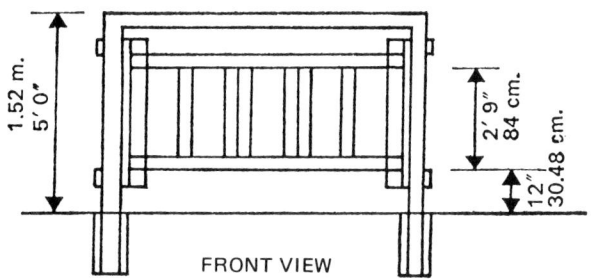

FRONT VIEW

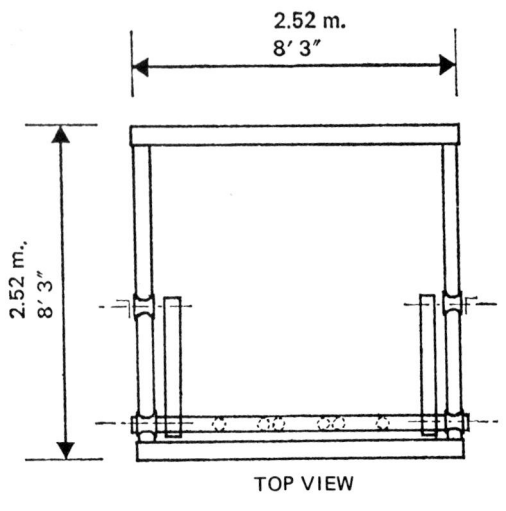

TOP VIEW

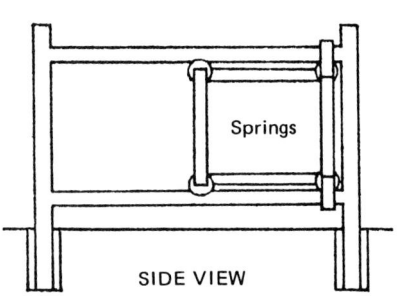

SIDE VIEW

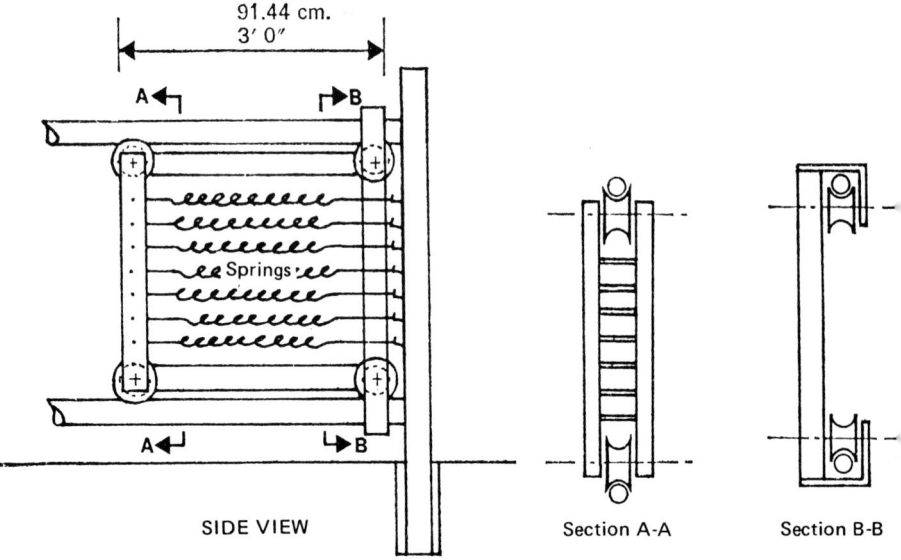

SIDE VIEW Section A-A Section B-B

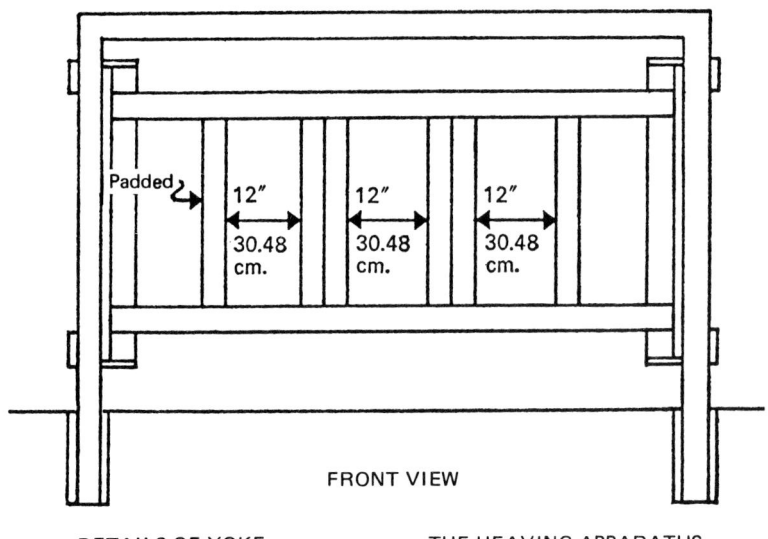

DETAILS OF YOKE   THE HEAVING APPARATUS

Lineout equipment with a tennis ball
This equipment is designed to teach forwards to stretch the entire body when jumping for the ball. Forwards can jump continuously in an attempt to strike the ball with their foreheads. The height of the ball can be varied. Forwards must take up their positions as they would in a line-out so that they will not use 2 or 3 short steps before the jump.

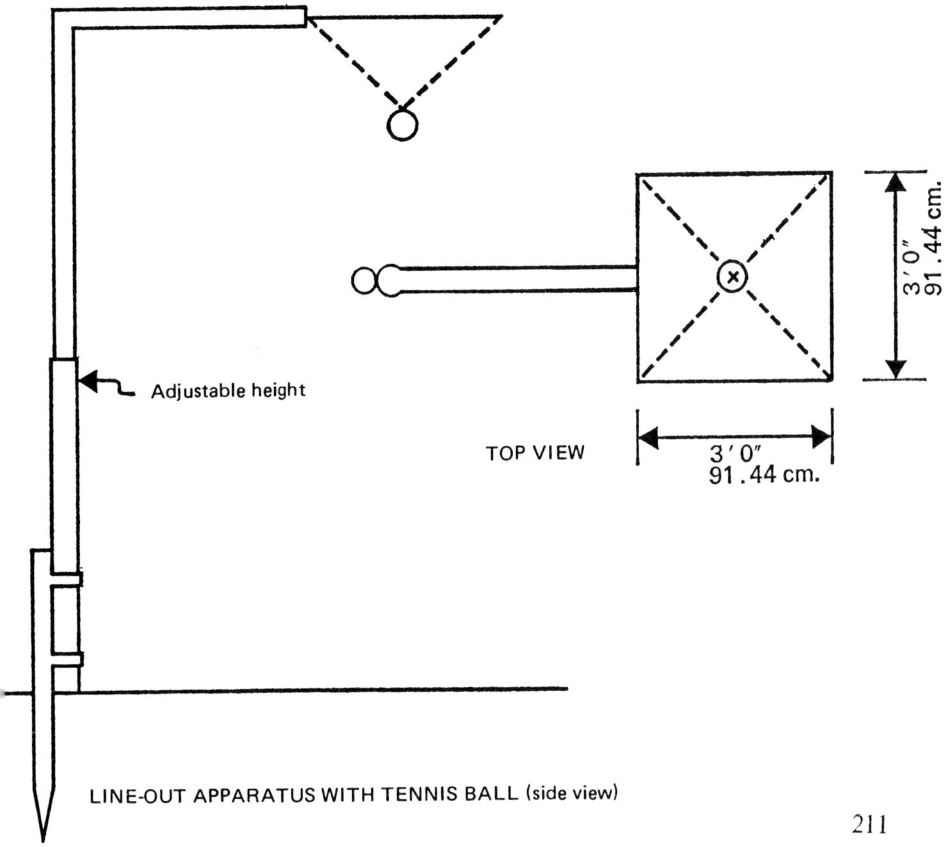

LINE-OUT APPARATUS WITH TENNIS BALL (side view)

Line-out equipment with a Rugby ball
This apparatus is aimed at improving the jumping achievements of forwards. Again, the height of the hanging ball can be varied. Forwards must use this apparatus by jumping off either foot and from both feet. The apparatus can also be used by 2 players jumping against each other. The ball need not be static but can swing.

LINE-OUT APPARATUS WITH RUGBY BALL

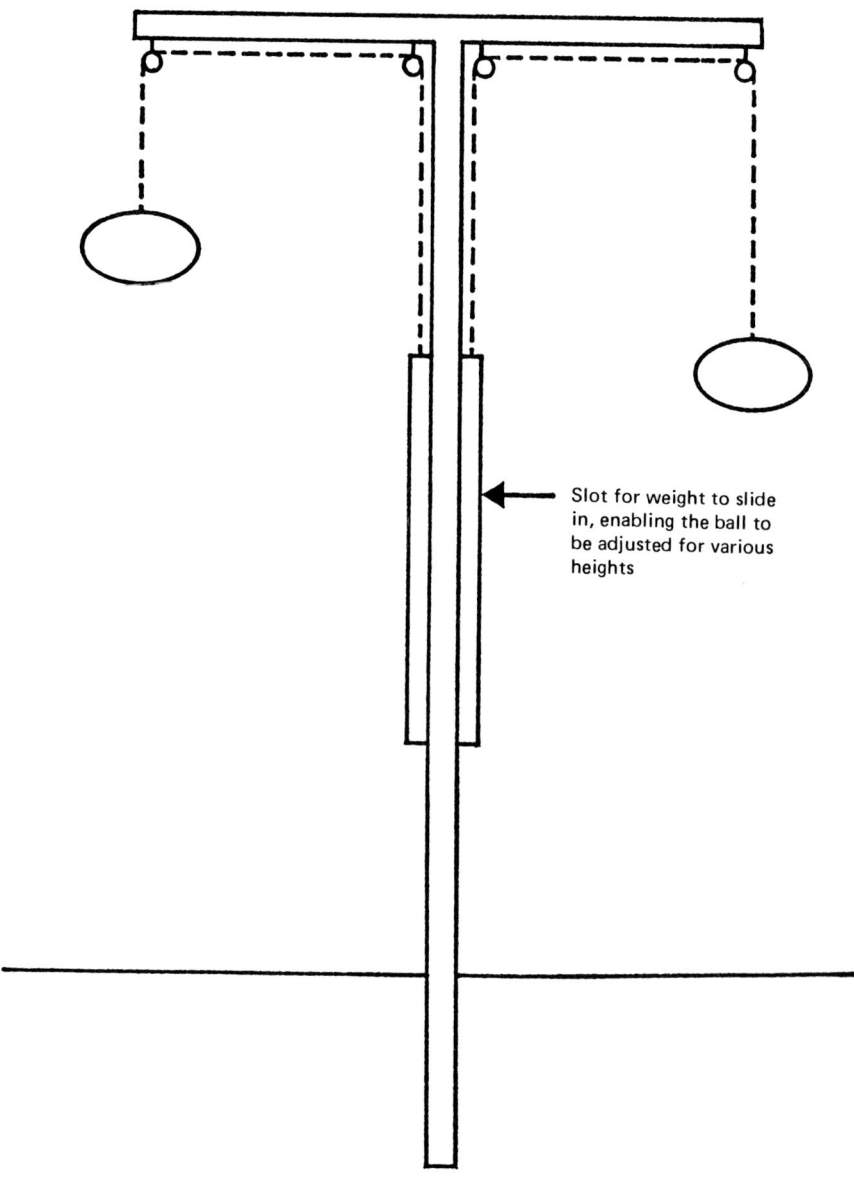

Slot for weight to slide in, enabling the ball to be adjusted for various heights

The Yoke
The yoke is used to increase scrummaging-power and general strength. The foremost part of the apparatus is placed on the neck of the forward who takes up his position either between the 2 ropes or, if the ropes are close together, with them passing between his legs.

The forwards can start in a standing position and run with the yoke, or they run along on all fours. The yoke can also be used for what is known as "crab walking" when the forwards crawl backwards (looking in the direction of the yoke). If 6 forwards pull the yoke with ease, the number can be reduced until only 2 forwards pull it.

Weight: The weight of the beam used by us here at Stellenbosch is 780 lb (353 kg). Bluegum stumps are used for this purpose.

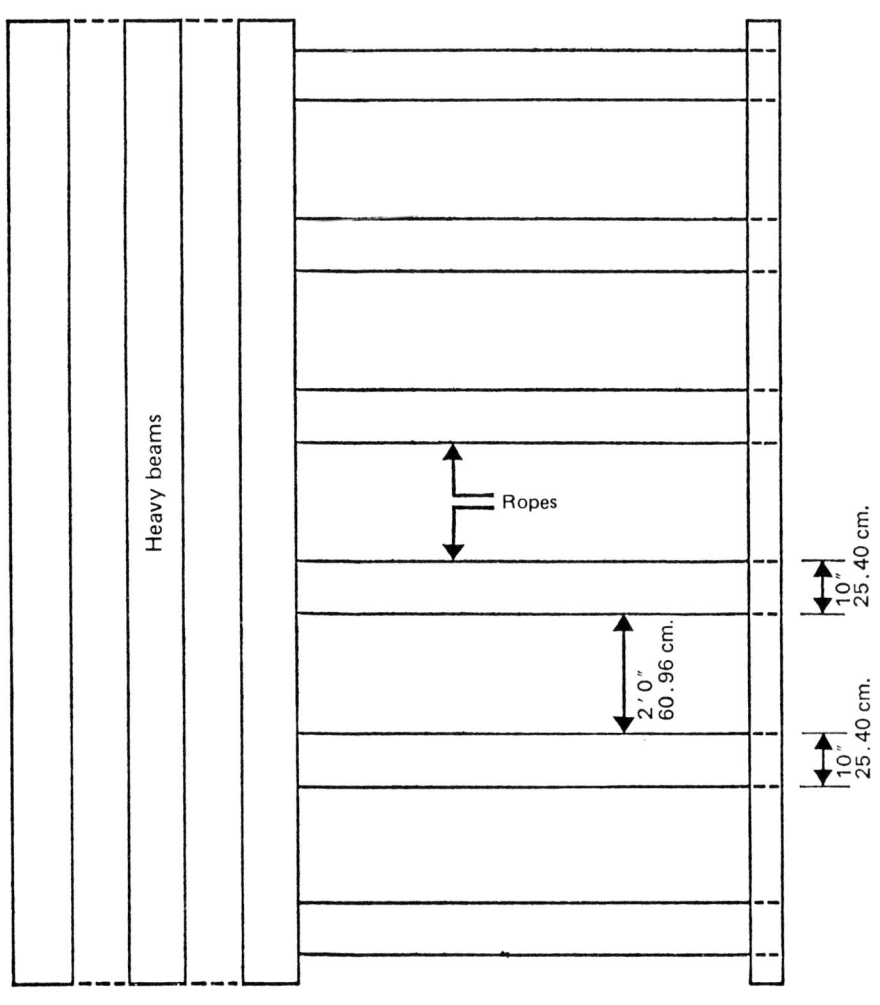

YOKE

Line-out throw-in apparatus
This is designed to help wings practise both methods of throwing-in the ball. The ring can be adjusted as it is screwed on to a pipe which can be turned. The height of the ring can also be adjusted.

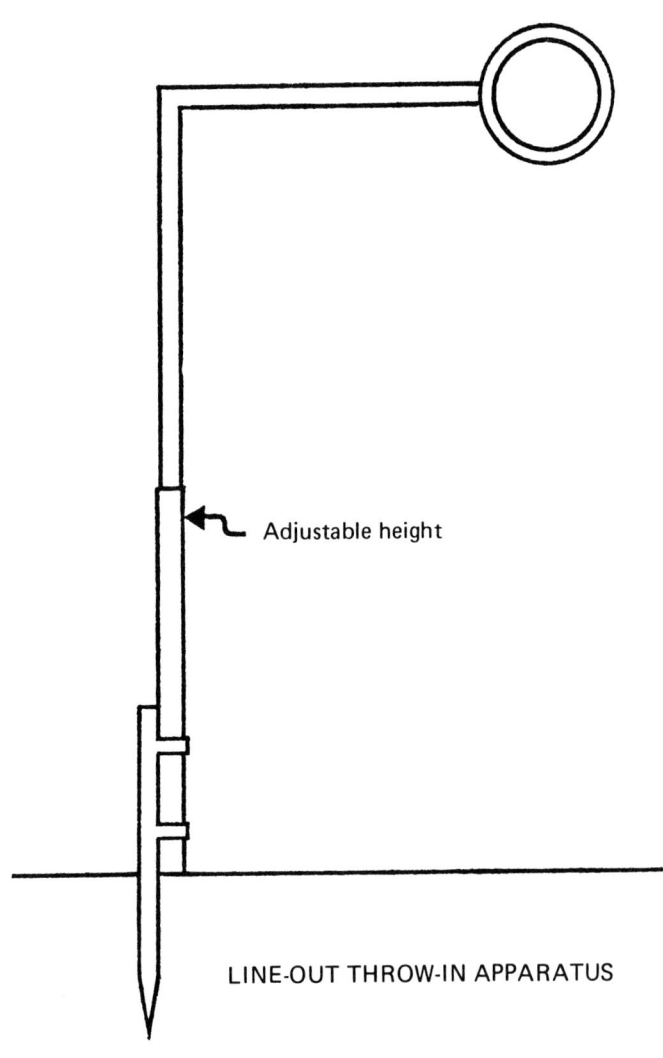

LINE-OUT THROW-IN APPARATUS

The tackling apparatus
The tackling-bag is suspended by strips of rubber so that it reverts to its original position after being used. To make sure that the rubber strips do not snap, they should be of equal lengths – before and after the tackle. To ensure this, they are tied – top and bottom – by means of elastic bands.

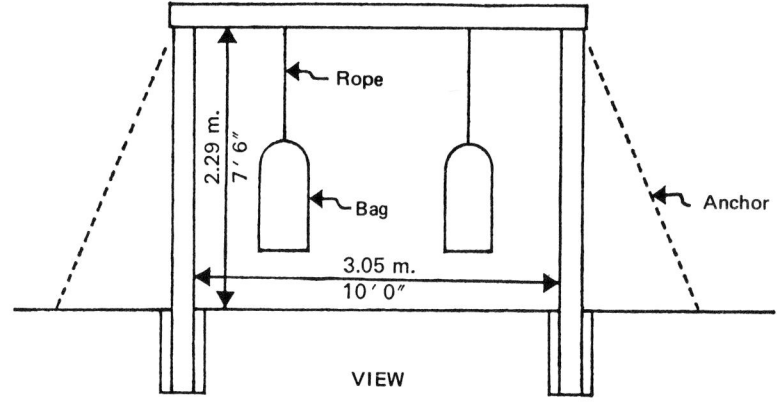

VIEW

Tackle-breaking apparatus
Inside the tyres are small plates, screwed to the posts. The tyres can be higher or lower, depending on the tackle being broken round the shoulders, sides, hips, or legs.

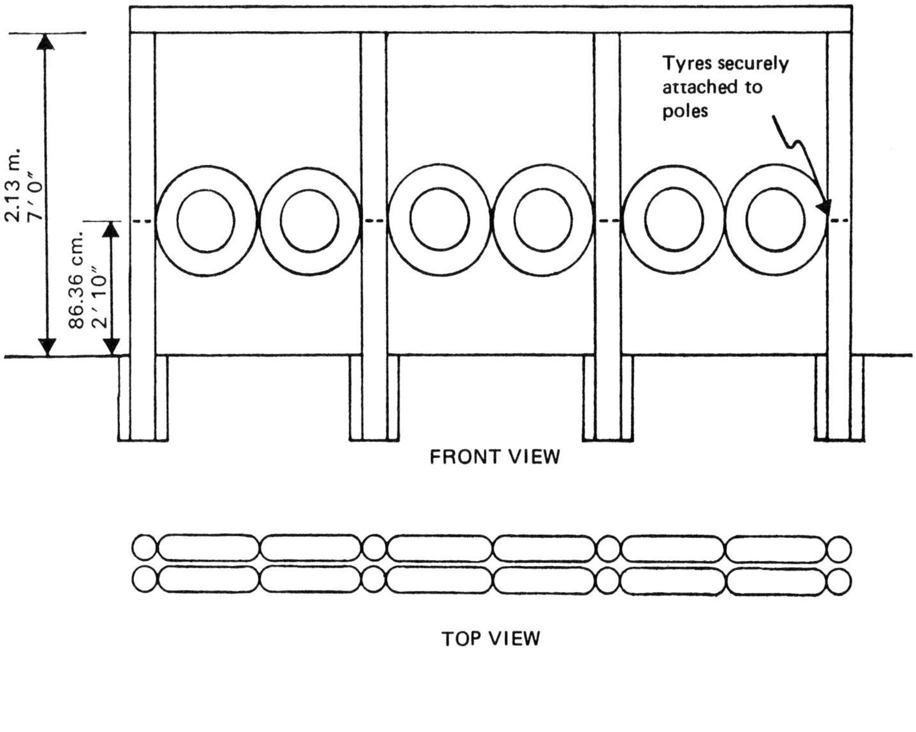

FRONT VIEW

TOP VIEW

Posts for loose forwards
This apparatus serves as support for 6 loose forwards – of 2 teams – and it is implanted next to the field. We envisage having a similar scrumming sledge for this purpose. The pattern of play is as follows:
The 6 loose forwards competing against each other take up their respective positions against the upright posts which represent the scrum. Balls, which are numbered, are placed in different positions all over the field. After the heave the loose forwards break away from the scrum and go full tilt for one of the balls in order to gain possession of it. A difference is made between attacking and defensive rucks, depending on where the ball is. Play continues until the ball has been won or the movement following upon it comes to an end.
The loose forwards return to the equipment and the exercise is continued with the loose forwards going after the remaining balls. Balls are also placed behind bags stuffed with sawdust, and the loose forwards must then form a ruck round the bag and gain possession.

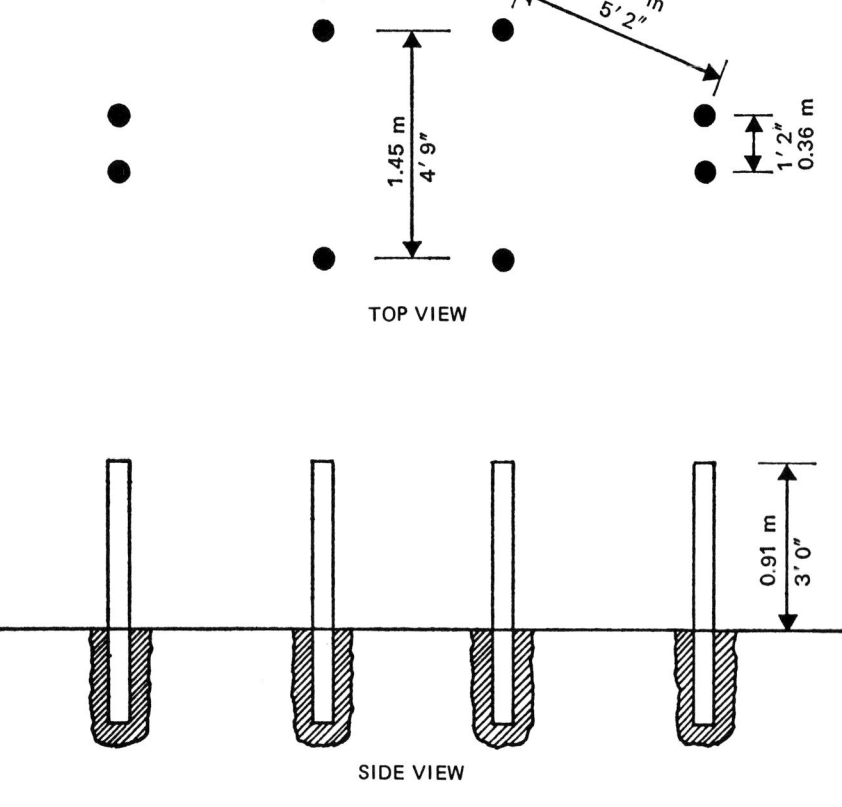

POSTS FOR LOOSE FORWARDS

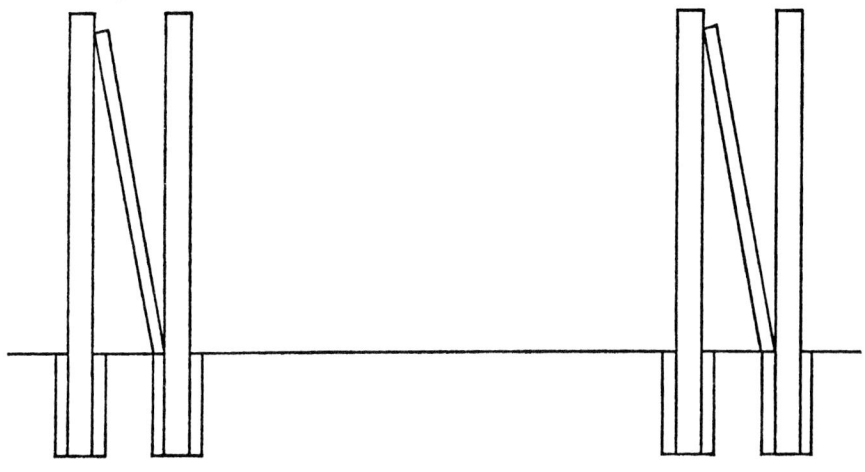

Front view

Handling nets
A ball rebounds off the handling net and gives a player the opportunity of improving his handling. The nets can be arranged in such a way that they deflect the ball upwards or downwards.

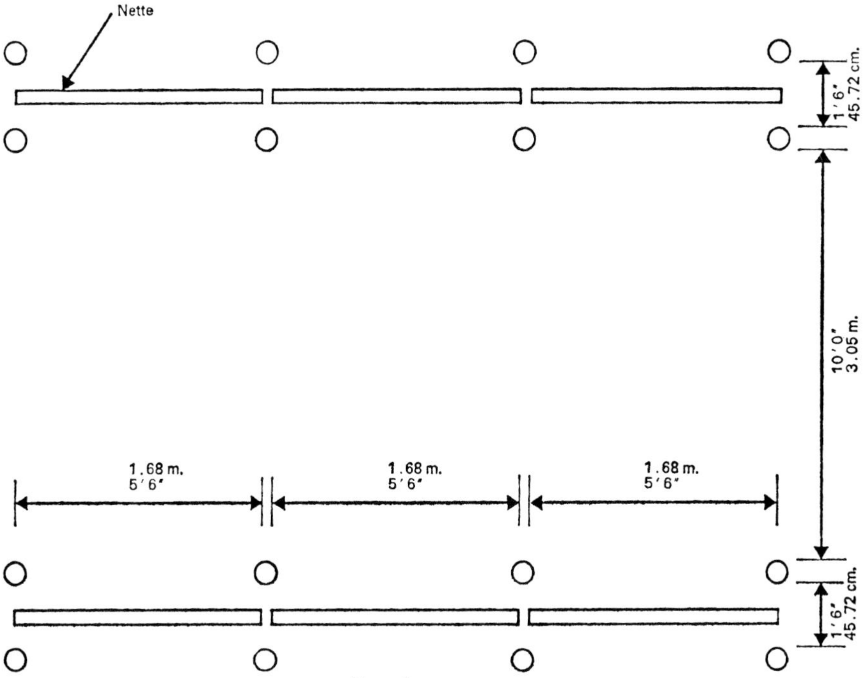

Top view

HANDLING NETS

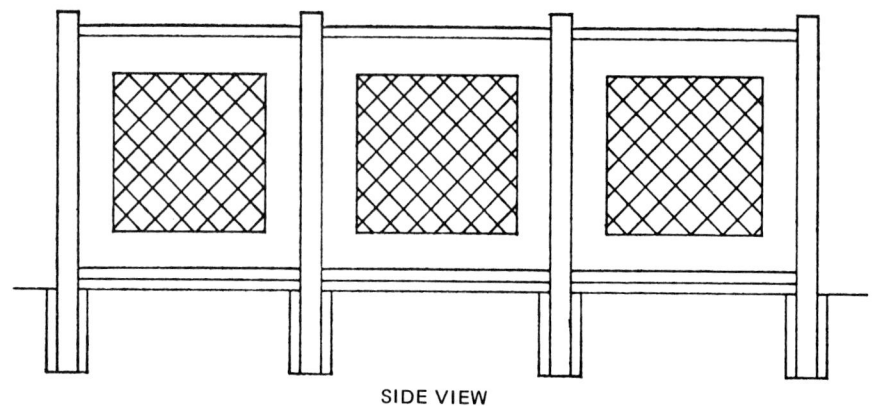

SIDE VIEW

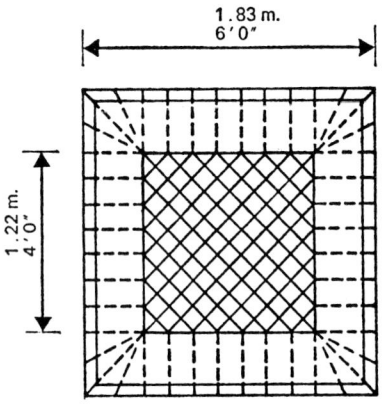

Nylon nets attached to steel frames with elastic bands

Description: Throw ball against nets

Schedule 2: Example of the use of the equipment as worked out for teams of Stellenbosch Rugby players, the "Maties".

Time	First Team	Colts
3–5 minutes	Warming-up, including rope climbing and heaving. (Whistle)	Warming-up, including rope climbing and heaving. (Whistle)
6 minutes	*Back-line players:* Seven or 8 pull against 7 or 8 with beam against colts, followed by double tyres with ball without walking. (Whistle)	*Back-line players:* Seven or 8 pull against 7 or 8 with beam, followed by double tyres with ball and tackling apparatus without walking. (Whistle)
	Forwards: Yoke tug of war against colts 2 to a yoke (each pair pulls 2 or 3 times). (Whistle)	*Forwards:* Yoke tug of war against first team – 2 to a yoke (each pair pulls 2 or 3 times). (Whistle)
3 minutes	*Back-line players:* Through maze carrying ball. (Whistle)	*Back-line players:* Handling at nets. (Whistle)
	Forwards: Three heaves and 3 steps taken with yoke. After this change round with colts and give 3 heaves at apparatus with springs. Change again with colts to give 3 heaves at scrumming sledge, etc. (Whistle)	*Forwards:* Three heaves and 3 steps taken with yoke. After this change round with first team and give 3 heaves at apparatus with springs. Change again with first team to give 3 heaves at scrumming sledge, etc. (Whistle)
3 minutes	*Back-line players:* Handling at nets. (Whistle)	*Back-line players:* Through maze with or without ball and without ever walking. (Whistle)
	Forwards: First team pushes against second team. (Whistle)	*Forwards:* Colts push against first team. (Whistle)
3 minutes	*Forwards:* Rucking beam and tyres and tackling-bags. (Whistle)	*Forwards:* Handling at nets. (Whistle)
3 minutes	*Forwards:* Handling at nets. (Whistle)	*Forwards:* Rucking and tyres and tackling bags. (Whistle)
3 minutes	*Forwards:* First team pushes against colts. (Whistle)	*Forwards:* Colts push against first team. (Whistle)
Rest of afternoon	*Forwards:* Individual exercises, as allocated to each player.	*Forwards:* Individual exercises, as allocated to each player.
	Backs: Individual exercises as allocated to each player. (Whistle from now on only for forwards.)	*Backs:* Individual exercises as allocated to each player. (Whistle from now on only for forwards.)

Schedule 3: Example of the use of the apparatus etc. for three teams.

Time	First team	Second team	Colts
10 minutes	Physical exercises with stones and benches. (Whistle to announce the following exercise.)	Physical exercises with stones and benches. (Whistle to announce the following exercise.)	Physical exercises with stones and benches. (Whistle to announce the following exercise.)
3 minutes	Twice up the slope, followed by heaving, followed by rope climbing. (Whistle)	Two heaves, followed by rope climbing, followed by twice up the slope. (Whistle)	Rope climbing, followed by twice up the slope, followed by heaving. (Whistle)
6 minutes	*Back-line players:* Eight pull against 8 with heavy beam and the rest against one another with light beam; after this they push against one another followed by double tyres with ball and tackling-bag without ever walking (Whistle) *Forwards:* Yoke pulling relay against second team – 2 per yoke. Each pair pulls 3 times (heaviest yoke). (Whistle)	*Back-line players:* Eight pull against 8 with heavy beam and the rest against one another with light beam; after this they push against one another followed by double tyres with ball and tackling-bag without ever walking. (Whistle) *Forwards:* Yoke pulling against first team – 2 per yoke. Each pair pulls 3 times (lightest yoke). (Whistle)	*Back-line players:* Eight pull against 8 with heavy beam and the rest against one another with light beam; after this they push against one another followed by double tyres with ball and tackling-bag without ever walking. (Whistle) *Forwards:* Heave and walk 3 yards with scrumming sledge, followed by heave at apparatus with springs followed by sledge then at apparatus with springs, etc. (They and the second team exchange roles every second week.) (Whistle)
3 minutes	*Back-line players:* Through maze with ball. (Whistle) *Forwards:* Three heaves and 3 steps with yoke sledge. After this they exchange with second team and give 3 heaves at apparatus with springs. After this they exchange again with second team to give 3 heaves etc. at scrumming sledge etc. (Whistle)	*Back-line players:* Through maze with ball. (Whistle) *Forwards:* Three heaves at apparatus with springs, after which they change round with first team and give 3 heaves and walk 3 paces with scrumming sledge. After this they exchange to give 3 heaves at apparatus with springs, etc. (Whistle)	*Back-line players:* Handling at nets. (Whistle) *Forwards:* Two per yoke – forwards in 2 groups of 4 (2 locks and 2 props on one side with heavy yoke, the rest at lighter yoke), relay race. Each pair pulls 3 times. (Whistle)
3 minutes	*Back-line players:* Handling at nets. (Whistle)	*Back-line players:* Handling at nets. (Whistle)	*Back-line players:* Through maze with ball without ever walking. (Whistle)

Time	First team	Second team	Colts
3 minutes	*Forwards:* First team pushes against second team. (Whistle)	*Forwards:* Second team pushes against first team. (Whistle)	*Forwards:* Rucking beam (2 work together – if beam begins to swing away, they run towards it to push it further and faster away) through 3 double tyres, etc. to start with rucking beam once more. (Whistle)
3 minutes	*Forwards:* Rucking beam and tyres and tackling-bags. (Whistle)	*Forwards:* Rucking beam and tyres and tackling-bags. (Whistle)	*Forwards:* Handling at nets. (Whistle)
3 minutes	*Forwards:* First team pushes against colts. (Whistle)	*Forwards:* Handling at nets. (Whistle)	*Forwards:* Colts push against first team. (Whistle)
Rest of afternoon	Individual exercises as given to each player.	Individual exercises as given to each player.	Individual exercises as given to each player.
Rest of afternoon	*Backs:* Individual exercises as given to each player. (Whistle from now on only for forwards.)	*Backs:* Individual exercises as given to each player. (Whistle from now on only for forwards.)	*Backs:* Individual exercises as given to each player. (Whistle from now on only for forwards.)

Example of a programme for special skill exercises.

	3 minutes	*3 minutes*	*5 minutes*	*5–10 minutes*
Props	Pulling beam and practising heave once every fortnight. Scrum sledge and beam for backs once every fortnight.	Halters.	Front-rows against front-rows and hooking without ball.	Front-rows against front-rows with ball and halves.
Hooker	Pulls beam and practises heave once every fortnight. Scrum sledge and beam for backs once every fortnight.	Hooking.	Front-rows against front-rows and hooking without ball.	
Lock forwards	Pulling beam and practising heave once every fortnight. Scrum sledge once every fortnight.	Jumping against tyres and grabbing ball once every fortnight. Jumping against tyres and striking ball with forehead once every fortnight.	A wing for one lock-forward throws in ball as at line-out.	In twos against each other, wings throw in ball as at line-out.
Loose forwards	Pulling beam and practising heave once every fortnight. Scrum sledge once every fortnight.	Picking up loose balls.	Three against 3 in picking up loose balls.	Three against 3 in picking up loose balls, or breaking through, or forming rucks.

	3 minutes	3 minutes	5 minutes	5–10 minutes
Scrum halves	Skipping.	Picking up balls and handling bad passes once every fortnight. Push-off and tackling once every fortnight.	Short punt and grubbers; 3 against 3.	With front-rows.
Centres	Skipping.	Picking up balls and handling bad passes once every fortnight. Push-off and tackling once every fortnight.	Short punts and grubbers; 3 against 3.	Scissors, dummy-scissors, shift-passes, short passes; 2 against 2.
Wings	Skipping.	Picking up balls and handling bad passes once every fortnight. Push-off and tackling once every fortnight.	Throwing in ball for lock forwards.	With lock-forwards; throw in as at line-outs; 2 against 2 lock-forwards.
Full backs	Skipping.	Picking up balls and handling bad passes once every fortnight. Push-off and tackling once every fortnight.	Kicking around posts.	Kicking around posts.

Chapter 7
Rounding off of Skills

THE SKILLS acquired in conjunction with satellites and team-mates, will determine whether the rounding off of skills will be successful. The individual now makes way for the team.

Pushing in the scrum is no longer practised, but it remains decisive. Jumping retains its value in that one is conscious of it, but without consolidation jumping will not have much value. Pushing-in-movement will be discernible only if it is better than that of the opposing team. Handling will be noticed only if it is exceptional, similarly with the push-off, with tackling, and with kicking. These skills, however, disappear in general play, in broken play, and in broken-down play, etc. Only in match situations will the skills, focal and satellitic, actually be applied. Skills, however excellent, will fail to come into their own without judgment.

The rounding off of skills falls in between skill building and the application of skills. More attention must now be paid to satellitic factors, so that they are already developed when the application of skill is required. It is, for instance, no longer required of a player who pushes off to straighten when breaking, because he has already made it part of his equipment for attack while practising the rounding off of skills. The building of skills, the rounding off of skills, and the applications of skills are concerned with the acquiring, refining, and applying of skills. Rounding off of skills thus emphasises the satellitic movements applied in sections (back-line players and forwards). Thus the two sections work, first of all separately, and then against each other.

In order to make the rounding off of skills possible, a coach should be fully conversant with the satellitic movements in Rugby and must see to it that they receive the necessary attention. Mistakes made and pointed out will be mainly of a satellitic nature and will involve teamwork. Mistakes in the application of skills will mostly include a wrong decision or an unwise course, such as players breaking when they should not break, kicking when they could have broken, or breaking too soon or too late, etc. On the other hand, mistakes in skill building will be technical mistakes.

As stated, rounding off of skills is crucial in all play. This means that those movements occurring most frequently in a match should receive the greatest attention. The following sequence is recommended:
1. Tight play and general play.
2. Broken-down play and loose play.
3. Broken play.
4. Special play.

In order to do full justice to each of the above, we should be fully conversant with the nature of each element of play and see to it that each is given attention. The exercises given make provision for all aspects of play, but the coach should also use them as background for assessing a player's merits.

Principle: In most cases a team – or its backs and forwards – will work apart before another team joins them. The exception is at scrum practice, where both packs of forwards are involved, unless, of course, scrum apparatus is used. The advantages of using such apparatus is that scrummaging faults can be ironed out more easily. The backs and forwards work separately on any new points, or points that need to be rounded off. The reason is obvious: a coach cannot pay attention to all the principles of attack and defence simultaneously, which is what he has to do when two sections are working together.

A coach can of course bring his backs and forwards together for the line-out, ruck, and for special play. This usually happens when a side is on tour and presupposes an advanced state of proficiency. A coach can also bring two teams together and let the forwards practise their own movements while letting the backs do theirs. This, too, is a good method and can be followed if rounding off is well advanced. It is a method often used for final rounding if one wishes to avoid injuries. It can also be used if forwards and backs wish to practise tactical moves without being hampered.

As the scrum, line-out and ruck have their own specific back-line formations, these two methods of using the forwards and the backs of a team simultaneously, or using two teams against each other without letting the two sections interfere in each other's activities, can often be used, especially if the teams have attained a measure of proficiency. The teams have the additional advantage that the scrum halves or wings can put the balls in at scrums and line-outs respectively.

Line-out and Scrum
1. We start with the line-out because for back-line play it has become more important than the scrum. The backs are 20 yards apart at a line-out whereas they are spaced only a few yards apart at a scrum. This means that whereas it is possible for backs to cross or to come close to the advantage line from a line-out, it is not so from a scrum.
2. There should be no running during line-out and scrummaging work. Running takes place later and it is best that it should be from one touchline to another.
3. In training for line-out work, care should be taken that either hand is used on the inside, because the major share of work in jumping and catching is done with the inside hand.
4. The younger the players, the more important it is that they should play in every position of the scrum or line-out. To a certain extent this applies to more mature players, but then it is more a case of line-out forwards switching positions, with their "protectors" remaining "protectors".
5. In senior Rugby, where scrum defences lie as shallow as the laws allow, the ball cannot reach the wings without a tactical move somewhere between the two extremities – scrum and wings. Only when the defence is uncertain might there be a possibility of the ball reaching the wing. In school Rugby the defenders still lie deep, but if a school side is unexpectedly confronted

by a team which does not conform to such defensive methods, they will be at a complete loss, apart from resorting to kicks. For this reason our proposal is that at the outset the same back-line movements are used from line-outs and scrums. The usual general attacking back-line play should later make way for tactical movements, of which the aim should be the overlap, breaking, circumventing, etc. Although these moves can be fitted in anywhere in the exercises, they are given a place with the scrum; but only after the knack of scrummaging, rucking, and mauling have been fully learnt. If the move breaks down, as frequently happens in a match, the ruck or the maul gets a place as part of the entire movement.

6. The time allotted to rounding off exercises – and for backs and forwards to complete their exercises before being brought together – is not stipulated. In this the teacher or coach must be guided by experience.

THE LINE-OUT AND LINE-OUT FORMATION

For backs and forwards working apart
Forwards

1. (a) Two packs work separately and a few yards apart so that the coach can watch both. Each pack forms a line-out and plays on a specific side. The hookers throw in the ball and then join the forwards. The ball is thrown for the no. 3s until the line-out works well and no. 3 can pass the ball out with ease. This entails that consolidation – covering of one of the locks by his team-mate, or covering by no. 2 of both locks, or covering of all players jumping – must be done correctly.
   (b) If both packs can apply the principles of line-out work satisfactorily at no. 3, the two packs change sides so that the outside arms become inside arms.
   (c) The ball is now thrown to no. 5 until covering, consolidation, etc. are satisfactorily done. The 2 packs change sides again.
   (d) The ball is now thrown to one of the loose forwards and then to number eight and no. 2, both of whom are later to be used for churning.
   (e) No. 3 now becomes no. 2 in both packs and the ball is thrown to them. In the same way no. 5 becomes no. 4, or they remain at no. 5 even if no. 3 is at no. 2.
   (f) The ball is now deliberately missed by the line-out forwards so that covering can be practised.
   (g) Churning at the front and at the rear of the line-out is practised.

Backs

1. (a) The two back-lines work separately but at the same place in the field. The scrum halves are at a point where the 5-yard line intersects the half-way line. One of the back-lines takes up its position accordingly. The blind-side wing taps the ball with his foot to the scrum half and the ball is passed until it reaches the open-side wing without any handling mistakes. In accordance with the principles of general attacking back-line play. The second back-line follows suit, after any mistakes made by the first back-line have been pointed out. The scrum halves now run across the field and start the movement again. In this way the back-lines move across the field until movement is uninterrupted and continuous with the open-side wing receiving the ball before he crosses the 10-yard line. In order to achieve this, he must receive the ball and have room in which to move before reaching the half-way line. He places the ball on the half-way line for his scrum half so that the movement can go back again.

N.B. The 2 back-lines can operate on both sides of the half-way line, but in this way too much space is taken up, as the forwards also require space and the coach has to watch both forwards and backs. For this reason the backs move towards the side occupied by the forwards.

225

| *Forwards* | *Backs* |

Backs

Test: The scrum half and the blind-side wing run in cover defence along the half-way line and see if they can cut off the open-side wing. Should they succeed, there is something radically wrong.

(b) The time taken by each back-line to move the ball across the field and back is clocked. Mistakes made disqualify them. The back-lines move from the intersection of the 10-yard line and the 5-yard line to the same position on the opposite side of the field.

Forwards

2. (a) The 2 line-outs are drawn up as they would be in a match. The hooker of each team has a ball, which they throw in simultaneously to no. 3, 5, or 8. Consolidation takes place simultaneously in both line-outs and a certain amount of bumping and jostling will inevitably be experienced.
(b) Each team works out its own signals and the balls are thrown in by the hookers to comply with the signals.
(c) Each team gets an opportunity to let its players practise deflection of the ball. Consolidation and covering still take place.
(d) One pack "churns" at the front and the other at the rear, and vice versa.
(e) Facets ending a line-out are practised. The ball is passed out, and the forwards catching it proceed with it across the line at which it was thrown in. For instance, the entire pack pushes the catcher over this line; the ball is placed on the ground between the feet of the players, or the ball is thrown over and beyond number eight.
N.B. The wings can also throw the ball in. If this happens, number eight takes up the wing's position with the backs.
(f) It might be advisable at this stage to let every forward switch to every position. The exchange of the line-out forwards should be from the front to the rear. Number eight becomes no. 1 in the line-out, for instance, and all the forwards move back 1 place. After the ball has been thrown in 2 or 3 times and everything has been done satis- factorily, the next switch takes place,

Backs

2. (a) The 2 back-lines are positioned as in a match, and although they operate separately they compete against each other. The scrum halves are on their own 10-yard line where it intersects the 5-yard line. The same positions, on the opposite side of the field, are where the open-side wings place the ball down after a movement. The 2 back-lines move simultaneously. The competition serves a double purpose: which back-line gets the ball to the open-side wing first – and, in what time. After this the aim should be – apart from winning the race – to improve on time. To break the record should be the aim of the entire club, not only for a season, but for all seasons.
(b) The competitions are extended.
(i) Instead of once across the field and back, the exercise is performed up to 4 times and more.
(ii) Instead of running, the backs remain standing. The wings start running only when they receive the ball to place it on the mark.
(iii) One movement takes place while the players are in a stationary position and then when they are running. The times for both are compared.
(iv) The fly half leaves out the inside centre, who doubles around to take the ball outside the outside centre.
(v) The blind-side wing comes into the line at different positions.
(vi) The full back slips into the line.
(vii) The open-side wing stops on the mark and returns the ball infield to one of the centres or to the fly half while the scrum half takes the wing's place in the back-line.

Forwards	Backs
taking the hooker to no. 3, and number eight to no. 2 position. (g) Between each line-out exercise, the forwards run – forward, backward and across the field – to given places.	(viii) Both the blind-side wing and the full back come into the back-line. (ix) When the wing puts the ball down the second movement is continued in the same direction as the first. After this the movement comes back. This means the movement goes twice in one direction and returns twice in another. For this purpose parts of the field over and alongside the touchlines can also be used, and if this space is insufficient, the exercise can be done across the field. (x) The backs are switched so that each plays in every position. Switching is repeated as follows: the scrum half becomes the left wing, who becomes the full back; the right wing becomes the right centre; the right centre becomes the left centre; the left centre becomes the fly half, and the fly half becomes the scrum half. After a few movements the switch, as indicated above, takes place again.

Forwards and backs of 2 teams working together but not against each other

1. (a) The 2 packs form a line-out on the half-way line and the backs take up their positions behind them. The ball is thrown in by the wings according to signals and it is kept while consolidation takes place before being passed out. A full threequarter movement follows with the open-side wings running to the intersection of the half-way line and the touchline. From there they throw the ball in to their forwards who have cut across the field.
   A mark is made on the half-way line 15 yards from touch, and only when all the forwards have crossed this mark and are in position do the wings throw the ball in. Again consolidation takes place before the ball is released. This time the movement goes in the opposite direction, back to the starting position. In this manner the movements can follow one another to and fro across the field.
   (b) (i) The forward to whom the ball is thrown deflects it to the scrum half.
   (ii) Vary the consolidation of the first movement with deflection in the second movement.
2. (a) A competition as described above takes place between 2 teams positioned as in a match. The teams may also be clocked. Two balls, thrown in simultaneously, are used. The first line-out involves consolidation. The second line-out involves deflection, but the ball is thrown in only after the forwards have crossed the mark which is on the half-way, 15 yards from touch. The time is clocked the moment the scrum half receives the ball from his no. 3 or his no. 5, or his number eight (stipulated beforehand) to the moment the wing, who has started the competition, places the ball on the original spot where the ball was thrown in, and when all his forwards are with him and across the touchline.
   (b) The same as above, but the number of movements to and fro is increased.
3. Two teams together. The forwards are again on the half-way line and the backs in position to be taken up at a line-out. On this occasion the forwards play against their own backs, but only after they have deflected the ball in a proper way to their scrum half. The forwards try to get to the backs and disrupt their movement before the ball reaches the open-side wing. The game is again played to and fro across the field.

As the open-side wings should receive the ball before they reach the half-way line, the 2 teams can collaborate. They must, however, be fully aware of the fact that they may not take play across the half-way line.

4. The 2 teams in either half of the field play towards each other but not against each other. The line-outs are taken on the 2 twenty-five yard lines, and if the ball is released the backs try to confound or beat the forwards. To do so they can run the ball back by the open-side wing stopping in his tracks and passing the ball to one of the centres. This leaves the scrum half to slip in between the backs to help make the move more effective. Use can also be made of outflanking an opponent by the inside centre and the fly half receiving the ball from the open-side wing on the outside. The game continues until the ball is dead. It can happen that the forwards gain advantage as a result of a mistake made by one of the backs. If this should happen the game goes on and the backs have to defend.

Backs and forwards of 2 teams working together and against each other

Forwards

1. The 2 packs are now brought together. One of the packs is allowed to catch the ball from the throw-in and the other team tries to break through the consolidation and gain possession. The ball is thrown to different forwards for consolidation. Each pack gets a chance to consolidate and to try and disrupt consolidation.

2. The ball is thrown in for one of the packs, and the opposing pack also tries to gain possession. The pack which succeeds consolidates while the other pack tries to rob them of the ball, or they try and push their opponents away in order to end the line-out. The pack gaining possession has a triple task: the ball has to be caught; consolidation must take place; and the players must see to it that they are not pushed away, which is actually part of consolidation.

3. The pack gaining possession consolidates and attempts to push its opponents away – a move which will, apart from causing uncertainty in the ranks of the opponents, prevent the players from being too loose.

4. Catching the ball is varied by deflecting – not striking – the ball and consolidation takes place again. The deflection brings the ball so close to their forwards that it should, together with consolidation, prevent the opponents from getting to the ball.

5. The 2 packs come together and one of them practises – with the aid of signals – catching and consolidation, deflection and consolidation, and "churning". The other pack tries to disrupt or prevent them.

Back-line players

Two back-lines are drawn up, one as attackers, the other as defenders.

1. The attackers start running only after the fly half has received the ball, and all take the same gap. The fly half throws a dummy but does not release the ball. The inside centre, however, catches a hypothetical ball and dummies and so on through to the wing. The dummy exercises have the benefit that all backs have to push off to the inside and are thus compelled to straighten in order to break. The receiver of the hypothetical ball can watch the passer to see if he is looking towards the direction in which the dummy is to be given, something which is neglected in most dummies.

2. This exercise derives from the previous one. The backs each have a ball. They each sell a dummy and break, and then kick a short punt or a grubber, following up to gather the ball.

3. The dummy to the inside is practised. Each player has a ball and begins his run when the fly half has received the ball from the scrum half.

4. Now that players have practised the push-off to either side, they all practise simultaneously swerving to the inside and to the outside.

5. The backs practise side-stepping to the inside and to the outside.

THE SCRUM AND SCRUM FORMATION

Backs and forwards of 2 teams. Backs together, and forwards against each other.

Forwards
"There is no exercise for scrummaging like scrummaging."

1. (a) Two packs scrummage with everything correct: packing down, taking the strain and shoving. This is done without a ball.
   (b) If the scrum is solid and stationary, the ball can be used. If everything takes place according to plan, the next step can be taken.
   (c) The scrum breaks up as quickly as possible after the ball has been hooked and is out. Another scrum is formed and the other pack is given the put-in.
   (d) Scrummaging, breaking up, and running to a given place for the next scrum is done repeatedly, forwards and backwards.
   (e) The ball is hooked, the flankers break and kick the ball away. All the forwards chase the ball and the forward first to it gathers it and a hand-to-hand movement or a ruck or a maul takes place. (These exercises will be most useful if rucking has already been acquired.)
   (f) The forwards switch positions as described, so that everyone can play in every position, or the 2 locks go to the front row, the props take over as locks, and the hooker as number eight. After a while the new locks (props) and flankers exchange positions, and later the original locks become flankers and the original flankers take over as props.

Without the ball
The first step towards acquiring the skill of wheeling a scrum consists first of using only the front row. At a signal the tight-head prop yields while the loose-head prop pushes hard to the inside. The hooker acts as pivot. Once they have acquired the knack, the locks pack down with them and, at a given signal, they wheel with both locks pushing in towards the loose-head side and withdrawing their heads at the correct moment. (This is quite an art!) The loose-head lock must help his partner by pulling him in. After this, the 3–3–2 formation is used and all forwards react at a given signal. From now on the ball is used.

Backs
The 2 back-lines work in collaboration, but they are drawn up against each other as in a match. Each player has a ball, except the fly half, who gets his ball from the scrum half and starts the movement. The 2 back-lines move towards each other and each player does the same thing. Each takes the same gap as is taken by his counterpart. At the conclusion of the exercise the back-lines exchange positions and repeat. The next exercises are as follow:

1. (a) The short kick: One back-line kicks to the outside gap, the other to the inside.
   (b) The back-lines change over.
   (c) The back-lines take short kicks alternately to the inside and to the outside.

2. (a) One of the back-lines kicks a grubber through the outside gap and follows up the kick through that gap. The other back-line kicks a grubber through the inside gap and follows up the kick through that gap.
   (b) The back-lines exchange roles.
   (c) The grubber is kicked alternately through the outside gap and the inside gap.
   (d) The short punt and the grubber kick are varied.
   (e) A back-line either kicks a grubber or a short punt, but their opponents are unaware of the type of kick to be used. The only stipulation made is which gap is to be taken.

3. A dummy to the outside and to the inside is practised alternately in the same way as for the short punt or the grubber.

4. The outside swerve and the inside swerve are alternately practised in the same way.

5. The side-step to the outside and to the inside are alternately practised in the same way.

6. Any of the abovementioned methods of attack are undertaken. The only "prescribed" exercise is that in which a specific gap has to be taken. Now every player does whatever he wants to do, but he must apply every method of attack while doing the exercises.

THE RUCK, THE FORMATION OF THE RUCK, AND LOOSE PLAY

Forwards acquiring a grasp of the ruck and maul
Two packs together but not against each other
The 2 packs work from the same spot, one following the other. A bag filled with straw is placed in front or behind the ball. The bag represents a player.

1. (a) The attacking ruck is practised.
   (b) The ball is gathered by the first player on the spot and the players practise an attacking maul.

2. (a) The defensive ruck is practised.
   (b) The defensive maul is practised.

3. (a) The neutral ruck is practised.
   (b) The neutral maul is practised.

4. The 2 packs work together and against each other.
   (a) One pack forms an attacking ruck, the other a defensive ruck. The roles are reversed.
   (b) One pack forms an attacking maul and the other a defensive maul. The roles are reversed.

5. (a) Both packs practise the neutral ruck.
   (b) Both packs practise the neutral maul.

Backs acquiring a grasp of formations at the ruck
Back-lines together but not against each other
The back-lines work in the same direction and one follows the other. The entire field can be used. The scrum half has the ball and kicks it along the ground, forward, backward and to the sides. He follows the ball, picks up and passes to his backs who have to be in position and not work against the stream.

The 2 back-lines work together and then against each other
The back-lines are drawn up as for a match in the centre of the field. One of the scrum halves kicks along the ground in any direction. Only the scrum halves give chase in order to gather the ball for passing to their respective back-lines. While the scrum halves are chasing, their 2 back-lines get into position. The back-line getting the ball tries to run it to the wing.

Forwards and backs of the same team together
One of the teams practises rucks and general back-line movements developing from them. For this they use 2 units of 3 forwards linked like a front row. One unit is positioned on one touchline while the other is in line with them on the opposite touchline. A ball is placed about 5 yards in front of each unit. The team's forwards take up a position about 15 yards behind one of the units and run full tilt into them in order to push themselves and the members of the unit over the ball so that it can be fed to the backs. After this the forwards run across the field to the unit and repeat the exercise.

The function of the unit is to serve as a basis for the ruck. As soon as the charging forwards make contact with them, the 3 players give way to cushion the impact, after which they offer as much resistance as they can. For this reason the ball is placed a few yards in front of them.

The position of the second unit can be changed to make provision for both attacking and defensive rucks.

Two teams together but not lined up against each other
The 2 packs go down for a scrum at the point where the twenty-five yard line intersects the 5-yard line. Both back-lines are drawn up defensively, one in front of the other. The foremost back-line gets the ball from the scrum and when it reaches the wing, he goes down and lies on the ball while his forwards form a ruck around him. They pass in the ball, which goes out to the other wing and he too forces a ruck to develop. In this way ruck succeeds ruck and the entire field is covered.

After the ball has been hooked from the scrum, the attacking forwards and the rearmost back-line remain behind and play together. A line-out is formed and from it the ball goes out to the wing. The same exercise as described above takes place. At the opposite touchline the last team to do the exercise joins the first and after a while the same exercise is repeated. Instead of forcing a ruck through the wing, the number eight receives the ball from the wing and all the forwards join him. At a signal, he has to tie up the ruck or maul. The ball is released and again the forward who takes the ball is joined by the others and a ruck or maul is called for. In this way both teams move down the field and back.

Forwards and backs of 2 teams together
The forwards of both teams work with the bag and practise rucks and mauls – as well as hand-to-hand movements. The forwards start with a line-out or scrum. The scrum half who receives the ball runs with it to the bag and places the ball at various distances in front of or behind it. The opponents try to stop him from doing so. Obviously the bag must be placed in a favourable position for the scrum half. At a line-out the bag can be quite a distance from him, but must be closer at a scrum.

The 2 teams together, drawn up in opposition but not playing against each other
1. (a) Each scrum half has a ball and puts it into the scrum. When it is hooked a full back-line movement takes place according to all the principles of general attacking back-line play. The open-side wings place the balls for the next scrum, on the intersection of the half-way line and the 5-yard line. Back-line movements follow from there.
   (b) The same exercise takes place but this time in the form of a race. The scrum halves put the ball in at a given signal, and the ball is hooked strictly according to the law, after which the movement goes across the field. On the opposite side of the field another scrum is formed, but the ball cannot be put in until all the forwards have packed down. The movement comes back again and a third scrum is formed. The race ends as soon as all 8 forwards of a pack have gone down into the third scrum.
   (c) The same exercise can be extended so that the movement goes 2 or 3 times, or even more, across the field.
   (d) The race or exercise starts with a scrum, but a line-out takes place on the opposite side, where the wings have to throw in the ball after all their forwards have crossed a mark on the half-way line 15 yards from touch. This exercise can also be extended so that the field is crossed several times.
   (e) The blind-side wing, or the full back, or both, can come into the line and the inside centre can be left out so that he will receive the ball from the outside centre, etc.

2. *Two teams against each other*
(a) One ball is used for the 2 teams. The ball travels from a scrum to the wing, who falls to the ground and holds on to the ball until all the forwards have formed a ruck over him. The ball is then hooked and travels to the starting point where the other wing falls to the ground and holds the ball. As soon as the ball is hooked, the whistle is blown. The exercise is clocked in the form of a race.
(b) A line-out instead of a scrum starts the exercise.
(c) The movements from the rucks are continued until a mistake is made. (At the outset many mistakes will occur, especially mistakes in handling, but eventually all movements should run smoothly.) The pattern is therefore that the movement commences with a scrum or line-out, after which rucks follow, first on one side and then on the other side of the field. The teams now no longer compete against time only, but they endeavour to see how many repetitions they can get in by counting the number of rucks. Scrums or rucks can be switched with line-outs. The wing throws the ball in when all the forwards are ready in position. The time can again be taken.
N.B. In order to win the race to the ruck, a pack may push its opponents away in the scrum, or it may wheel the scrum in the opposite direction to which the movement is going. This means, at the same time, that the "game" does not become too loose. In the line-out they may tie up their opponents by pulling them in. They may also "churn" or push through to where the ball is.
(d) The same exercise but instead of holding the ball, the wing passes back to his number eight, who tries to launch a passing ruck among the forwards. When they are stopped a ruck or a maul takes place and the ball is run out to the wing again.
(e) The teams play against each other and a back of the team winning the ball places it on the ground. The backs, as well as the forwards, can pick up the ball if they are the first to arrive at it. The game continues as in a match.

Two packs together and against each other

1. Two packs play against each other with the line-out as the basis. If they "churn" and succeed, the game continues. If they consolidate, it must be quality possession so that they can push and dictate when the ball is to be let out to the hooker or the number eight, who breaks. If the ball is lost, their covering should be so good that the disadvantage can be turned to advantage. If the ball is dead, a new line-out takes place. Rucks and mauls must be practised as part of the game following the line-out.

2. Two packs play against each other across the field between the half-way line and the goal-line, with the scrum as the starting point. Number eight throws the ball in and the first player to get it breaks. If the ball goes dead, a scrum is formed. If the ball goes out, a line-out is formed. If a try is scored, a scrum is formed in the centre of the field and the team which has scored puts the ball in.

N.B. Let the scrum halves and one of the wings sometimes play with the forwards and let the number eight take up his position among the backs.

Two back-lines together and against each other

1. The 2 back-lines are drawn up on either side of the half-way line as in a match. One back-line attacks and the other defends. The attackers apply general attacking back-line play by sending the ball out to the wing while the players try and find a gap. The defenders apply general defensive back-line play. This means that they come up correctly according to the 2 methods of defence without neglecting basic defence.

2. Each attacker has a ball and tests the defence. The attackers decide beforehand which method they are going to use, and every player applies it the same way; for instance, a dummy to the inside, a side-step through the outside gap, a grubber kick through the inside gap, a punt, a swerve through the inside gap, etc. Their success will obviously be limited, but they can nevertheless deceive the defenders by giving a dummy to the outside, followed by a short punt. They can also dummy to the outside and slip through the inside gap. They can dummy to the outside and kick a grubber. They can dummy to the inside and take the outside gap, etc. The defenders tackle as they would in a match.

3. The attackers combine forces against the defenders, but they use only one of their players to break or kick etc. He is supported by his team-mates.
 (a) The attackers, preferably the centres, kick a short punt or grubber.
 (b) The fly half kicks a corner or hooked kick.
 (c) The inside centre kicks a grubber kick.
 (d) Tactical moves are used.
 (e) One of the backs breaks.

4. On receiving the ball, each attacker looks up towards his opposite number. Later he looks about to see what is taking place. Observing, in this connection, goes hand in hand with deceleration of speed.
 (a) The 2 back-lines practise without a ball but they come up as if one of them is handling. The players scrutinise their opponents' footwork until they can ascertain if the outside or inside foot of the opposing player is in front.
 (b) The same exercise is done with a ball. A player who notices that his opponent's inside foot is in front, breaks to the inside.

Two back-lines separately
In order to teach the backs to support

one another, the following exercise is used. The player in possession dictates what has to be done by his team-mates. The fly half is the first to receive the ball. He holds it and either moves to the left (the centres and wing also moving to the left), or to the right (when they too move to the right). If he stops in his tracks, they follow suit. If he retreats, they do likewise. If he stops in his tracks and turns, they all move towards him because this signals that he wanted to break but was prevented from doing so. His team-mates therefore come to his assistance.

Two teams together. The team in possession against the backs of the other team

1. The forwards hook the ball from a scrum. They may also wheel the scrum or the scrum half may break to form a maul. Their opponents try to push them away if they have hooked the ball, or, should the scrum wheel, try to stop the movement. Back-line movements follow after possession has been won. The forwards who have gained possession play together while the other pack withdraws from the game.

2. If a line-out is formed, they must consolidate before letting the ball out. They can also deflect it or start a churning movement and keep the game going by means of rucks and mauls. As long as one pack has the ball the opposing pack takes an active part in the game, but as soon as the scrum half passes the ball out, the losing pack withdraws from the game.

3. *A scrum or a line-out is formed*
(a) One of the attackers breaks. If he goes through the outside gap, he feeds the ball through to the wing. If he goes through the inside gap, his forwards link up with him for hand-to-hand movement. If the back fails to penetrate, the forwards help either by starting a hand-to-hand movement or by forming a ruck or a maul. If the ball is gained from there, the back-line takes up the position best suited for attack from a ruck and the ball goes out to the wing, who does everything as he would in a match. If he cannot round his opponent, he cross-kicks. If he is checked near the goal-line, he holds the ball for either a ruck or a maul.
(b) Tactical moves, in which the forwards join, are practised.
(c) Tactical kicks are practised and the forwards join to give a hand.

HANDLING (AND ATTACK) AGAINST DEFENCE

1. *Forwards against backs*
The forwards try and stop the opposing backs in possession. The game starts in midfield from a scrum and continues until the ball is dead. The blind-side wings and the scrum halves help their forwards while the full back helps either his forwards or his backs.

2. One of the teams hooks the ball from a scrum then moves the ball out to the wing, who tries to cross over. In the team losing possession, the loose forwards, the half backs, the blind-side wing, and the full back have to defend. If the scrum is on the half-way line, the wing should not be able to cross over. If the scrum is on the defending team's twenty-five yard line, however, the wing ought to be successful. The same exercises can be followed by making use of short punts or corner kicks and bringing in the open-side wing as a defender. As soon as the wing is tackled, a scrum is formed on the other side of the field and the opposing team now attacks with tight forwards and the 2 centres of the defending new team also running. The movement may be continued in this manner as long as the coach wishes or until the cover defence performs effectively.

3. A scrum is formed on the half-way line and with the back-lines drawn up deep in attacking formation. The backs who receive the ball feed it to the wing. The forwards

of the team deprived of the ball try to cut off the backs by running across the field on the half-way line. Should they succeed, some or other principle has not been properly applied. The backs of the team not gaining possession do not participate. If the defending forwards are otherwise occupied, the blind-side wing has to do the work of cutting off the attackers after the ball has been raked from the scrum.

4. A scrum is formed at the corner of the twenty-five and touchlines. One of the back-lines takes up a position in a shallow line with the scrum nearest to the goal-line. On gaining possession they let the ball out as fast as they can to the wing. The wing then feeds it back to the centre, to the inside centre, to the fly half, and to the scrum half, who sends it out to the wing once more.

As soon as the forwards have hooked the ball they break up and run straight to the furthermost goal-line to see if they can arrive there ahead of the backs who are handling the ball. The backs should get there first as they have been lined up shallow and are supposed to be faster than the forwards, but they must receive and pass the ball at top speed. However, it is sometimes difficult for the backs to emerge as the winners!

The forwards robbed of possession – and their backs – run to the opposite twenty-five yard line where a scrum is formed and from which they gain possession, therefore becoming the next to race against their backs.

Continuous tight play and loose play by 2 packs of forwards

The purpose is to have line-outs, scrums, rucks and mauls in quick succession. The scrum halves join in and, if they are not available, the number eight takes their places and the places of the wings at line-outs.

1. The scrum, plus wheeling, serve as the starting point, with or without the scrum half breaking. The game continues until the ball is dead.

2. Churning from the line-out serves as the starting point and the game continues until the ball is dead.

3. The scrum half or number eight who receives the ball from a scrum or a line-out passes it out in different directions to another player or person positioned near a bag. The player or person places the ball next to the bag and moves away. If the distances are too far for passing, the ball can be kicked by the scrum half or it may even be rolled out.

Formation exercises for back-line players

The backs play against one another and use the formations at the line-out, scrum and ruck alternately as starting points. The ball is passed out to one player in the attacking team who launches the attack, be it a straightforward or a tactical move.

Attackers against Defenders

1. The full length of the field and 2 balls are used.

Two teams are used as in a match with one the attacking side and the other the defenders. Both must be given sufficient opportunities as attackers and defenders to practise general play and loose play.

Line-out: Two line-outs and one general back play for the backs. The ball is thrown in at a line-out on the half-way line for the team who is to attack. For all practical purposes a line-out tussle takes place between the 2 packs. Should the attackers get quality possession, the ball goes out to the wing. The forwards take no part in the general back-line play. The team practising defence throws in the ball at a second line-out on the half-way line and if they gain possession, the ball is let out to the scrum half, who runs back towards his 10-yard line. Here he places the ball behind a bag filled with straw, where a ruck is formed – an attacking ruck for the attacking forwards and a defensive ruck for the defending pack. Whichever team wins possession, sends the ball out to the wing. This means that the backs must be in position already. The ball comes back to the forwards by means of a centre kick by the wing and the line-out series continues.

Two line-outs are taken on the defending team's 10-yard line followed by a ruck on the twenty-five yard line. After this 2 line-outs take place on the twenty-five and the ruck is formed near the goal-line. For every ruck a bag can be used. The 2 teams change their roles.

2. The same exercise is done with the scrum as the starting point, although 1 scrum – as against 2 line-outs – may serve the purpose.

3. Scrums and line-outs follow one another. For instance, 2 line-outs 5 yards from the goal-line, a ruck on the twenty-five, 2 scrums on the twenty-five, a ruck on the half-way line, 2 scrums on the 10-yard line, a ruck on the twenty-five, 2 line-outs on the twenty-five, a ruck on the goal-line, 2 scrums on the goal-line. After this the teams change roles.

KICK-OFFS AND DROP-OUTS

Two teams separately

1. (a) A team works together. One of the teams takes either kick-offs or drop-outs and the forwards try to catch the ball. They form a quick maul from which the ball comes out quickly and goes through the back-line – which is drawn up in formation for a ruck – to the wing who centre-kicks for the forwards. They start a hand-to-hand movement, form a maul, and pass the ball out to the back-line.
   (b) When the ball is handled by the backs, one of them either goes down with the ball to form a ruck, or stops and turns, giving his back for a maul.

2. (a) A quick tap penalty kick is taken and the entire back-line is used.
   (b) Tactical moves from a penalty are practised.

3. A team member either kicks off or kicks a drop-out towards his team-mates and then takes up his position with them. Again a maul is formed and the ball is tied up by the forwards before being let out.

Two teams together

1. One of the teams takes either a kick-off or a drop-out and tries to get the ball to land in a "box" or to get the opposing team into difficulties.

2. One of the teams takes either a kick-off or a drop-out. A maul is formed and the team to receive the ball tries to get it out to the backs as far as the wing. The kicking team try to catch the ball themselves. If they fail they then attempt to nullify the maul.

Chapter 8
Application of Skills

AT THE SUMMIT of the scale of exercises is the application of skills. All other exercises aim towards this ideal. First of all the body is built, after which the skills in situations are perfected.

In skill building each skill is fully developed. In rounding off of skills these have merged into the general play.

In the application of skills we again use, for obvious reasons, two teams performing as they would in matches, but they play either in or with the different facets of play. One of these will always be tight play while the other could be general play, broken play, broken-down play, or loose play. Tight play – the scrum and line-out – is the starting point of the application of skills with general play following and then broken play, broken-down play and loose play. The team winning possession from the tight play has handling, push-off and kicking as allies. The team losing the ball has tackling, and handling if attacking kicks are used against them.

Here we have four combinations of the above:
1. Tight play followed by general play – if handling plays the major role.
2. Tight play followed by broken play – if push-off plays the major role.
3. Tight play followed by broken-down play or loose play – if tackling plays the major role.
4. Tight play followed by loose play – if attacking kicks play the major role.

Broken play takes place by means of exception, and broken-down play leads inevitably to loose play. Consequently the most frequent forms of play are tight play, general back-line play and loose play.

But how frequently does the ball actually go out to the wings? Not often, which means that general play in matches is also an exception. Moreover, the two plays mostly used in matches are tight play and loose play. According to usage, the different types of play in hard matches runs in the following order: tight play, loose play, broken play and general play, and special play.

This does not mean that there are plays which we can afford to neglect in the exercises. The forwards are made to realise that their first task is tight play and their second task loose play, but that neither can be neglected. It will also show them that they must take the blame if their opponents get to the loose ball first. The opponents' achievements in the loose reflect on our forwards' ability in the tight. If the opponents are well held in the tight, they will not have continued success in the loose. A good performance by the opposition in the loose also means that our backs will have to cope not only with their opposite numbers in the back-line but also with the opposing forwards as well.

This all boils down to the following: ensure that your tight play is first-rate and that possession is quality possession. This is achieved by consolidating in the line-out and shoving in the scrum so that the opponents are on the retreat – and a pack retreating is hard put to get to the loose play.

This warning is necessary because the energy used in the tight is often conserved for loose play, and as a result both aspects suffer. This is what happened in South African Rugby. Forwards became so loose that they were virtually backs; we found ourselves cultivating "back-line forwards" instead of tight forwards. Be on guard against this. In the application of skills the margin between forwards and backs after tight play must be kept, even should a great deal of loose play follow.

The aim of forward play must be apparent in all the exercises. For the team who has the throw-in, quality possession is essential. At the same time they must keep the opponents' forwards away from their backs and see to it that the opposition are last to arrive at the loose play. This can be achieved by possession, which is linked with consolidation and shoving. This need not necessarily be practised in every scrum and line-out. Churning and wheeling, the two most important methods of attack forwards can launch, should also be practised.

The forwards' rhythm may consequently be: consolidate (line-out), push (scrum), letting the ball out immediately (scrum and line-out), wheeling (scrum), churning (line-out), letting the ball out (scrum and line-out) etc. There must be uncertainty about this rhythm in the minds of the opposing team; uncertainty creates aimless play, which is always fraught with danger for the opposers.

The team not putting in the ball should fight for possession. Should they fail they should concentrate on pushing the scrum away, or shove so hard that the ball is held up and the plan of the opposing team goes awry. It is easier to push a pack away which has the ball than to push a pack away without the ball. In the line-out the aim should be to end it as soon as possible so that the backs can come up on defence beyond the 10-yard off-side line. This can be achieved by disrupting the consolidation efforts of the opponents. One of the best countermoves against consolidation is to push the consolidation open, or to push it across the line of the line-out. Pushing is therefore one of the most powerful weapons at the disposal of the forwards who do not have the throw-in It helps them to prevent their opposing numbers from linking up with their backs or from arriving first at the loose play.

This piece of Rugby philosophy is more than a philosophy; all that remains is for the coach to see to it that the forwards know this truth and keep it constantly in mind in skill building, in rounding off of skills, and in the application of skills.

What about the backs who, according to the order and frequency of phases used in matches, are only in third position, with tight play and loose play coming before general play and broken play? What the backs have to bear in mind is that the order and frequency of phases are actually up to them. If, for example, they are effective on attack, broken play will take the place of loose play. If their attacking ability and handling are poor, loose play will be more prominent than broken play. If they make frequent use of attacking kicks, they can see to it that loose play is more prominent than broken play. If their tactical kicks are poor, they create more line-outs and, as a result, more tight play, and also cause frequent kicking by their opponents.

Tactical kicks, however, are absolutely necessary, and care should be taken that they serve their purpose. In the first place the kicks should be well placed in the boxes or empty spaces on the field. As soon as the kicks land there the opponents will want to ensure that there are no more empty places, but in doing so they will neglect something else. A wing who has to come up on defence, for instance, will hang back. The blind-side wing will cover too soon, and the full back will take up a position at the cost of neglecting another. Usually the "boxes" are not big at the start of a match because there are few teams which make use of their wings – and wings are the players mainly used for closing the boxes.

For this reason it is frequently necessary for a tactical kicker to create boxes. This can be done by compelling the wing to come up on defence and compelling the full back to guard both touchlines instead of the touchline towards which the movement is going. For this the hooked kick can be used; blind-side movements can cause the full back and the blind-side wing also to keep an eye on that touch-line, causing divided attention. A dummy kick in the direction of the one touchline and a kick in the other can also help in this connection. The open-side wing can also be lured into moving to his touchline by means of a dummy kick and then placing a short punt in the "box" he has left. It is the job of the inside centre to kick these short punts. If the outside centre takes the short punt, he kicks it right over the head of his opponent and not obliquely, as his inside centre would have done.

Once the boxes have been created, the time is ripe for broken play. The back whose opponent has left the box, breaks. This creates uncertainty. In other words, attacking punts are important because they lead to broken play. The broken-play attacks can be direct, meaning that a back tries to get past his opposite number, or indirect, meaning that tactical moves are executed. Tactical moves must be made to increase uncertainty among the opponents so that they will not know exactly where to close up all the boxes. If this can be achieved, the opponents will no longer come up on defence so fast or as directly as they would wish. This, in fact, is the primary aim of a back.

Sometimes fatigue and uncertainty combine to cause the opposing back-line to come up slowly. We can set fatigue aside and concentrate on uncertainty. At the start of a match the ball is sent out deliberately to the wing, even if it should lead to broken-down play. If the opposing team is unworried by this move, the ball is next kicked into empty boxes, a move which is bound to change the opposing team's attitude if the balls are correctly and effectively placed. This tactic is continued until the opposition thinks that all is well. A direct or indirect attack is then launched on their goal-line and should it succeed, uncertainty is once more their bedfellow.

A team can also assume that the opponents' back-line will start off with *panache*, doing everything correctly and speedily. For this reason the team can start with short punts instead of beginning with general play. If the boxes are guarded, the team goes over to general play or broken play. General play entails that the ball goes out to the wings and this, in turn, extends the opposition's line of defence, in the process of which the gaps between the players are widened – something which can be exploited by means of direct or indirect attacks.

If the forwards wish to gain the upper hand up front, they must see to it that their opponents are not only made to work hard in the tight but that they must run about in between. There is nothing more tiring for a forward who is losing the struggle up front than to have to work hard in the tight and then be made to run long distances afterwards. This is the reason why backs help forwards and vice versa. The best assistance forwards can give backs is by arriving first at the loose play, thus ensuring that none of the opposing forwards are in the backs' way.

The aim of back play is therefore: breaking the line of defence by causing uncertainty among the opposing numbers, which can be achieved by judiciously varying play. For backs on defence the aim should be to see to it that the defensive measures are adequate to counter any attack. Only with this in mind should application of skills be approached, otherwise it would serve no purpose. It is a duel between the backs and forwards – separately and combined – of one team against those of another. It can be likened to a boxer in the ring, confronting his opponent all by himself. In the case of Rugby, however, it is like boxing with assistance, because the backs can come to the aid of their forwards and the forwards can come to lend a hand to the backs. This is absolutely essential.

What has been said so far is the ideal, but we all know that matters can take an entirely different course during the match. What can happen?

A pack is too light or too small to take on another pack, but their backs are good or quite good. Should they concentrate more on back play and on loose play? The answer is "yes", because this is the only hope they have, and if their opponents allow them to do so it would be foolish to do anything else. On the other hand, their opponents would be foolish if they did allow this. Not only would they ignore a Rugby truth, but they would also fritter away their own power or strength. Is this not, however, what we see so frequently in Rugby?

It must be remembered that forwards and not backs win matches. If a pack is beaten, their backs seldom win the match. If a pack is hard put to hold its own, but succeeds nevertheless, the backs may still manage to win the match. For this reason I firmly believe that even if forwards are on the light side and comparatively small, the pack need not concede victory. With correct coaching any light pack can take on a heavy pack and, even if defeated, can keep their opponents fully occupied. If the eight light forwards combine and play as one, they can defeat a heavier pack which uses a number of its forwards in back-line play. This, too, we see frequently nowadays. A good pack can be wasted because five forwards do the work while the remaining three are bent on running about.

If a team has a good pack but weak threequarters, should it play with its pack? The answer is again "yes", but with a proviso: supremacy up front means supremacy in the loose. These 2 aspects – supremacy in the tight and supremacy in the loose – are inseparable. Having the upper hand in the loose is also to have the ability to score tries, usually by the threequarters. For this reason a back-line may be weak in attack but it should be able to handle a ball and get it out to the wing. There is no justification for neglecting a weak back-line because it does not contain any stars in attack. They will keep on doing general back-line play, in and outside match situations. As stated previously the aim must be realised in the application of skill or else we get what we have today – match practices consisting of aimless play. The question is this: how does a team know that it is achieving, or has achieved, its aim? The answer is simple: if a team knows what it is striving for, it will soon realise whether its goal has been attained.

In order to help players, a few symptoms are outlined – the word "symptoms" is used because a weak team has some flaw or other which is responsible.

Forwards: They become soft. *Backs:* They no longer come up fast.

I am not bringing any episodes or incidents into this book, but I may be pardoned for saying something about "softening up" or "becoming soft". I introduced the expression of "softening up" as a result of reading the book by Joe Louis, the former heavyweight boxing champion of the world. He followed the policy of not starting his fights with his opponent's chin as his target, but keeping it for the last, for the knockout blow. Before going for the target he used to maul his opponent's body and he called this the "softening process". As a result of this I shaped the policy of the 1955 Springboks on this concept. The policy of the Springboks therefore consisted of softening up the Lions forwards, after which the knockout would be delivered by the Springbok backs.

I was strongly criticised for this phrase and it was argued that one could soften up one's opponents only by means of infringements or foul play. Today, however, we understand what is meant by the expression, viz. the opponents are rendered worn out and are dispirited. The symptoms of softening are: 1. They yield up front, in the scrums; 2. they can no longer jump well and their consolidation, if still there, is wasted; 3. they are the last to arrive at rucks and are consequently not in the way of the backs. In other words, they are paralysed in three plays or departments.

As far as the backs are concerned, the signs that you are beating your opponents are that they no longer come up fast, and when they do come up a certain uncertainty and sluggishness can be discerned. The result is that your own mistakes are less noticeable. If, for instance, you run too far, you may not pay the penalty for your errors; if the ball is dropped, it is not so dangerous. Even a badly placed kick may be effective. If, however, your team is being beaten, the identical symptoms will be discernible in their efforts. The captain should therefore be able to recognise the symptoms of both his own team and those of the opposing side and be able to decide on, or prescribe for, the "medicine". This is indeed his biggest task on the field.

To proceed now to the realisation of the aim in the application of skill, we must tackle the latter in two stages: 1. Match situations must be created. 2. Matches must be played with this in mind.

Match situation must be created
Why is this done? To make players think.

This means that they must make observations, read situations and react accordingly. They must be able to judge and outmanoeuvre their opponents, and then use the correct weapon in their equipment.

How are these situations created? By accentuating that which must be stressed: tight play must serve as starting-point, and that which follows it will be reconstructed according to match situations which are known to us.

N.B. Attack, push-off and kicks follow only after handling, and each of these must serve as a basis for creating situations. Tackling, on the other hand, plays a part every time an attack is launched and consequently always forms part of the exercise.

One should bear in mind that the game continues until the ball is dead or until it becomes unplayable, i.e. everything happens as in a match.

The following exercises are suggested, starting with the line-out because back play follows it.

1. (a) Line-out followed by general play, i.e. attacking by one of the teams (forwards and backs) and defensive action by the other team. The movements of the forwards are watched, even if the game has to be stopped, and the position of each forward noted. The game continues, i.e. the ball goes further along the back-line, and the game is stopped once more, etc.

   (b) When these two basic plays are done satisfactorily, other situations are created. To make the exercises interesting and to teach the players to keep their eyes open, the aim of the attackers should be to outwit their opponents, not only as regards clever play, but also by making deliberate mistakes. At the same time the defenders must make the task of their opponents as difficult as possible.

Forwards
   (i) The ball is struck in the line-out.
   (ii) The scrum half tarries with the ball.
   (iii) The ball is thrown to the full back close to the goal-line.
   (iv) The forward vary line-out positions as a surprise move.
   (v) The ball is thrown over the line-out to the backs.
   (vi) Churning in front or at the rear of the line-out. If checked at the rear, the blind-side is tested. If the churning movement is successfully carried out in front or at the rear, hand-to-hand movements follow.
   (vii) A forward in front of the line-out plays the ball back to the wing.
   (viii) A deep throw-in and the scrum half breaks round at the back of the line-out.
   (ix) A rhythmic pattern is followed, e.g. consolidate, deflect, churn at the back, etc.

Defenders try and disrupt the plans of the attackers
   (i) They strike the ball towards either side. (A jump in which one hand is used gains more height than a jump in which both arms are used.)
   (ii) They surreptitiously push or pull those forwards jumping for the ball.
   (iii) They get hold of the arms of the line-out forward.

(iv) They allow the line-out forward to take the ball and then try to pull him through to their side.
(v) They push the maul away in order to have the line-out repeated.
(vi) They fling themselves over the forwards, who consolidate towards the ball when the line-out forward has brought it down.
(vii) They kick through the legs of the line-out forward in an attempt to kick the ball from his hands.
(viii) They see to it that they are not drawn into the line-out by consolidation and play loosely, by which they can spoil back play.

Backs

If general play is good, one back-line must try to outwit the other, but in a particular manner. The defenders must try to catch the attackers out by deliberately doing incorrect things to see if the attackers are quick to spot them and act accordingly. The following will serve as examples:
  (i) The fly half does not come up. If the opposing fly half does not break, the latter is at fault.
 (ii) A centre hangs back. If his opponent does not break, the latter is at fault. If he forfeits his satellitic movement, i.e. if he also fails to straighten his line and create the impression that he is going to pass the ball out, he is also called to account.
(iii) A centre or a wing comes up faster than his line. If the outside centre or the inside centre does not break, and break correctly, he is at fault.
(iv) The wing comes up with his line from the start. If the opposing fly half does not cross-kick or if the inside centre does not kick a short punt, a mistake has been made.
 (v) The blind-side wing either stops in the line or moves away before the ball is let out by a line-out forward. If he has done this previously and the forwards have not been advised to consolidate before letting out the ball, and the blind-side kick or hooked kick is not employed, both sections are guilty of having made serious mistakes.
(vi) The full back takes up his position in the middle of the field. If the fly half does not aim towards the outside and kick a hooked kick to the opposite side, the defenders are the winners.
(vii) Number eight goes to help his back-line on defence. If the opposing forwards do not start a churning movement at the back, and – if they are checked – the backs fail to go blind-side, or if the forwards do not consolidate and the scrum half does not break, they have erred.
(viii) The backs are widely spaced. If their opponents use grubber kicks or tactical moves, but individual breaks are not attempted, they have made a mistake.
(ix) The backs come up in line, but the line is not oblique. If a grubber kick or punt is not used, the chance has been missed.
 (x) The outside gap is given to one of the inside backs. If he fails to straighten and break, with or without a grubber kick, it is a clear indication that there is something wrong with his game.
(xi) The outside centre tackles the inside centre, or the wing tackles the outside

centre. If the player who is tackled fails to swerve out when the ball comes to him and either to break or send his partner away, he will run into further trouble.
(xii) The entire back-line takes up a deep position. If the opposing back-line does not line up shallower, and if it does not attempt crossing the advantage line, it is unaware of the value or significance of the advantage line.

2. The defenders try to do everything correctly and the attackers attempt to point out their mistakes by means of successful play, or they try and force them into making mistakes. They now play as they would in a match and as has been explained previously in this chapter. This means that they try and disrupt the line of defence and strike at the point where it buckles.

N.B. It is clear that many line-outs are required to allow all the above situations to develop. For this reason an entire afternoon can be devoted to the line-out as a starting point. It must be borne in mind that there are at least 60 line-outs in an average match; sometimes there are 100. It is also clear why the game must go on until the ball is dead or unplayable, otherwise the forwards and the backs will work as separate entities.

3. *The scrum as starting point:* The forwards gaining possession deliberately try and outwit their opponents or highlight their mistakes:
(a) They hold the ball and push, and then let the ball out.
(b) They allow the ball to shoot out so that the scrum half has to run back to gather. They continue pushing their opponents.
(c) They wheel the scrum.
(d) The scrum half breaks and plays with his number eight or with his flank forward while the opponents are being pushed.

Back play
(a) The defenders are lined up deep and the same competition between defender and attacker takes place as in the line-out.
(b) The defenders are lined up shallow and the attackers attempt to compel them to come up slowly by means of tactical moves and kicks.
(c) Each back is given the opportunity of breaking and, if their efforts fail, the result is loose play.
(d) Each back gets the opportunity of taking an attacking kick.
(e) With either the line-out or the scrum as a starting point, the backs kick only for a period, followed by tactical moves and then breaking.

N.B. Skill building is drilling in technique. Rounding off of skills is drill in the satellitic movements and in teamwork. Application of skill is drill in situations.

4. Kick-offs, drop-outs and penalty kicks are used as starting points, followed by the play resulting from them.

5. The players have reached the stage where they are conversant with their duties. Applying the duties when playing against the best players is better than

when applying them against a weaker opposition. For this reason the first and second team players are changed over. The three tight-head forwards – and the hooker – of the first team exchange positions with their counterparts in the second team. The left centre, the right wing and the fly half also switch to the second team.

N.B. Sooner or later changes will be made in a first team and by the above method any new players will have already been blooded.

Matches are played
The aim should be to make everything as realistic as possible. The players are now prepared in every respect and they can apply what they have been taught.

Here follow some of the things that should be done:
(a) A referee controls the match strictly according to the laws. Penalty kicks, conversion kicks, kick-offs, and drop-outs are taken as in a match.
(b) The captain leads his team. The coach is on the touchline, and if he wishes to participate he does so through the captain.
(c) The 2 teams play in easily-distinguishable colours.
(d) Players should not pull their punches. They must get stuck into the rucks, tackle hard, etc.

A PATTERN OF RUGBY AND EXERCISES FOR IT

Principles
1. In order to play well, players must be *drilled* to do so. This means that in their exercises they must repeat their duties in the game over and over again.
2. In order to have a sound and healthy club, as many teams as possible should be involved in the exercises. Three or 4 club teams can practise together, take part in the same exercises and on the same field.

Drilling
Forwards are drilled in:
1. The scrum.
2. The line-out.
3. Loose play. (a) The ruck.
   (b) The maul, which is preceded by driving.

Backs are drilled:
1. To get the ball out faultlessly to the wings from a line-out and from second-phase possession, i.e. ruck and maul. (A ball can reach the wings from a ruck, from a maul, or from a line-out.)
2. To ensure linking with their forwards after gaining possession from the scrum by means of blind-side and tactical moves close to the forwards. (A ball cannot reach the wing, nor even the outside centre, from a scrum.)
3. To find gaps, to take them, and link with other backs if the outside gap is taken, and link up with the forwards if the inside gap is taken.

N.B. After possession from a scrum a back-line should try to link up with the forwards and bring them into play for second-phase possession. Possession gained from a line-out, however, means that forwards should try to link up with their backs.

The pattern
Why do we drill players? To put them in readiness for our Rugby pattern, which consists of the following:
Forwards: Forwards soften up their opponents in the scrum by pushing them away, even if it can be done only by means of heaves. Should they succeed in this, they will be able to break up more quickly and arrive first at the loose play where the softening process is continued.

The softening process is continued in the line-out, in which the opponents are tied up. The rhythm here consists of the following: tie up, release ball, tie up.

The softening in the 3 facets of the game in which the forwards are involved – the scrum, the line-out, and loose play – will see to it that the opposing team's loose forwards are not in the way of the backs. This is the forward's primary aim in the game next to winning quality possession.
The backs: Backs must disorganise their opponents, and they do so by disrupting their line of defence. They do this by stretching the line out, mainly by means of long passes and by causing uncertainty among the defenders. The game is varied so that the opponents are uncertain about what they are going to have to cope with.

This varied play must bring the forwards back into the game after a scrum.

From a line-out the ball must first go out to the wings in order to assist the forwards in the softening process. This means that they cause the opposing forwards to run as far as possible.

From the loose play (ruck and maul) the ball is also sent out to the wings. If the ball has already gone out several times to the wings, the centres strike in the middle or elsewhere.

Therefore: from a scrum, keep the ball close to the scrum by means of forced breaks, movements and short punts in order to bring the forwards into play. From line-out and from loose play, get the ball out to the wing, and later any back who has his opponent summed up should take the gaps. Should his breaks not come off, his greatest allies, the forwards, will link up with him. If the backs have broken a few times, they start from the beginning again – they send the ball out to the wings. Rhythm: to the wings, break, to the wings.

Exercises: Here is a simple exercise containing all the elements of play required by a team. There are many others, but it is better to do one exercise well and to know why it is done, than to do many exercises haphazardly and without purpose.

First exercise of the week – if practices are held twice a week – for three teams.
Explanation:
Step 1. The forwards of team A form a scrum against team B, and A sees to it that their backs get the ball.
Step 2. Their inside centre breaks to the inside and is tackled by the inside centre of team B. The centre who is tackled sees to it that he turns round and

keeps the ball free for his flank forward, and he starts the driving movement through pack C. All the forwards of team A drive through C, who remain in their position and do not advance.

If A cannot drive any further, the players form a maul by packing round the forward who has been checked and see to it that the ball emerges, or they form a ruck after forcing the ball on to the ground. The backs of team A move with the ball emerging from either the maul or ruck, and send it out to the wing.

Step 3. Four of the forwards of team B sprint – directly after the termination of a scrum against team A – straight ahead to a position outside the opposite twenty-five yard line, to serve as basis for a ruck by the A team forwards. When A has completed the driving movement against team C, they ignore the ball used for driving and sprint towards, and into, the rucking base supplied by the B team, pushing their way across to free the ball. The backs of the A team move with the ball and send it to the wing.

Step 4. All the forwards in team B sprint up to the goal-line for a line-out against the forwards of team A, and the latter, after completion of the ruck, sprint towards the line-out in order to take the ball.

The wing of team A throws in the ball. The forwards of team A have to catch it and consolidate. Team B must attempt to break through in order to try and rob them of it. (They do not try to catch the ball.)

As soon as team A has completed the round, its players exchange places with team C, and team B goes through the drill against team C. If team B has finished, the players exchange places with team A (the players of whom form a row) and team C goes through the drill against team A. See to it that A performs against B and C; B against A and C; C against A and B.

Technique: The exercise starts with the drill. If the players are tired, specific attention is paid to the scrum – two packs – and to the line-out with two packs. In both cases they are used with the back-lines, one moving with the ball while the other defends. Forwards and backs work together and separately, but the forwards must see to it that scrum and line-out work is perfected, while the backs comply with the principles of getting the ball out to the wings. The backs also practise tactical moves, especially from scrum possession. Consequently the forwards do not join the backs after having fulfilled their functions in the line-out or scrum.

Drills for the scrum: One of the packs partially locks the scrum and pushes off one foot against the other pack which is stationary. Each team is afforded the opportunity of giving a heave. If this is done satisfactorily, the two packs heave simultaneously. The ball is put in at every scrum. Backs of the team not being drilled sprint one length of the field along the touchline.

Drills for the line-out
(a) One of the packs takes the ball and closes up until everything goes smoothly. Each team gets a chance.
(b) One of the packs takes possession of the ball and ties it up while the other team tries to break through. Each team gets a chance.
(c) Each pack tries to catch the ball, and if they succeed, they tie it up. If they fail to gain possession, they attempt breaking through.

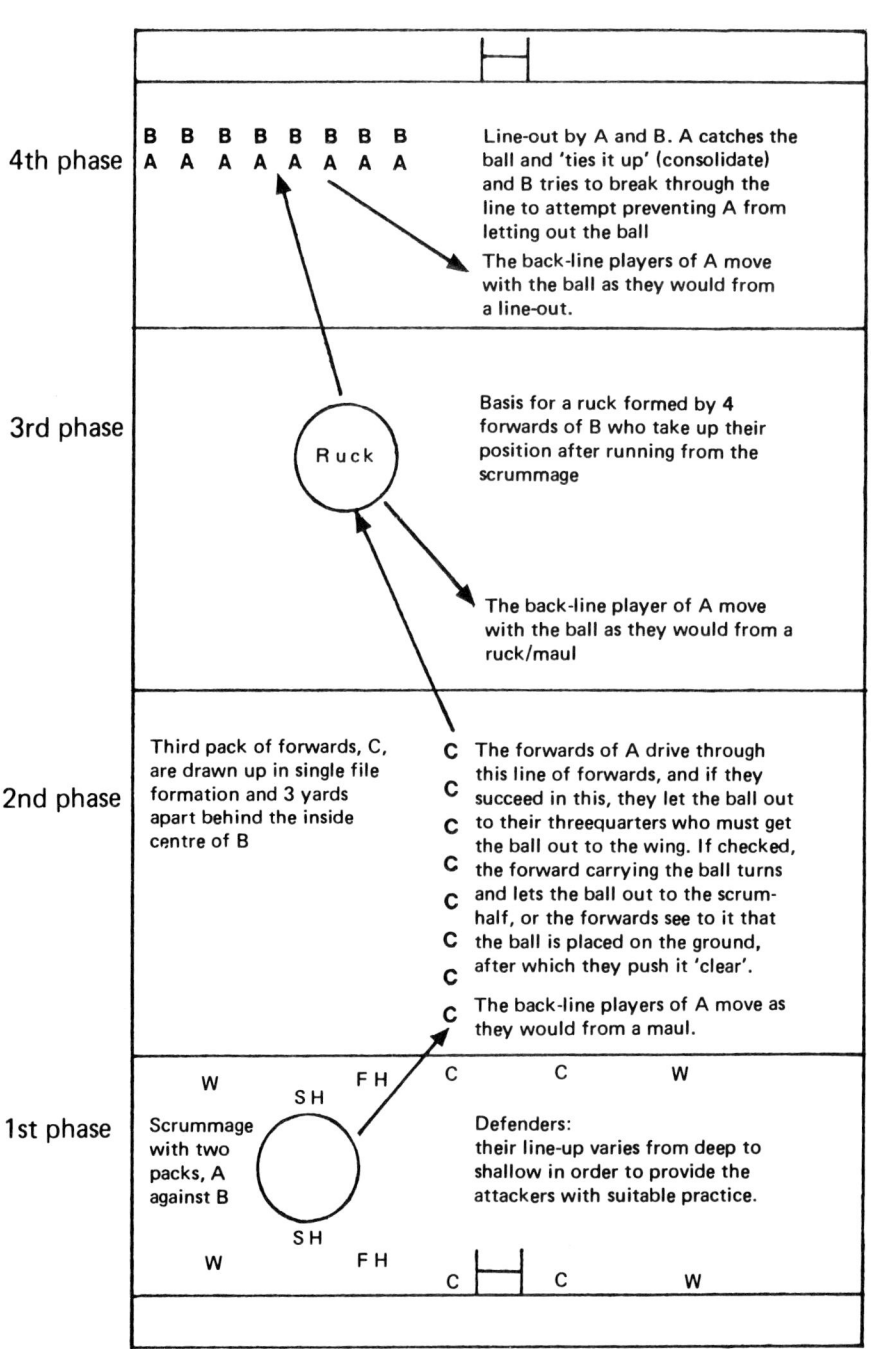

3 teams A, B and C exercising together

Backs
Linking-up with forwards after gaining possession from a scrum
1. Use the blind-side movement when the fly half receives the ball in line with the scrum. (A scrum in the centre of the field has two blind-sides.)
2. (a) The fly half goes blind-side, but the blind-side wing takes the ball on the open-side field in line with the scrum.
   (b) The fly half goes either to the left or to the right of a centre-field scrum and one of the centres takes the ball in a line with the scrum on his opposite side.
3. (a) Scissors movement between the fly half and inside centre.
   (b) Scissors movement between the fly half and scrum half.
4. A short punt straight ahead by the fly half or inside centre.
5. Forced breaks by the scrum half, fly half and inside centre.

Remember that there are occasional breaks to be made if the gaps are waiting to be taken. There are forced breaks when no gap exists and an attempt is made to force one or make a breach.

Second Practice
1. Play begins with a scrum near one of the touchlines and continues until the ball is dead. This play is repeated from one twenty-five to the other with attackers and defenders playing as in a match. See how long the ball can be kept going. Repeat near the opposite touchline. Repeat with scrum in centre field.
2. The same principle but with the line-out as starting point.
3. The same principle but vary the line-outs with scrums.
4. Start the game with a kick-off and with a drop-out.
5. Start the game with a penalty tap-kick.

If three teams practise simultaneously, two of them play against each other while the third practises behind the posts or on one section of the field. The entire field need not be used for the practice – they can start with a hypothetical scrum or with a hypothetical line-out and the game proceeds from one of these set-pieces. If four teams are used, they play in each half of the field, and then two of the teams exchange positions at frequent intervals.

What is driving and how is it done?
Forwards drive or play forward. In actual fact only one player drives and when he is held and is on his feet, he has to see to it that his team-mate behind him receives the ball. His team-mate's first object is to get the ball, and his second object is to run through his opponent. Driving thus means to attempt to run through an opponent, and the driving movement continues until the driver is blocked.

In order to drive, the player lowers his head and clasps the ball under his arm. If he is blocked, he can either turn or hold the ball at the ready for a team-mate to take it.

Forwards drive if they churn in the line-out and if they take the ball from their backs who have been tackled.

N.B. If the forwards do not attempt to run through their opponents, they run with the ball in the manner in which the backs run. If, as a pack, they push the other pack away in a maul (ball in their hands), we speak of "walking" with the pack.

If forwards drive through the row of forwards and are held, the forward holding the ball turns and the others pack down next to him and push. The ball is let out directly to the scrum half, or if this is not possible, the ball is rolled out.

If the defenders hold on to the ball and pull at it, the "drivers" must push the ball to the ground and form a ruck. This means that they push to get across the ball.

The basis for ruck drilling

Four forwards stand in a row and bind round one another. They have their backs turned towards the team which is being drilled. As soon as no. 1 of the pack runs into them, they yield. They do the same when the first pair of forwards pack down against no. 1, but after this they brace themselves so that the pack can acquire the knack of pushing itself across the ball without touching it.

How do the backs get the ball out to their wings?
1. Backs get the ball to their wings from a line-out by doing the following:
   (a) The fly half stands behind the 10-yard off-side line to pass the ball out on that "line". He thus receives the ball behind the hypothetical line.
   (b) The fly half starts running only when the ball is on its way to him. The scrum half passes the ball about a yard in front of him. The inside centre starts running when the fly half catches the ball, the outside centre starts running when his partner catches the ball, and the wing sets off with the outside centre.
   (c) The same deep-lying position is maintained for the passes, i.e. every threequarter passes the ball backwards to his team-mate and not in line with himself.
   (d) The ball is caught and passed within the distance of a yard.
   (e) The inside centre straightens the line, standing far away from the fly half.
   (f) Long passes are given in order to help every threequarter to run straight.
2. If the forwards get possession from the backs for second-phase play, they move in a straight line and in line with the ruck or the maul in order to cross the advantage line as soon as possible and in order not to allow the opponents to reorganise themselves.

General
1. If only one team is practising, they form a hypothetical scrum in order to introduce the drill. They form a line-out by themselves. They drive through their own backs, of whom the first three form the basis for the ruck. Obviously there will not be any back movements.
2. If four teams are used, one of the teams runs round the field while the other three are working. The team doing the drill take their places after the drill and form the row through which the churning is done, e.g.

A is drilled.

B scrums against them, forms the basis for the ruck and does line-out work against them.

C serves as buffer against which driving is done.

D jogs round the field.

If A has finished, they take D's place. D takes C's place. C takes B's place, and B takes A's place.

After this: B jogs round the field, A forms a buffer, C is drilled, and B works against them, etc.

3. If the players do the scrum and line-out drills satisfactorily:
   (a) Every forward pushes in every position in the scrum and every back is made to play in every position in the back-line.
   (b) Players of the third team, for instance, are exchanged with players in the first team.
   (c) The row through which driving is practised no longer remains a row, but the players take part in the ensuing ruck or maul.
4. If scrums and line-outs are drilled with more than two teams, each team must practise against the other. If four teams practise, two teams can use one half of the field and the other two teams can use the other half. They exchange their backs after some time.
5. Half-locking means that the locks and loose forwards are rigidly straight in the scrum with one foot a few inches in front of the foot whose leg is straightened.
6. Instead of starting the drill near the left touchline, it is started near the right touchline or in the centre of the field. The pack to be used for driving through must sometimes be positioned behind the scrum, and the bases for rucking must be placed behind the row of forwards used for driving practice.
7. Each team can go through the drill more than once before exchanges are made.